Advocating

Answering

Breathing

Building

Confronting

Connecting

Constructing

Containing

Countering

Crafting

Creating

Cultivating

Destigmatizing

Dismantling

Educating

Enabling

Enhancing

Envisioning

Establishing

Expanding

Fabricating

Facilitating

Forging

Fostering

Futuring

Helping

Improving

Increasing

Inspiring

Institutionalizing

Inviting

Mapping

Procuring

Promoting

Prototyping

Raising

Reconceptualizing

Removing

Repurposing

Reviving

Rooting

Sharing

Strengthening

Transforming

Understanding

Editors	**Mariana Amatullo** **Bryan Boyer** **Jennifer May** **Andrew Shea**
Assistant Editors	**Isabella Gady** **Jenny Liu**
Editorial Data Assistant	**Vasuta Kalra**
Editorial Case Study Assistant	**Andrea Noble**
Editorial Research Assistants	**Nidhi Rathore Singh** **Mohammad Sial** **Stephanie Soussloff**
Book Designers	**TwoPoints.Net**

This project was produced with support from Sappi's Ideas that Matter program

sappi | **ideas**
that
matter

First published 2022
by Routledge
605 Third Avenue, New York, NY 10158

and by Routledge
2 Park Square, Milton Park, Abingdon, Oxon, OX14 4RN

Routledge is an imprint of the Taylor & Francis Group, an informa business

© 2022 Taylor & Francis

The right of Mariana Amatullo, Bryan Boyer, Jennifer May, and Andrew Shea to be identified as the authors of the editorial material, and of the authors for their individual chapters, has been asserted in accordance with sections 77 and 78 of the Copyright, Designs and Patents Act 1988.

Library of Congress Cataloging-in-Publication Data
A catalog record for this title has been requested

ISBN: 9780367898441 (hbk)
ISBN: 9780367898427 (pbk)
ISBN: 9781003021360 (ebk)

DOI: 10.4324/9781003021360

Typeset in Helvetica and Sabon
by TwoPoints.Net

Publisher's note
This book has been prepared from camera-ready copy provided by the editors.

Design for Social Innovation

Case Studies from Around the World

Edited by Mariana Amatullo, Bryan Boyer, Jennifer May, and Andrew Shea

Routledge
Taylor & Francis Group

NEW YORK AND LONDON

Contents

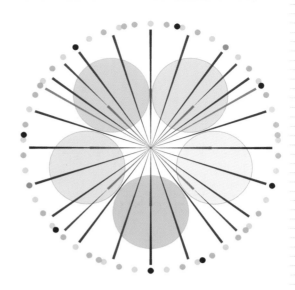

Geographies
of
Power

Case studies are listed with the name of the organization that led the design work. See case study pages for full details on the partnerships that enabled these projects. In every case the lead designers are just the tip of the iceberg.

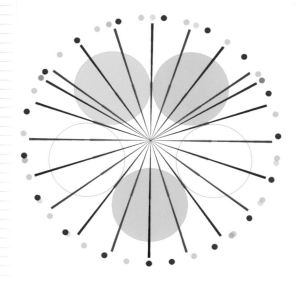

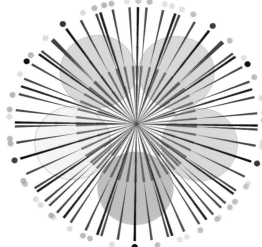

Trajectories of International Development

Organizing the Work

Case Studies

Case Studies

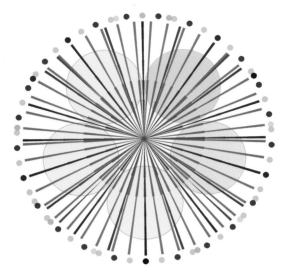

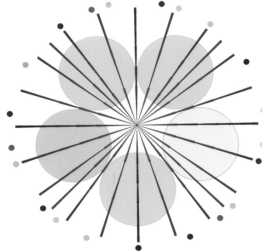

Navigating
Partnerships

Mediums
of Change

Case Studies

Case Studies

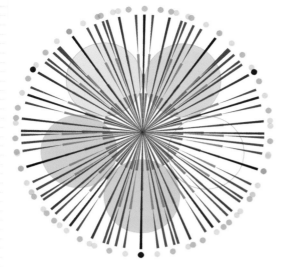

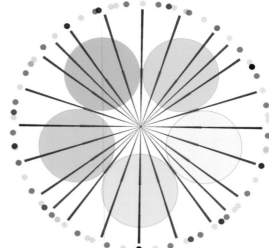

Measuring
Impact

Positioning
for Growth

Case Studies

Case Studies

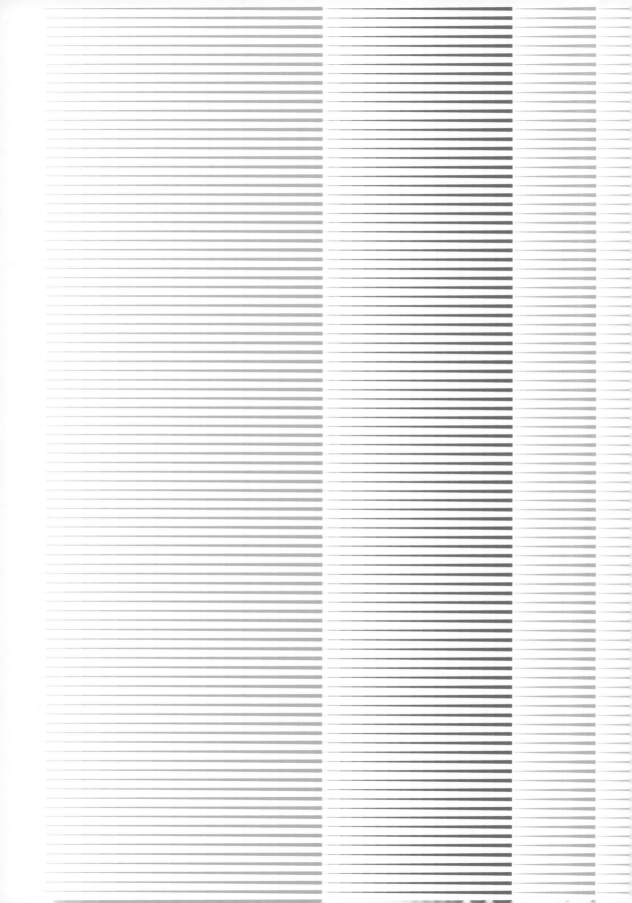

Introduction

Writing a new constitution is one of the most important and difficult things a people can do, but if you want to turn up the level of difficulty from high to insanely high, try crowdsourcing it with 9 million of your neighbors. In 2017 the megalopolis of Mexico City adopted a new constitution, taking the momentous step to convert from a federal district to a city-state. While a document such as this is often drafted by political insiders behind closed doors, Mexico City sought wide public input.

Gathering ideas and suggestions from a population of 9 million demands careful planning and creative thinking in equal measure, so the City asked its creative team Laboratorio para la Ciudad (*Laboratory for the City*) to lead the crowdsourcing effort. The result was impressive: some 300 proposals and almost half a million signatures in support. From this, 76% of the ideas were incorporated into the final document, which became law in September of 2018. With this remarkable success barely behind them, the Laboratorio ceased to exist just a year later. Poof! Gone. What happened?

The Laboratorio had a short existence. Miguel Ángel Mancera, Mayor of Mexico City, appointed Gabriella Gómez-Mont Chief Creative Officer in 2013 and she founded Laboratorio shortly thereafter with the goal of bringing new problem-solving approaches and a wealth of creativity to government. Most of the Laboratorio's work was bottom-up, meaning the lab's 20-person team were collaborating with citizens, entrepreneurs, and other "unusual suspects" in addition to the expected work with fellow government officials. The Lab used its sidewalk credibility to do things that had previously been beyond the ability of government, like creating a map of the informal network of micro-buses that crisscross the city. In another project, Laboratio's strengths in mapping and participatory processes helped the government of Mexico City bring new levels of attention to the city's 3 million youth. They developed tools to map children block by block and then correlate that with green spaces and other public services, resulting in indices of segregation and marginalization that revealed "hotspots." This allowed the government to be more targeted in their efforts to address spatial justice in a city that struggles with inequality.

Five years went by in a flash, and then a different government took over from Mayor Mancera with new priorities and the Laboratorio was closed. In Gómez-Mont's telling, the Laboratorio's closure was "not a disappearance, but the afterlife." Gómez-Mont is sanguine despite what might be perceived as a setback. She asks rhetorically, "Even though there is an institutional carcass on our hands, is there an idea that has persisted?" Indeed, many of the Lab's alumni are now applying their perspective and skills in other settings, continuing the mission of the Lab beyond the formal container of the organization.

In that sense the "afterlife" of the Lab may someday prove to be more important than its five year lifespan, with those 20 alumni sparking changes in yet more contexts both in Mexico City and beyond. Still, it's hard not to wish that the Lab had been maintained in its productive and inspiring form. How would Mexico City be different today if the Lab were continuing to do good work, employing a team, and producing a stream of alumni? How much larger would the ripples of change be? We cannot know the answer to these questions, but we can and should use this story to ask how future efforts that share some resonance with the Lab can be made more enduring.

This story is about government, but the implications are more broad. It is relevant to anyone who is interested in meeting the needs of society with creativity and care through design for social innovation (DSI).[1] Are those designers working in social innovation forever condemned to see labs, centers, pilot projects, and other vessels of their work, come and go on short-term cycles? This is not a question but a call to action.

If you believe that government is important, that business cannot continue to function in pursuit of predominantly financial goals, that the wicked challenges of society require new ways of doing things—then the story of the Laboratorio[2] invites us to examine the sustainability of design for social innovation practices. What would increase the likelihood that the next Laboratorio exists for 10 years, and the one after that for 20?

Design for Social Innovation

Though the accomplishments of Laboratorio para la Ciudad were singular, the story is, unfortunately, not unique. Working outside the boundaries of traditional ways of doing things weds exhilarating freedom to existential fragility. The Lab is just one of many examples showing how difficult it is to change the way governments, businesses, and non-profit organizations meet the needs of contemporary humans and make them more effective against the demands of the day. With countless pilot projects, startups, and labs that have come and gone, the question is how the sustainability of design for social innovation practices can be enhanced. If that's a question you care about, this book is for you.

To understand the sustainability of DSI around the world, we conducted a global survey that resulted in 45 succinct case studies. Each one presents a project, describing both the outcomes and the setup that allowed the work to be possible. This survey was created via a bottom-up process that also surfaced a slate of thematic issues related to the future of design for social innovation, each of which you will find addressed in a roundtable discussion. The organizing principle behind our book, and the two years of effort that went into it, is a hunch that design for social innovation as a field of practice is at a unique moment of maturation. It's time to move beyond the attempts to explain or justify the role of design within social innovation processes and instead put more emphasis on how the field is growing and evolving. It is time to focus on identifying the approaches that enhance the sustainability of this practice.

We use the word "sustainability" in its most basic sense: the ability of design for social innovation work to continue. Our hypothesis is that sustainability is the result of perceived legitimacy, which grows when the outcomes of design work are perceived to be positive, which itself requires that the work and its goals be legible.

Legibility ➡ Impact ➡ Legitimacy = Sustainability

We explore this hypothesis through case studies, data analysis, and roundtable discussions. The cases are structured in a manner that will make projects legible on a very basic level, describing who was involved, how it was supported, and what happened. We have also asked each of the case study teams to describe their own approach to measuring impact. With only 45 case studies, this book provides more data points than it does conclusions, but our hope is that presenting the cases in this format allows the reader to get to know the work in a deeper way with regard to both impact and questions of business and organizational models. Too often these dimensions are left out of case studies in this field.

While we acknowledge that different political, economic, social, and cultural contexts make it difficult to create a depth of comparison between projects in different regions, we also recognize that practitioners of design for social innovation can still feel isolated. As the DSI field is maturing, we must strengthen the many communities of practice that are forming within it, and knowledge sharing among designers is key. The ability to compare and contrast one's experiences with that of others to identify reference points and find patterns of similarity and difference fuels the collective confidence and potential of DSI overall as a field. The sustainability of a field comes easier when those in the thick of it feel that they have a cohort of peers who they can learn from, collaborate with, and even compete against.

As you will see when reading the cases, the distinction between designer and non-designer (and in some cases also the line between service provider and commissioner, client, or partner) is waning in relevance as the nature of this type of design work becomes increasingly collaborative and participatory. Regardless of how one identifies professionally, our goal has been to help readers contextualize their understanding of social innovation within a global context. It used to be the case that a philanthropic foundation or government who hired designers was a rare occurrence indeed. Fortunately, the world has changed and that is no longer the case, as can be seen simply by scanning the impressive list of organizations that are highlighted as "clients" (in the broadest sense) in these cases. Nevertheless, because the design process asks those who commission it to be comfortable outside the common logic of linear, quantitatively inclined ways of working and top-down strategic planning and decision-making processes, it puts individuals commissioning design work at risk of being perceived by their peers as acting in a manner that is risky and untested. To counter this, it is important to aggregate a wide variety of examples showing how design has been applied to very complex challenges with grace—and concrete results. Sustainability involves organizations happily commissioning future design or social innovation work and hiring their own designers; this book includes examples of both.

There is also a historical impetus for our interest in focusing on a selection of case study projects. In 2016, the editors of this volume penned *LEAP Dialogues*,[3] a book that captured a polyphony of more than 80 individuals, mostly working in the United States, describing how they were able to build a career in design for social innovation. The focus of *LEAP Dialogues* was often intensely personal, even including "day in the life" essays that illuminated the professional rhythms of a handful of practitioners. What we found during that project is that design for social innovation had many small footholds across a wide variety of organizations as disparate as Nike, the Bill & Melinda Gates Foundation, and the federal government of the United States, but that these examples sometimes felt tenuous in ways similar to the story of the Laboratorio.

The LEAP dialoguers each fought in their own way to convince managers, clients, partners, and peers that design had a meaningful role to play in philanthropy, business, government, and civil society. Personal fortitude features prominently throughout that book. Many if not all of the individuals whose stories are highlighted came to design for social innovation with formal training in some other subject, such as the traditional design fields, because, by and large, they started their careers before design for social innovation was formalized into programs of study. By the time the *LEAP Dialogues* book was released, however, the world was different and there were already a variety of places to study design for social innovation or related perspectives, as well as deeper and diversifying research on the subject.

As authors, we are also design and architecture educators, and we are encouraged by the evolution of design education curricula and educational offerings. With descriptions such as service design, strategic design, social design, transdisciplinary design, and transition design, some of the most effective programs today manage to avoid the trap of design "solutionism" that has become synonymous with human-centered design. In place of easy answers, "critical pedagogies"[4] enable students to become reflective practitioners and principled citizens. The best programs keep idealism and a sense of purpose intact while teaching against the reductive seduction that "doing good for others" can so easily invite. We cannot quite claim that the current generation of graduates is leaving our schools with a fully embodied comprehension of the grit, patience, and humility DSI demands—such learning comes from the doing. That said, these are individuals who are entering the field with a healthy dose of criticality, self-awareness, and much more than an inkling of the systemic complexity they will be encountering head-on.

We see in our students a widespread desire to engage in socially meaningful work, though not all are fortunate enough to find a supportive place to practice in this way immediately upon graduation. Anecdotally, it would seem that there's a deeper well of design talent interested in social innovation than there are organizations yet seeking that talent. Likewise, among design practitioners we see a broad interest in mission-driven work and applying design methods and mindsets at a strategic and systems level of intervention. Alas, connecting that intention to real projects still takes some doing. Acknowledging this reality of design for social innovation today, we set out to assess the ongoing maturation of the field so that, in part, we could confidently tell our students that the future they see for themselves is a legitimate and growing option.

It's not just our students who are asking questions about the effectiveness of their tools and methods, and contending with the limitations of the mainstays of design education today, such as human-centered design and participatory practices. Practitioners and students alike are aware that many of our popular design and social change narratives remain riddled with problematic asymmetries of power, class, race, gender, and geography. As we watch the centers of gravity of our globalized world diversify and become displaced, the shortcomings of the 20th-century industrial era's design canon, dominated by the Global North, are coming into full view. The good news is that we can point to encouraging signposts that a more inclusive approach to DSI is emerging.

Focusing on projects that have been implemented in some manner usefully directs our attention toward examples where the teams doing the work have sought validation of their hypotheses, which is another area where design for social innovation is showing new maturity. Examples like Kuja Kuja (p320) and the Financial Literacy for Ecuadorian Microentrepreneurs project (p170) demonstrate how designers are integrating quantified validation in their work, alongside qualitative self-reflection that has been pervasive in design practice for some time. Validating the outcomes of one's project demands that the project actually transitions off the whiteboard, which in turn brings the details of implementation more clearly into the core of the project. As a colleague put it rather more poetically,

"innovations will wither on the vine without a clear path to implementation."
We're seeing less patience for blue sky thinking and more of an appetite to get design practice out under actual blue skies, tested by the real world but also having a clear impact in the real world.

As demonstrated by the projects we highlight, designers appear to be much less naive about walking into contested spaces claiming some kind of neutrality. Through highly transdisciplinary and multi-stakeholder initiatives such as the Civil Society Innovation Hubs (p364), we see that building trust between all of the actors involved in design for social innovation is not a side effect of the work but a primary enabler. Social innovation is the work of answering society's old questions in new ways, and it is seemingly impossible to do so in a transactional mode. This makes the traditional mystery that surrounds design practice and methods untenable. None of the projects in this book involve magical efforts by designers which are then revealed to astonished clients, like a sparkling new kitchen unveiled at the end of a home makeover television show. Instead, projects like Equity by Design Immersive Series (p74) and the Edmonton Shift Lab Collective 1.0 (p66) show us that design for social innovation is increasingly being used to break open the precious "sealed box" process previously used to exclude many from the acts of design and the decision making that happens therein. Where genius exists in this book, it is not personified by lone creatives, but embodied by trusting collectives.

Executing projects that directly touch the lives of some of the most marginalized members of society amplifies the stakes of design for social innovation, and the partners that fund and commission this work are right to be careful about adopting new practices. The cases in this book demonstrate the extent to which the buy-in of funders and partners makes or breaks a project. The cycles of reciprocal learning with design teams become heightened when projects recur or grow over long durations, as in Paddy to Plate (p262), Solo Kota Kita (p358), and The Human Account (p120). Unquestionably, this deeper alignment between DSI practitioners and their partners across sectors should be a source of optimism. The manifestation of projects that are operating at mounting scales of intervention and involving multiple actors is an indicator of the growing adoption of design by players across the spectrum of social innovation.

That's the positive story, but design for social innovation is still finding its footing in numerous ways. All too many DSI projects remain high-cost experiments and bespoke solutions that struggle to move beyond the pilot stage of implementation. When this reality is acknowledged by the team, as in the case of Nest co-study spaces in Tel Aviv (p220), it can be a productive learning outcome, but when this tendency is swept under the rug it perpetuates the image of design as an ineffectual and resource-intensive way of working.

While the cases in this book employ 37 different methods of measuring the impact of design for social innovation work, truly identifying and understanding the unique contributions of the design process and the role of the designers involved remains a less than obvious task. This difficulty partially stems from the highly collaborative nature of work, but the ambiguity here is further amplified by the gap between the technocratic and often mechanistic orientation of the structures in place which are opposite of the free-form and generative organizational environments that typically nurture creative processes and enable innovation to flourish. Is it reasonable to use the logics of yesterday to assess outcomes that represent elements of tomorrow?

Every One Every Day (p180) provides a useful example through which to consider this rhetorical question. The project presents a possibility of community activation that is outside or parallel to the status quo of economic and governance structures of the UK. It asks us to ponder what success and growth look like in such a project. Does growth equate with more money, more jobs, and a bigger footprint, per many of our accepted norms? Or is it possible through a project such as this to see new ways of understanding growth and progress, not on the terms of industrial society but as determined by members of a community themselves.

The contradictions lingering in this brief assessment of the current state of design for social innovation are why we felt compelled to mark this moment in time with a survey of practices around the world. We set out to understand it from two angles: by gathering a broad set of representative, concrete examples in the form of cases; and by inviting a diverse mix of thinkers to join roundtable discussion reflecting on themes emergent from the case study research.

With DSI efforts being multi-stakeholder, intensely collaborative, and social in nature, one of the challenges of writing about it is that parsing exactly what was done and how it was accomplished can be difficult. In an attempt to keep the research grounded, we focused the case studies on projects rather than organizations or teams. Projects as the unit of analysis offer a ripe nexus between teams of "doers" and their clients or commissioning bodies, as well as between intentions and impact. This allowed us to get more specific about the details of who did the work, critical contextual factors that enabled the efforts, what was done, and the impacts. In recognition of the contours of each project, we've chosen to present the cases as narratives. We crafted these over several iterative and collaborative rounds of writing from survey data and the insights provided by the teams whose work is featured.

In addition to the written narrative, we collected metadata about each of the cases. Our intention in presenting the metadata is to get concrete about the details of the work in a format that is standardized across very disparate contexts.[5] However imperfect this approach may be, it gives the reader the ability to compare and contrast the case studies more directly so that points of difference and convergence become easier to spot. Indeed, visualizing the cases in a literal sense became a fascination for us as well. Each case is presented with a "flower" graph that is generated using the data we collected about the project, explained in more detail on page 38.

We sourced case studies through a bottom-up process that started with an open call via the web to submit projects that the submitter considered to be a recently completed (or ongoing) exemplar of design for social innovation, defined in whatever way they saw fit. This effort was bolstered by the contributions of an International Editorial Advisory Board[6] with deep and diverse knowledge of the work happening in their regions and around the world. In addition to the requirement that the projects be implemented in some fashion, we sought case studies that were lesser known to the international community. The result was nearly 200 submissions.

We spent long hours winnowing this large pool down to a set of 45, while using the projects as lenses onto the world—what do they tell us about design for social innovation practice right now? Where are the hotspots of interest, excitement, or struggle? What causes the threads of similarity that we see streaking through these projects? Seemingly simple questions such as the location of the designers compared to the location of the client or partner organization became entry points into more complicated issues. Understanding the geography of a project in more discrete terms leads quickly to questions of power. From where and to where does the money flow? Who's making decisions and how well do they understand the context? Knowing more about who was involved and the type of their organization allows us to begin to understand modes of partnership and collaboration. Getting precise about what was created during a project represented an invitation to confront the strengths and also the edges of DSI practices.

In other words, the intention has been to capture projects through these case studies that, while singular and specific endeavors, allow us to start gaining a more integrative view of DSI practice overall, especially when viewing these projects as a set. The metadata analysis and the complementary insights that emerge in the roundtable discussions engage with the tension between projects and practice, between parts and wholes.

Once we made the final selection of case studies, it was energizing to zoom out and look for thematic veins that ran across them. A handful of themes emerged: power, international development, organizing models, partnerships, mediums of change, measuring impact, and growth. We chose to organize the book's chapters with each of these themes and anchor them with roundtable discussions that brought together academics, practitioners, and case study contributors. Needless to say, while these seven themes are critical to the future of DSI, they are far from simple to capture, let alone resolve, by gathering just a few individual perspectives for a single discussion.

In the section that follows, we summarize the chapters of the book while presenting findings from our study of the quantitative data that emerged from the aggregate view of 45 case studies from around the world.

Geographies of Power

Power is ever-present in social settings, yet often hard to identify, and harder still to talk about, which is why it is a critical topic for the future of design for social innovation. Mariana Amatullo, Fatou Wurie of UNICEF, Ahmed Ansari of NYU, and Shana Agid of Parsons School of Design at The New School address power and its embodiment and distribution across varied geographies in this discussion. Interrelationships across space, people, institutions, and political economies is at the center of this roundtable.

How does power play out in problem-definition, problem-solving, and in the narrative of the project and solution? Who is given credit in a project and whose voices are lifted up? What shapes the directional flows of power, including education, perceived or promoted expertise, tools and resources? To date, many of these things have flowed from the Global North (and, more specifically, Western Europe and North America) into the Global South.

Anchored by three educators, this roundtable also delves into design education and its relationship with practice and community-based work, including themes of colonialism and the legacy of design's formal emergence as a discipline in the industrial era. They question a pervasive myth in design education, challenging the notion that it is possible for the designer to ever be neutral. Design for social innovation, with participatory practices at its core, is inherently relational. Design education must not only shed the myth of neutrality but also must look to new texts, histories, and contexts as they seek to find an ethical and truly successful way forward. Designers, this discussion tells us, should also widen their understanding of what it means to "be a designer" and to become more inclusive of multidisciplinary and community expertise in that regard.

HOW DOES ONE BECOME A SOCIAL INNOVATION DESIGNER IN YOUR COUNTRY OR REGION?

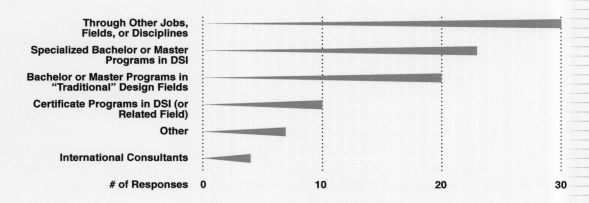

In addition to providing information about their projects, we asked case study respondents to tell us about the state of design for social innovation in their region. The majority of contributors responded that designers enter into social innovation through other fields or disciplines. As one respondent explained, "There are numerous routes into teams like ours in the UK. Whilst practical design skills are important, they are not a prerequisite for the strategic design and policy work we do in our team. We are more likely to recruit for potential and mindset rather than specific or accredited design skills."

Trajectories of International Development

Design for social innovation has grown as a practice in international development with the adoption of design methods and designers in key agencies such as UNICEF Innovation; the Airbel Impact Lab at IRC (International Rescue Committee), and the Amplify Program at DFID (the former UK Department for International Development), to name a few. Due to its complexity, international development is perhaps one of the trickiest areas for designers to navigate as effective contributors, making it essential to address as we think about the future of DSI.

Isabella Gady and Jenny Liu speak with Ayah Younis of the Airbel Impact Lab at the IRC; Sarah Fathallah, who applies her design practice to projects in the social sector; and Robert Fabricant of Dalberg Design. Together, they explore the extent to which design is recognized and practiced in international development, and its relevance. They reflect on the interplay between established practices of traditional international development that are rooted in the social sector, including community organizing and participatory research. They also discuss human-centered design, agile practices, and tried-and-true techniques such as prototyping in the context of this work.

Central to this discussion are the limitations of traditional funding models in the international development space. Project-based funding models hinder the ability of designers to address root causes. This funding model often stymies long-term interventions that strive for more significant impact. While competition can spur improvement and development, the panel explores how competition between designers also detracts from creating a culture of shared knowledge and best practices. The discussion further touches on money flows within the social sector and international development, and a certain dependency upon—and complicated relationship with—philanthropy. The reality is that funding is what makes international development work possible. And yet the complex mosaic of financing sources (government allocations, international donor funds, and philanthropy) and the process of securing funding can be incredibly cumbersome and resource intensive. In the worst-case scenarios, these dynamics lead to a cycle of grant-chasing that further entrenches problematic power dynamics between funder, grantee, and community members.

CASES BY LOCATION OF THE WORK

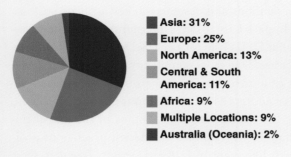

- ■ Asia: 31%
- ■ Europe: 25%
- ■ North America: 13%
- ■ Central & South America: 11%
- ■ Africa: 9%
- ■ Multiple Locations: 9%
- ■ Australia (Oceania): 2%

CASES BY LOCATION OF WORK COMPARED TO ORIGIN OF TEAM

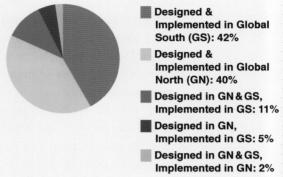

- ■ Designed & Implemented in Global South (GS): 42%
- ■ Designed & Implemented in Global North (GN): 40%
- ■ Designed in GN & GS, Implemented in GS: 11%
- ■ Designed in GN, Implemented in GS: 5%
- ■ Designed in GN & GS, Implemented in GN: 2%

This chart represents the projects in our survey and not some greater claim about the distribution of design for social innovation activity more broadly. Nonetheless, what's clear is that DSI can be found just about everywhere today.

When analyzing the projects to understand what they can tell us about the relationship between Global North and Global South, some 82% of cases were completed by teams within their own hemisphere.

Organizing the Work

Design is a team sport, and as the field of design for social innovation matures, those teams are getting larger and taking on more diverse forms. In places with active and predictable regulation and taxation systems, the form of legal entity or organization one uses to do their work can have an impact on who they get to work with and how they collaborate. Non-profit, for-profit, government, non-governmental organizations, civil society collectives, and a thousand variations are all possible, but the work of design for social innovation often does not fit neatly within these structures.

Dependent as it is upon a broad spectrum of relationships, different kinds of resources, long and fluid timelines, and open-ended methodologies, the question of how to organize as a legal entity takes on more profound meaning in the context of social innovation design efforts, and so it became the subject of a roundtable discussion in search of loopholes and other promising avenues yet unexplored. Bryan Boyer (who splits time between a for-profit and academia), Alexandra Fiorillo of GRID Impact (a social enterprise), Christian Bason of Danish Design Centre (a mostly government-funded non-profit), and Tessy Britton of the Participatory City Foundation (a charitable organization) consider the day-to-day work of design for social innovation and the gaps between the transactional, top-down structures of industrial society and the more nimble, relational approaches favored by many in the design community and growing within industry and government.

The panel addresses their desire to build longer-term relationships with partner or client organizations, and the need across the board to continue working to improve the perceived value of design. One way to index perceived value is through the volume of work that is funded via fee for service and that which is funded by government, which together account for approximately 50% of the cases in this book.

CASES BY SOURCE(S) OF FUNDING

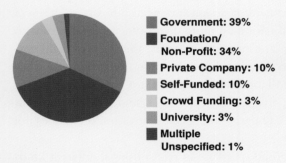

- Government: 39%
- Foundation/Non-Profit: 34%
- Private Company: 10%
- Self-Funded: 10%
- Crowd Funding: 3%
- University: 3%
- Multiple Unspecified: 1%

Projects represented in this book are heavily reliant on government and/or third sector dollars, with a less significant investment from the private sector.

CASES BY TYPE OF DESIGN ORGANIZATION

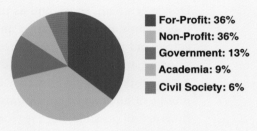

- For-Profit: 36%
- Non-Profit: 36%
- Government: 13%
- Academia: 9%
- Civil Society: 6%

For-profit and non-profit design organizations accounted for the majority (split in equal measure).

CASES BY MECHANISM(S) OF FUNDING

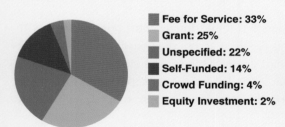

- Fee for Service: 33%
- Grant: 25%
- Unspecified: 22%
- Self-Funded: 14%
- Crowd Funding: 4%
- Equity Investment: 2%

Though much of social innovation is still grant funded, we found that a significant amount of cases (33%) are funded by fee for service. This is promising because it signals a clearly perceived value proposition by the organizations paying for services.

CASES BY PROJECT COST

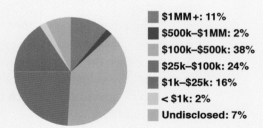

- $1MM+: 11%
- $500k–$1MM: 2%
- $100k–$500k: 38%
- $25k–$100k: 24%
- $1k–$25k: 16%
- < $1k: 2%
- Undisclosed: 7%

Contributors estimated the costs of their project, including salary. 42% of the cases feature projects with budgets of less than $100,000. Only 11% or five cases worked with budgets of more than $1 million.

Navigating Partnerships

Collaborations are integral design for social innovation, occurring as it does at the intersection of sectors, disciplines, and models. None of the 45 cases in this book—indeed, none of the 182 projects that were submitted to the initial call for case studies—feature designers working in a vacuum. Each case in this book describes some form of collaboration: formal or informal, with universities, corporations, governments, NGOs, non-profits, community organizations, advisory boards, committees, subject matter experts, and community members.

Jennifer May, Nandana Chakraborty, and Vivek Chondagar of Digital Impact Square, Jesper Christiansen of State of Change, and Fumiko Ichikawa of Re:public look at the ins-and-outs and ups-and-downs of partnering up. They examine the models, scale, and scope of the partnerships each participant is engaged in, as well as how they set clear expectations at the beginning of their collaborations. Like the ground beneath our feet, expectations inevitably shift, and what to do in those instances is a topic of lively discussion in this roundtable.

To understand partnerships on a more operational level, we asked case study respondents to tell us about the teams working on their projects. Were they small or large? Of the overall team, what was the "design quotient" or the percentage of members who identify as designers? Understanding the make-up of project teams more discretely helps the reader refine their understanding of where a "difference" is being made by designers (or not).

CASES BY TEAM SIZE

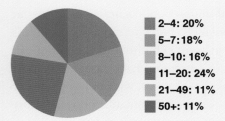

- ■ 2–4: 20%
- ■ 5–7: 18%
- ■ 8–10: 16%
- ■ 11–20: 24%
- ■ 21–49: 11%
- ■ 50+: 11%

Close to 80% of the cases consisted of small to mid-sized teams with fewer than 20 members. Only five cases feature teams of 50 or more. For the purpose of this survey, "team size" is the total number of people actively contributing to the work, regardless of which organization they belong to.

CASES BY DESIGN QUOTIENT

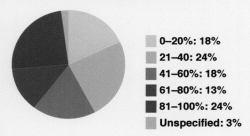

- ■ 0–20%: 18%
- ■ 21–40: 24%
- ■ 41–60%: 18%
- ■ 61–80%: 13%
- ■ 81–100%: 24%
- ■ Unspecified: 3%

We also asked teams what percentage of the total were designers, which we refer to as the "design quotient." Teams with a majority of designers represented about 42% of all cases, which reflects the trans-disciplinary and collaborative nature of the projects. Respondents were invited to define "designer" as they see fit.

Design for Social Innovation

Mediums of Change

The purpose of design for social innovation is not to make things, but to facilitate social change, so designers must carefully and deliberately connect intention with outputs. Bryan Boyer, Debbie Aung Din of Proximity Designs, Jan Chipchase of Studio D Radiodurans, and Professor Ramia Mazé of University of Arts London dig into the many "mediums" through which design for social innovation is executed. They explore how to balance the creative and exploratory aspects of the design process with funder expectations to produce work that has a clear timeline, budget, and impact.

When the work of serious social innovation includes unconventional outputs, like a bottle of bespoke moonshine which you will read about in this round-table, how do the project partners put a value on that output and ripple effects? The group sensitively teases apart the value of unexpected objects and experiences that invite stakeholders to participate in new ways, including opening their thinking to novel possibilities.

Ultimately, we learn, it requires defining and assessing the *outcomes* of a project beyond the *outputs*. Project deliverables may live on a shelf, but the most powerful examples of design for social innovation are able to make space for new knowledge, processes, methods, and questions in the hearts and memories of those who engage with it.

CASES BY DESIGN MEDIUMS

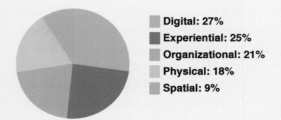

Digital: 27%

Experiential: 25%

Organizational: 21%

Physical: 18%

Spatial: 9%

Cases were analyzed to identify the "mediums" utilized, based on self-reports from case study teams describing the outputs of their work. From this analysis, the editorial team identified five categories listed in the graph above. The breadth of different outputs is a humbling reminder that creativity in how social change is manifested is critical to matching intentions and outcomes within the unique context of each project.

36 MEDIUMS WERE FOUND ACROSS ALL CASES

Digital (8)

App
Chatbot
E-Book
Network
SMS
Social Media
   Communications
Software
Website

Experiential (4)

Education
Event
Training
Workshop

Organizational (6)

Business
Policies
Incubator
Innovation Lab
Non-Profit
Service

Physical (14)

Beehive
Billboard
Book
Calendar
Device
Furniture
Game
Information Guide
Journal
Medical Device
Poster
Rainwater Harvesting
   System
Teaching Aid
Training Manual

Spatial (4)

Exhibition
Interior Space
Repurposed Building
Urban Design

Design for Social Innovation

ORGANIZATIONAL, EXPERIENTIAL, AND DIGITAL MEDIUMS ARE MOST COMMON

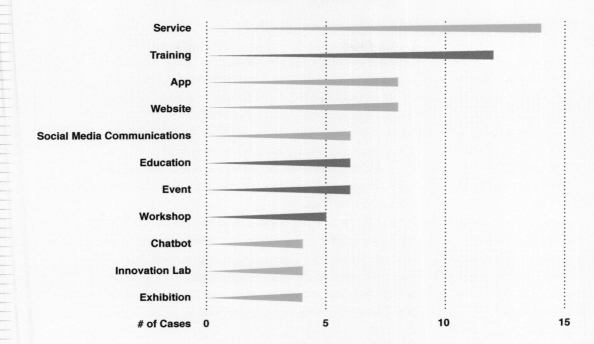

KEY
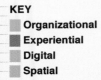
Organizational
Experiential
Digital
Spatial

Almost one third of the projects involved the creation of a new service in some form, indicating that service design is an essential medium for contemporary design. Unsurprisingly, digital mediums such as websites, apps, social media, and chatbots were also highly indexed.

Measuring Impact

Design for social innovation does not matter unless it creates an impact in the world—and not just any impact but a positive and desired one. Mariana Amatullo, Stuart Candy of Carnegie Mellon's School of Design, Chris Larkin of IDEO.org and Joyce Yee of the School of Design, Northumbria University, convened to discuss how designers assess whether their work is producing positive outcomes by design. Through their multifaceted conversation, the panelists surface three key barriers to measuring impact.

First, design for social innovation occurs at the intersections of sectors and disciplines and involves many stakeholders. Practitioners are often working through ambiguity, defining problem statements, research methods, and other project factors as they go. Taken together, this makes it difficult to identify clear theories of change and parameters for success.

Second, consultancy-based work is often mismatched to goals of design for social innovation initiatives. Developing and deploying methodologies for measuring impact takes time, especially for projects aimed at behavior change or social outcomes that take time to be adopted at scale. When design work is done under a consultancy model, the ideas are usually handed over to a partner to implement, subverting the possibility (and, some argue, imperative) to learn and adjust from the process of delivery.

Third, evaluation methods for design practices are immature, and the typical frameworks and methodologies used in international development, philanthropy, and social sciences do not always capture the intricacies of designed outcomes. Additionally, whether working across the globe or in one's own neighborhood, power and cultural dynamics inevitably shape what success looks like, and for whom.

PRIMARY IMPACT CATEGORY

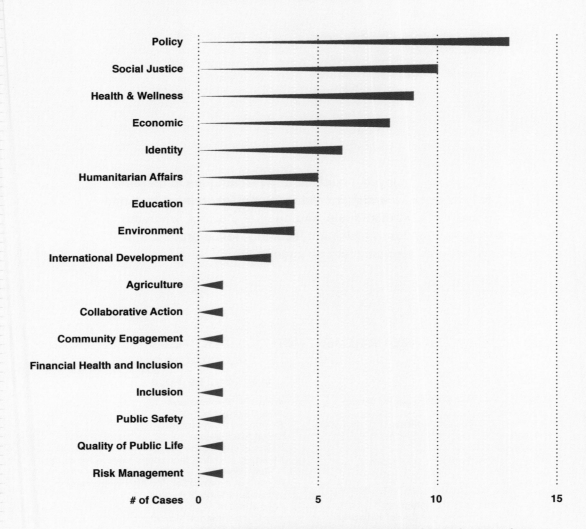

Category	# of Cases

Policy
Social Justice
Health & Wellness
Economic
Identity
Humanitarian Affairs
Education
Environment
International Development
Agriculture
Collaborative Action
Community Engagement
Financial Health and Inclusion
Inclusion
Public Safety
Quality of Public Life
Risk Management

# of Cases   0   5   10   15

Case study contributors were asked to select a primary category of impact for their projects among Health & Wellness, Environment, Education, Social Justice, Identity (gender, culture, race), Economic, Policy, International Development, Humanitarian Affairs and Other, with some write-in responses noted in the graph above. Contributors were also able to select a secondary category of impact, which is included on the case study pages.

CASES BY IMPACT MEASUREMENT APPROACH

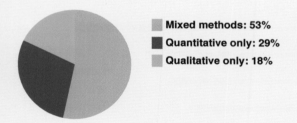

■ Mixed methods: 53%
■ Quantitative only: 29%
■ Qualitative only: 18%

The majority of cases employed mixed methods techniques to measure the impact of their work. Quantitative methods of measurement included surveys, randomized controlled trials, and number of users, whereas qualitative methods included participant feedback, focus groups, and stakeholder interviews. See full chart on page 31.

TABLE OF ALL IMPACT MEASUREMENT METHODS IDENTIFIED

QUALITATIVE METHODS

Adoption by the Organization and/or Other
  Organizations
Assessment of Change to Internal Organizational
  Practices
Awards Received
Evaluative Case Study
Focus Groups
Mystery Client Visits
Observational Research
Observed Community Participation
Observed Formation of New Social Networks
Observed Impact on Policy
Participant/Client/User Feedback
Stakeholder Interviews
Surveys
Team Reflections

QUANTITATIVE METHODS

Academic Publications
Cost Savings
Evaluative Assessment
Event Attendance
External Impact Evaluator
Financial Viability, Including Funding/Revenue
  Generated
Growth in Product/Service Adoption or Usage
Headcount/Time of Participation
Jobs Created
Key Environmental Indicators
Number of Financially Viable Projects
Number of Inquiries
Number of Projects Initiated
Observed Formation of New Social Networks
Participants/Stakeholders Trained
Project Replication/Citation by Other Groups
Quantity or Area of Spaces Created
Randomized Controlled Trial
Response Rate
Surveys
Verified Sharing of Learning Experiences
Volume of Media Coverage
Web/Mobile Analytics

Design for Social Innovation

MOST COMMON WAYS TO MEASURE IMPACT

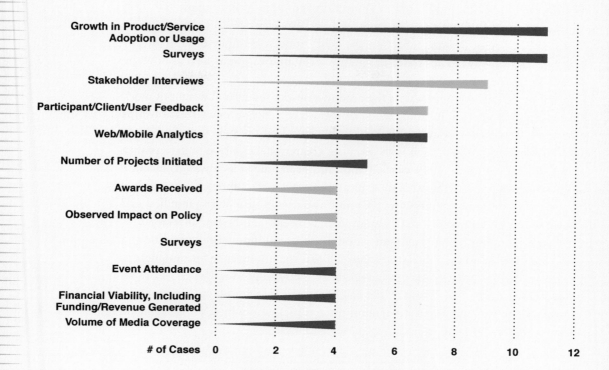

| # of Cases | 0 | 2 | 4 | 6 | 8 | 10 | 12 |

Growth in Product/Service Adoption or Usage
Surveys
Stakeholder Interviews
Participant/Client/User Feedback
Web/Mobile Analytics
Number of Projects Initiated
Awards Received
Observed Impact on Policy
Surveys
Event Attendance
Financial Viability, Including Funding/Revenue Generated
Volume of Media Coverage

KEY
■ Quantitative
■ Qualitative

The diversity of methods of measuring impact reveals that project teams are still exploring new ways to track design for social innovation activities, which we take to be a broadly positive finding. Among the methods, the top three were a common-sense approach of monitoring product/service adoption and use, surveys that result in some form of quantitative summary, and stakeholder interviews.

Positioning for Growth

Finally, Andrew Shea, Indy Johar of Project 00 and Dark Matter Labs, Gabriella Gómez-Mont of Experimentalista (whose story also kicks off this introduction), and Panthea Lee of Reboot reflect on the field's trajectory. They discuss the current plurality of ways to approach design for social innovation as well as how the field is evolving.

Central to this roundtable is the need to consider the ethical weight of working within broken systems and, when doing so, to redefine one's relationships to such systems. This point highlights a goal shared by the panelists (and many designers in this book), which is to promote greater participation in governance and self determination. While participation has been lauded as a way to increase responsiveness of government, that aspiration comes with subtle challenges. Is it fair to ask community members to take time away from their work, families, and lives to participate in fixing systems they didn't "break" in the first place?

The panel interrogates whether design for social innovation could be anything but small-p political in nature; they address the importance for designers to be involved in the creation of new governance, knowledge, and design of organizational structures. They point to the role that designers are playing to facilitate conversations and collaboration around these topics, and why it's important for them to embrace their agency during these processes.

Design for Social Innovation

WHAT ARE THE KEY CHALLENGES WITHIN YOUR REGION TO DESIGN FOR SOCIAL INNOVATION?

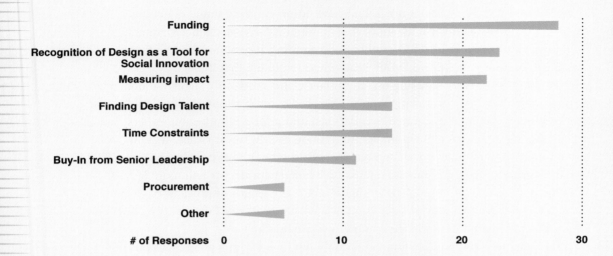

Funding

Recognition of Design as a Tool for Social Innovation

Measuring impact

Finding Design Talent

Time Constraints

Buy-In from Senior Leadership

Procurement

Other

\# of Responses   0   10   20   30

Across the 45 cases, funding, recognition of design's role in social innovation, and measuring impact were the most common challenges noted. Though few in number, the write-in responses to "Other" are indicative of the future of design for social innovation, and so we list them here: access to design education, white supremacy and institutional racism, finding designers who understand behavior or cognitive science, complexity [of the work] and lack of precedents, politics and regulations, and proper scoping of projects.

The End of the Beginning

Let us go out on a limb and imagine that you won't be satisfied by knowing that compelling examples of design for social innovation can be found on six continents, with goals as diverse as improving community dynamics in apartment buildings, to supporting LGTBQ+ rights, to expanding access to clean drinking water. We suspect you will nod your head when reminded that college degrees are offered in (or largely focusing on) the subject, and show only slightly more interest in the fact that organizations including the United Nations, national and local governments, globally active foundations, and a long tail of many others are employing designers to help make progress on the thorniest issues. If these assumptions of ours have proven correct, it's because the type of people who are drawn to design and social innovation alike are hungry for deeper and more lasting change. If you've been working in this area for any length of time, all of the facts stated above will likely be reassuring, but still not satisfying. Sure, design for social innovation has some legitimacy now... so what next?

The answer to that question is precisely why we felt this project was important. In focusing on articulating the impacts of design for social innovation efforts, we hope that this survey will contribute to the growing and necessary discussion about the forms of evidence that designers use to know when their efforts are successful or not. Though true that the qualitative, relative, and often indirect outcomes that designers value cannot be readily reduced to numerical metrics, we owe it to ourselves as practitioners to build scaffolding between ways of knowing and doing, between regions, and between disciplines. In short, more discussions of what's working and what's not.

Humanity has some thousands of years of cumulative experience tabulating activities in the neat columns of a financial ledger. If it's hard to figure out how to measure the impact of social, emotional, non-human, or environmental impacts (just to name a few alternative priorities), this should not come as a surprise. Rather, it's an opportunity for continued, careful innovation with as much creativity as is applied to the projects detailed here.

This survey also hopes to prompt a discussion of how we draw comparisons across work that is so necessarily situated in the ontological and epistemological contexts of individual communities and unique geographies. As important as it is to apply an intersectional analysis, we also seek ways to draw comparisons across vastly different groups without capitulating to universalist frameworks. Pairing case study metadata and free-form narratives is our attempt to balance these competing lenses.

Every book is an artifact of its time. As this one goes to press in 2021, we see the world slowly emerging from the throes of the global pandemic. It is too soon to imagine the post-Coronavirus world fully. Still, it is already clear COVID-19 has only emphasized existing weaknesses in the systems of everyday life. This global health catastrophe has illuminated how interconnected everything is: health, social, environmental, and economic impacts all spill into each other. The pandemic has precipitated a unique cultural and social moment—a time of reckoning around the world that is bound to have ripple effects for the future of the field of design for social innovation.

Though named for the year 2019, the impact of the novel coronavirus that recently reshaped the globe is sure to last far longer. Likewise, when considering this survey of global DSI practices, it is apparent that the field has matured in ways that seemed far-fetched even just a decade ago. With vaccinations now being distributed and the grip of the virus apparently loosening ever so slightly, the global public health situation and the state of design for social innovation share one thing in common: in both regards it feels as if we've only just reached the end of the beginning.

1   For clarity, we have adopted the phrase "design for social innovation" in the title of this book to connect with the established term (and the acronym "DSI") that refers to a maturing subset of design practices, research, and education applied within the multidisciplinary field of social innovation. The cases selected in our book refer to social innovation both as an intentional process that involves interactive learning and leads to social change. This kind of so-called innovation work can be found today in government, business, and civil society around the world. Ezio Manzini, the founder of the DESIS Network (Design for Social Innovation and Sustainability), offers a useful articulation: "In the twenty-first century, social innovation will be interwoven with design as both stimulus and objective. That is, it will stimulate design as much as technical innovation did in the twentieth century, and at the same time social innovation will be what a growing proportion of design activities will be seeking to achieve. As a matter of fact, design has all the potentialities to play a major role in triggering and supporting social change and therefore becoming *design for social innovation*. Today we are at the beginning of this journey and we still need a better understanding of the possibilities." See Ezio Manzini, *Design, When Everybody Designs: An Introduction to Design for Social Innovation*, trans. Rachel Coad (Cambridge, Mass.; London: MIT Press, 2015).

2   Other high-profile peers that applied a design-led approach to public sector innovation, are also no longer in existence. This is the case of the Helsinki Design Lab, established by the Finnish Innovation Fund Sitra, which closed in 2013, and MindLab in Denmark, which closed in 2018 after 16 years in existence. Considered one of the first public sector innovation labs to apply design methods, Mindlab was housed at the intersection of the Danish Ministry of Industry, Business and Financial Affairs, the Ministry of Employment and the Ministry of Education.

3   Mariana Amatullo et al., *LEAP Dialogues: Career Pathways in Design for Social Innovation* (Pasadena, Calif.: Designmatters at ArtCenter College of Design, 2016).

4   The concept of "critical pedagogy" was first introduced by the Brazilian philosopher and educator Paulo Freire in 1968 in his foundational text, *Pedagogy of the Oppressed*, published in English by Herder and Herder, New York, 1972.

5   The data gathered was self-reported by the case study contributors and then processed by our editorial team for clarity and consistency. For details of this process, see the Methodology section (page 391).

6   For a full list, see page 405. We also invited a handful of our international advisors to contribute their perspectives as roundtable discussants. We are indebted to Ahmed Ansari, Christian Bason, Jesper Christiansen, Fumiko Ichikawa, Gabriella Gómez-Mont, and Joyce Yee for their dual contributions to our book.

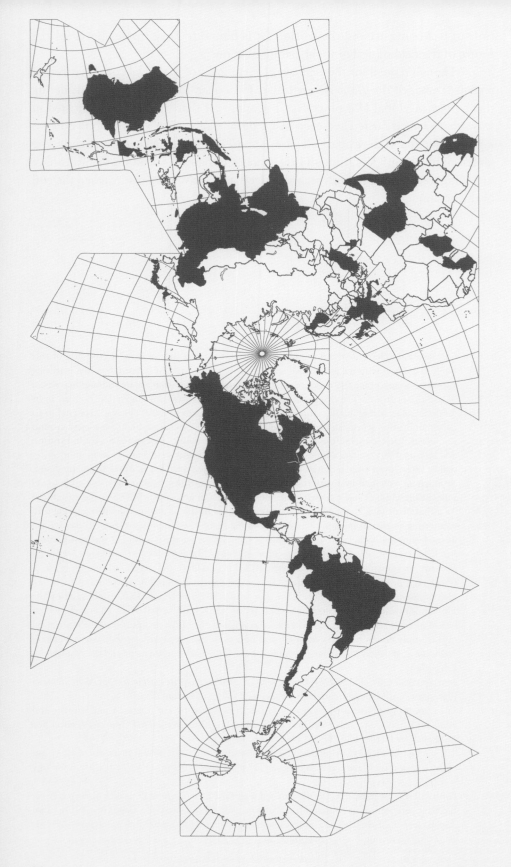

CASES BY CONTINENT

Flower Diagram Key

Accompanying each case study is a page of data describing the who, what, and how of the project. This has been visualized in a unique "flower diagram" using data about team, funding, and outputs of the project. Below is an explanation of how to read the flowers at a glance.

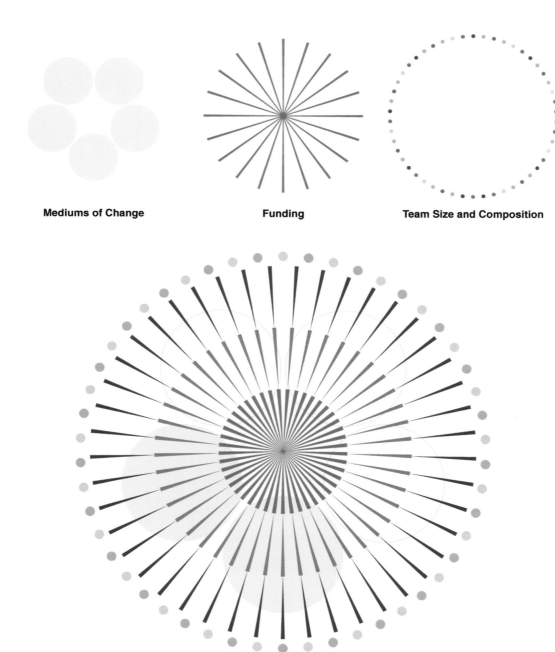

Mediums of Change   **Funding**   **Team Size and Composition**

Example: a project with sizable funding from three sources, executed by a team of many collaborators who are approximately 50% designers operating in a non-profit fashion, resulting in physical and experiential outputs

Scale of Funding

Case study teams reported the cost of the project on the scale below, reported in US Dollars. Costs is defined as salary and project expenditures or the total fee for consultancy-based projects.

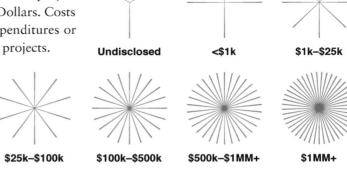

Undisclosed	<$1k	$1k–$25k

$25k–$100k	$100k–$500k	$500k–$1MM+	$1MM+

Source of Funding

The lines of the diagram are colored in based on the source(s) of funding. Where multiple sources are present, the lines are broken into sections. Teams did not report the relative percentage of each funding source, so multiple line segments indicate the presence of multiple sources but do not describe proportionality.

Foundation / Non-Profit / Endowment Government Private Company

Crowd Funding Self-Funded University

Multiple Sources

Mediums of Change

Each of the five pale circles represents a different category of design medium. If that medium is present in the case, the flower diagram will show it as filled in.

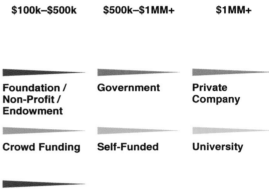

Digital Organizational

Physical Spatial

Experiential

Team Size and Composition

Information about the team is represented by an array of dots around the outside of the flower. The quantity of dots describes the approximate team size based on seven self-reported categories from 1 to 50+. More dots, more people. The color of these dots describes the composition of the team as non-designer or designer, with the latter group further described with one of five different types of organizations. Teams did not report the relative percentage of each type of design organization where multiple are present, so colors indicate the presence of multiple types but do not describe proportionality.

- For-Profit Designer
- Non-Profit Designer
- Government Designer
- Academic Designer
- Civil Society Designer
- Non-Designer

Geographies of Power

Shana Agid, Ahmed Ansari, and Fatou Wurie, with Mariana Amatullo

At the heart of the definition of power is one's ability to influence an outcome or an action. Richard McKeon, the American 20th-century philosopher responsible for drafting the Human Rights Declaration, emphasizes the capacity that power brings in generating change, for better or for worse. Power becomes the act of "influencing the actions of others or in forestalling the effects of their actions."[1] On the other hand, geography is commonly understood as the study of places and the relationships between people and their environments. Geographies also signal interrelationships across space, people, institutions, and political economies. The distinguished critic of development, Colombian-American anthropologist Arturo Escobar is a critical reference in this roundtable. Escobar's concept of the pluriverse—a world in which many worlds fit—one where the relational becomes core to the design act, provides a helpful lens vis-à-vis the provocation that frames this discussion.[2]

Fatou Wurie, Ahmed Ansari, and Shana Agid are colleagues working locally and globally. Each of them is deeply committed to addressing power and its embodiment and distribution across varied geographies. The reflections they offer touch upon design education, design practice, and their intersectionality with international development and community work. Their critical observations and the many entanglements they surface serve in many ways as a through-line that informs and extends the insights we glean from all 45 case studies in this publication.

Several salient take-aways emerge from the roundtable that are worth highlighting. In no particular order, ten stand out:

#1: The "romance" of design education with neutrality and the associated myth of the designer's neutral stance

#2: The importance of paying attention to "directional flows" of knowledge production, particularly in transnational exchanges and in community-based work

#3: The recognition of ever-present power-laden dynamics that reveal unequal expressions of power, whether it may be based on race, age, gender, sexuality, language, class, or geography

#4: The responsibility to name one's own privilege and acknowledge structural inequities

#5: The limitations of well-meaning human-centered design methods

#6: The Western, patriarchal, and Cartesian logics that often remain entrenched in design as a legacy of the discipline's emergence in the industrial era

#7: The reckoning with the problematic legacy of the "Colonial project" and a new-found awareness about the systematic erasing of difference that logics of development and globalization perpetuate

#8: The opportunity to widen our understanding of "what it takes to be a designer" and recognize multidisciplinarity and community expertise

#9: The fundamental relational aspect of design and participation: it is about building relationships—and trust—with people, "making power" in solidarity

#10: The call to imagine and reimagine a world where different worlds can exist

This is an honest, reflexive, and clear-eyed discussion. It reminds us that design mediates all of our realities and that there is ongoing hard work and humility called for when we engage in design for social innovation projects that have an aspiration for positive impact.

The discussion took place at the end of August 2020 and was edited for clarity and length

Fatou Wurie

My name is Fatou Wurie. I am from Sierra Leone, currently based in New York and on my way to relocating to UN Headquarters in Geneva. I work for UNICEF as the emergency specialist leading on digital engagement. I specialize in how to leverage the use of "the digital" and various technologies to improve our people-centered approaches to emergency responses. Outside my role at UNICEF, I consider myself first and foremost a storyteller and a social justice activist. For over a decade prior, my work has been based out of the continent of Africa, where I am from, and which has always been situated at the intersection of gender, health, and innovation—issues that continue to shape my professional interests today.

Ahmed Ansari

I am Ahmed Ansari, an industry assistant professor at the Integrated Digital Media Program at New York University in the Department of Technology, Culture and Society within the School of Engineering. My work unfolds at the intersection of design studies and history, decolonial and post-colonial theory, and the history and philosophy of technology, with an area focus on South Asia.

Shana Agid

My name is Shana Agid, I am an associate professor of Art, Media, and Communication at Parsons School of Design at The New School. My work in design focuses on a kind of use/application/research into service design and participatory design. More specifically, I look at the relationship of design to social movements, and to collaborative practices for working with community-based organizations including public schools. I think about what it means to engage in "self-determined design" as a means to consider relational practices and building practices with people.

Mariana: What does the phrase "geographies of power" prompt for each of you in the context of your practices and the focus of this book?

Fatou: These days I am participating in a variety of conversations where we are interrogating power. I am reflecting on what it all means from both a personal and professional perspective. In the context of UNICEF as a multilateral institution, there seem to be many more opportunities to have these discussions, and more vigorously than in the past. It feels quite important, because we don't necessarily always engage with notions of power, its location, and its fluidity with the heightened awareness we are showing now.

Some of the critical questions for me are about how power is interrogated, and where it is perceived and/or located in the way we design. I am interested in how power plays out in our presentation of solutions and whose voice(s) are those that emerge as most prominent in these narratives. I believe we can interpret "geographies of power" to mean more than the physical location of where power and powerful ideas reside. It is also about understanding the flow and combinations of where social innovation solutions and practices are coming from, how they are advanced, what sort of limitations and opportunities we see emerge. In sum, I look forward to interrogating how we think about power, who gets to create what for whom, and what this transnational exchange looks like.

Shana: Geographers such as Ruth Wilson Gilmore help us to interrogate the relationships between space, place, and power, and time, especially in relation to the control of people and resources. I think this has incredible resonance for design. How do we understand and read those relationships of power, how do we acknowledge and work with them, in design? This can take the shape of engaging power in relation to space or place, absolutely, and also lead us to think critically about time and temporality. We frequently lose sight in design of the fact that what the present looks like is deeply influenced by the past. Design is often oriented toward creating "a better future." Who gets to decide what is "better"? And how is that determined—through what lenses of time, place, space, etc.? This is one of the consequential questions.

We tend to privilege the idea of innovation in design as an attachment to the novel. We like to celebrate the notion of replacing things and the idea that there's always something better. Fully embracing geographies of power in design means to upset somehow the very notion that design has the capacity to create things that are better. In fact, I think it raises questions about design as inquiry. Accepting this position necessitates a willingness to be interrupted and the humility to be wrong.

There's something really compelling about the ways in which power relations are present, no matter where we are. I am reminded of this community where I have been working with the same group of people for six years—teachers and students at the Washington Heights Expeditionary Learning School (WHEELS), a regular district public school in New York City—in one neighborhood. All of our interactions and work happen within a radius of ten to 20 blocks. The ways in which these ten blocks or so represent people's movements in and around the world are deeply implicated in what people need, what we make, and in the knowledge that people bring with them. The discipline of geography becomes a useful framing to understand the relationship of space, of borders, and of movement. Taking the time to theorize and to work from a systems perspective in a grounded manner, in this case, is very helpful.

> **Ahmed:** My work deals with geographies in wide-ranging ways. I tend to think of power as emerging out of, and produced through, relations and by things that are done when people are in relation to each other. This includes the history of knowledge production, practices, materialization, making, and of course design. One of the threads that I pay a lot of attention to is how power unfolds through relations of colonization, through policies, and through acts of design and the designing of infrastructures such as technology in different parts of the world at various junctures of time.

> I am also interested in geographies of power vis-à-vis attending to the complexity in the relationship between the local and the global. The phenomenon of globalization that we see unfolding over the last few hundred years raises particular issues today in relation to matters of difference and of knowledge production. It also leads to quite a few anxieties, especially about how knowledge discourses flow from one part of the world to another. The direction of these flows enacts, builds, and develops particular relations of power. For example, the arrival of "design thinking" in places like South Asia illustrates how design methods that were initially constructed and framed with certain Western, North American, and European knowledge models landed in this corner of the world. That does things—both locally and globally. It prefigures the way design education and design practice are set up in many parts of the world. Paying attention to how power flows in and across the global and the local opens up multiple vantage points to understand these dynamics. The courses that I teach often address these questions by inviting a reflection about how our present modern world system, by and large capitalist (but not homogeneously so), came to be.

Naturally, this kind of inquiry also entails thinking through what are the other geographies that could exist. This measure of speculation is the hope embodied in design, and why I see design as a very hopeful discipline. Design can imagine geographies of power to be otherwise. Design is a discipline that imagines future terrains, future landscapes, and future geographies. While many designers are not necessarily trained well in understanding power, they do excel at the work of imagination.

Mariana: Fatou, would you build on the notion of directional flows that create specific power relations? Have you seen these dynamics play out in your work, and, if so, how?

Fatou: What stands out for me from the humanitarian context of multilateral, national, and non-profit institutions is a default position that seems to dominate whenever we engage with the notion of power. We assume, or we are told to assume, a sense of neutrality. We are to believe that our organizational systems are based on principles of impartiality, equity, and so on. This is one of the insidious ways in which colonialism and a colonial lens are completely reproduced, actually. It is within this imaginary system of impartiality, supposedly built to benefit everyone, that these power dynamics play out. It happens in the guise of a grounded, rational, and patriarchal logic. As a Sierra Leonean, and as a woman of color working within this system especially in the Global South, I'm being told that the principles and the values that I work with and reproduce are neutral. And, of course, this is not the case and it troubles me.

These assumptions play out, for example, in a brainstorming session about a project that aims to bridge the digital divide, and we are trying to think with the team about potential digital technologies. We're trying to bridge the digital divide, so we're able to collect their information, because we say we want to use it for change. The intention is admirable and the rhetoric of participatory methods such as co-design and human-centered design all sound great. But the fact is, when you experience this work from the location of the Global South, where many of us are being told that we are helpless and other people are here with certain expertise and tools, and resources to help us get better, the dynamic can become problematic. Instead of the true agency we aspire to, we are creating dynamics of disempowerment by design. We are basically working behind a façade because, no matter how hard we may wish to believe that we are part of a neutral system, we know it isn't true. We have to be more aware of directional flows, realizing that the global is often Western and Euro.

Shana: Fatou, I'd like to build on the point you made about this idea of a presumption of neutrality. In the context of the United States, this is all very familiar to me. I am a white middle-class queer and trans-identified person. I am a community organizer working primarily around imprisonment and policing, and the work that I do is rooted in, and with, communities that are impacted by different forms of violence. My position(s) are not neutral, and they are always, necessarily, present in my work. This matters for how I understand both my privileges and my political stakes in the work I am doing with people who are targeted by these systems in ways that I am not. None of this is neutral.

As someone who teaches in a design school but came to design through many side doors (I was not trained as a designer but have a background in liberal arts, fine arts, and visual and critical studies), I would go so far as to say that in design education we have a certain romance with the idea of neutrality. We want to believe not just that designers are neutral, but that the discipline of design itself is neutral. We want to believe that there's something about the processes of design that produces neutrality. This presumption of neutrality furthers the colonial lens.

"We want to believe not just that designers are neutral, but that the discipline of design itself is neutral. We want to believe that there's something about the processes of design that produces neutrality. This presumption of neutrality furthers the colonial lens."

I frequently come back to the function of design education in producing the idea of neutrality and wedding it to this idea of "doing good."

Years ago, at my institution, the tagline "You can do well and do good" used to appear in marketing materials to prospective students. I remember being horrified! In many ways, this is a marketing technique that we still often encounter when design claims a connection to social practice. This narrative perpetuates those dynamics of power in which either white, or male, or straight actors—and the accompanying ideas that center design in whiteness, masculinity, and hetero-patriarchy—are the ones we invest in. These become the lenses through which we filter our understanding of what makes sense, what "works," what's doable or viable, and designable.

Instead, there's something incredibly important about being able to have a much more nuanced conversation about what viability means. What is it that is really needed in the particular context at hand? Is the thing that's needed just a container to be able to move ideas forward to the next place? Is the thing that's needed an actual object or a system? Is the thing that's needed the time and focus to prioritize local knowledge? In other words, shouldn't we be creating space and resources for what we already see within an existing framework rather than insisting on intervening with something new? Following this direction requires that we widen the scope of our understanding of what it takes to be a designer. It sort of demands a counter-intuitive gesture, taking down a notch the act of designing as making, if that makes sense.

> **Mariana:** The idea of widening our scope is a good segue into a key domain we must touch upon: the decolonizing design movement and the plural discourses it is inspiring. Ahmed, how do you see this body of work impacting design education? To use Shana's qualifier, are there more "nuanced" practices emerging as a result?

Ahmed: I've certainly seen a shift in the past half a decade or so. The shift entails an acknowledgment that the artifacts that designers make, and the practices and processes they engage in, are not politically and ethically neutral. It is a reckoning that I find heartening, even though challenges remain.

How we define design, historically, follows what I refer to as "logics" that often seem to go unquestioned. This stems from the fact that design is a modern discipline with a relatively young history tied to industrialization, which we can trace from its beginnings to Europe. As a result, 20th- and 21st-century design follows by and large logics connected to an Anglo-European history and genealogy. Design today is deeply tied to the kinds of modern logics that pervade and enable things like "development," "globalization," and "modernization." These logics enable and are part and parcel of the kind of world that we live in today.

Decolonial and post-colonial thought and practice in design attempts to illustrate that these logics, which emerge from colonization, do not end with the Global South becoming independent from their European colonizers—this is what we call "coloniality" today. It is important to recognize that coloniality has many different dimensions to it, including the Eurocentricity and Anglocentricity of thought that underpins how we think about gender, heteronormativity, patriarchy, the construction of race, and socioeconomic segregation. These logics, insofar as they provided ways of organizing societies, were, in many cases, quite foreign to many cultures and civilizations prior to colonization. As we know, coloniality as a phe-

Design for Social Innovation

nomenon still exists globally. It presents a big issue and there should be an imperative for designers to figure out how to deal with it in the same way as they need to address productively climate change and other large existential threats.

Doing this requires, firstly, realizing how design has been shaped into what it is today and, secondly, rethinking what design is. We need to rethink design separately from what it is today and imagine what it could be. We must foreground a different set of practices, discourses, and new approaches to design education that are not as closely tied to technology and material things. In the realm of design education, I'm arguing for a shift away from purely focusing on making artifacts towards considering what things do, and towards the larger sort of conditions under which things are created and prefigured, and within which they do their work.

> **Mariana:** So if we consider this concept of the relational in design and the geographies of power, how might we understand how these dynamics play out in the field of design and gender? Fatou, you have been working with girls and young women in the Global South who are often at the receiving end of well-meaning designs that are aspiring to "empower" them. What are you seeing happen?

Fatou: As we said before, there is a discourse in the development and humanitarian sector that we're really trying to do good by being human-centered. The type of good that we are after claims to capture people's voices; this is the case as well in the work we do with women and girls. In fact, I reject that notion. If we were truly centering the voices of the people in our programming and humanitarian responses we would be de-colonizing our frameworks for how we design, how we adopt technologies, and how we do good. Of course, it does become critical to weave a people-centered approach and be accountable to those we are trying to impact for the better. I am just not sure we can be effective if we're not ready to decolonize. I hate the term "neocolonialism" because my perspective is that we never decolonized, to begin with. We started the process, and it was too difficult, and so we got lost. Fast-forward to the present legacies that we face today.

And so, behind the work that I do in international development, I always start by acknowledging my privilege. I may be a Black Muslim woman from Sierra Leone, but I am also the product of a certain socio-economic background and had access to a Western, liberal education in gender studies (in my case from the University of British Columbia) that makes me privileged. I also try to keep front and center the fact that I work within a heteronormative system. It can be very easy for colleagues of mine to rely on me for credibility and say, "Well, you sound a certain kind of way.

We can have a safe conversation with you, and therefore you can be the voice of the people." This is not true. I emphasize that we cannot center the voices of people in how we design programs and choose to respond if we do not decolonize the house itself from an economic, historical, and political perspective. My point is: we haven't dismantled the house. You've given us the house, you've moved the furniture around, and you've said, "Well, we've moved the furniture around, we've allowed you to put some of your furniture in here, we've made sure that you can sit in the living room, so you should be happy." But the house is still problematic.

Another goal is to interrogate what we mean by "empowering" someone, for example "empowering women" often used to describe the verb of "doing something" for women from the Global South or black and brown communities in the "North." I hate the word "empower." To give power to someone—as though women and girls (black and brown bodies) are passive agents, without ideas, dreams, actions, movement, creation. I'm talking here about activating their agency—equity, creating pathways for their already activated selves to thrive in.

"I hate the word 'empower.' To give power to someone—as though women and girls (Black and brown bodies) are passive agents without ideas, dreams, actions, movement, creation. I'm talking here about activating their agency...creating pathways for their already activated selves to thrive in."

What does that mean very, very concretely? I do think we are at a point where there are many of us preoccupied with social justice and aware that there is an urgency to push the decolonization agenda, for ourselves, for our women, and for our people.

> **Mariana:** It is an important take-away to recognize that in co-design, power is not necessarily always diffused. Shana, can you reflect on what gives you hope from the approaches we have at our disposal for engaging with the community and learning from the community? How do you personally navigate these dynamics as a mediator and as a practitioner?

Design for Social Innovation

Shana: As Fatou was talking about the house, I started thinking about Audre Lorde, the Black American lesbian feminist writer, and civil society activist. I would argue that a lot of what Audre Lorde's work has surfaced in terms of addressing injustices of racism, sexism, classism, heterosexism, and homophobia could be, and should be, central to design education. I also believe this question of tools and "the master's tools" is such a critical one. I think one piece that has been happening over the last maybe ten years, certainly in the last five to six years, is to try to interrupt the idea that there are methods that are simply replicable. There is a fallacy in believing that what designers do is create good methods, and then once you have those methods you can pick them up and use them anywhere. I would add that we must go beyond the idea that the methods just need to be made "appropriate" to the environment where they are being used. The idea that the method will stay roughly the same, but needs to be made sort of workable from place to place and in "cultural terms," falls short.

There are a number of design researchers, such as Yoko Akama, Andrea Botero, and many others, who have been thinking a lot about what it means to understand design practices as embodied. Drawing on their work, and building on feminist theory that points to design as embodied, is one way to become more aware of a constant engagement with the dynamics of power among people. To your prompt about hope, what I find useful and important is the act of imagining how to be in relation when we work with people and to actually introduce ways of shifting existing dynamics. As Fatou was talking, I was also thinking about the role of capitalism, both in the kind of formation of design and vis-à-vis industrial practices as Ahmed was referencing earlier. In many ways, this begs a much larger question about the extent to which capitalism has to be unsettled in order for many of these ideas we're talking about to actually stand a chance of taking root. I bring this up because I believe that capitalism as a set of dynamics is also what dictates the idea that you can have "non-designers" and "designers" in a room together working according to a set of practices and following a set of interactions that usually involve things like emotions, and reason, and logic, and research, and what have you. In these situations, like the proverbial fuzzy front-end design diagram, we are typically expected to come out on the other side with "a solution."

There are alternatives to this model—work happening that is using feminism, Black feminism, decolonial theory, and frankly other long-standing practices. I'm thinking right now of the international Participatory Design Conference (PDC 2020) that was organized this year in Manizales, Colombia (before it moved online due to the pandemic). A huge theme of that conference was inspired by the body of work of the late Colombian sociologist Orlando Fals Borda, one of the founders of the participatory action research framework. Many of the discussions touched upon the idea of re-shifting the whole relationship that we have to how knowledge is made, how it's produced, and introducing the idea of reason and rationality that is constructed in a different way.

I bring this up as to say that to me there is still something immensely valuable, fundamental, in building relationships between people. And I think that the way that we have seen change happen over time is by people building relationships and shifting dynamics of power and access to resources. The geographer I mentioned earlier, Ruth Wilson Gilmore, writes that sometimes we think of power as something that people take from one place and move to another, as if it were a sort of absolute thing. She argues—and we know this from Michel Foucault, as well—that power is in fact diffused in a different kind of way, and is produced in multiple ways. Gilmore says that we need to think in terms of "making power." This argument inspires me to consider participatory design practices as ones that might facilitate or produce circumstances where the question is no longer one of taking power, but rather one of making power. In thinking about the ways in which participation happens, what's exciting about participation is that it invests in building relationships over time that are sometimes unpredictable. Participatory design invests in the knowledge and experiences of people, no matter where they are. When done with intentionality, it also recognizes that those locations are differentiated in ways that will produce conflict and may manifest forms of difference that sometimes are deeply complicated. What it takes to produce ideas, next steps, and even things out of those relationships, is precisely the kind of anti-oppression work that gives me hope.

Doing this work requires an understanding of history, and a willingness to listen. It also requires refusing timelines to a certain extent, and/or making timelines that are dictated by very particular things that are not always in the designer's timeline. If I remain drawn to participatory design it is because of this willingness to engage with all of this complexity and reject a blanket sentiment that co-design or human-centered design can sometimes invite. There's something important about being able to stay grounded in what's necessary in the moment while also not getting in the way of future moments. There's a balance between those two things that requires a deep engagement with the relationships of power we've been discussing.

> **Mariana:** By connecting the notion of participation with the observation that the timeline of the designer does not always fit, you're leading us, Shana, to an area that I've certainly experienced in my own practice. It has been a profound dilemma, since I am determined to make design more accountable and I am interested in measuring the value of design not simply as methods but as a cognitive mindset that might advance opportunities for social innovation.

Shifting gears slightly to pick up on Fatou's great metaphor of the house and the need to go beyond a superficial rearrangement of its furnishings, I wonder if I can invite you, Ahmed, to point to some of the structural issues that are perhaps provoking some of these dilemmas. Where do you see a potential for change? ... What are the levers for change that we might find?

Ahmed: I'd like to build on the previous question around participation, not necessarily participatory design, but participation. I will make two points.

First of all, there's a really interesting problem when designers working with communities engage from the get-go from a position that acknowledges that historical injustices and existing systems need to be accounted for as potential sources of oppression. Starting from here entails a reflexivity, an attention to systemic injustices, and that is a good thing. However, one of the problems that working in a participatory manner raises is the issue of negotiating incommensurabilities, i.e., how do I help the community in such a way that both I and the community preserves and respects our differences? Here I'm talking about differences not as shallow but as deep, where being different entails a distinct worldview and relation to reality. In a cosmopolitan society, this can become an issue, right?

Take the example of a white Anglo-European male living next to a Muslim Pakistani immigrant in the US. You are not Muslim, nor Pakistani, nor a first-generation immigrant, and will thus experience your reality completely differently from them—how do you coexist with others radically different from you? This is but one scenario that poses a set of particular challenges to participatory design. Where and how do we preserve and respect differences? How do we do it while still enabling societies to exist as cohesive units? And how do we make sure that the voices and the wishes of all are truly heard, and respected, and privileged, including those who are historically marginalized and disadvantaged, those whose voices have been silenced, or who have just been rendered invisible? For me, this means negotiating incommensurabilities.

"Where and how do we preserve and respect differences? How do we do it while still enabling societies to exist as cohesive units?"

Secondly, in terms of your questions of where we might find levers of change, we need to address again how we choose to imagine a global world. We cannot undo globalization. But how we imagine a world where different worlds can exist in difference is a promising direction we can move towards - this is the idea of the pluriverse, as per the Zapatistas and Arturo Escobar. I believe this particular view entails a different kind of stance and set of sensitivities where participatory designers need to only be very self-reflexive, but also foster reflexivity within the communities that they are working with, while recognizing that different communities might want very different things. At the same time we might also want some of those things to change in the service of issues we are collectively facing as societies. I would like to challenge participatory designers to think about the kinds of logics that prefigure the different wants and desires of communities. We must move towards new, more emancipatory logics, and think about materializing these logics via new socio-technical enabled conditions.

Shana: Ahmed, this brings to mind the kind of imagining and making of futures that are endemic to social movements and to the living practices of lots of people who are subject to exactly the kinds of power systems that we've been discussing together. I am thinking about folks who do work around transformative justice, for instance. This is work that does not look to re-engage the state in producing justice but seeks to produce relationships of justice and capacities for accountability outside of the state. It requires a kind of thinking about things that are both future-oriented, but also deeply observant of daily practice. So, to expand upon this particular example of transformative justice, the key question is how to create relationships that are grounded in accountability that do not involve, for instance, calling the police. People answer this question all over the world by creating common-sense capacities to solve problems, address conflict, at all kinds of scales, without following the accepted norm of calling the police (a norm, as we know, that for a lot of valid historical reasons may correlate police with unsafety, not safety, etc.). And so, if we look at the work of Black, queer, and trans feminists in particular, in the United States but also internationally, or if we examine practices of sex workers, and focus on all of the systems that people build to produce other forms of safety, I think we're seeing already alternative forms of envisioning futures. And not just the envisioning of the future as an imagination, but as something that is active, and that is prototyped, to borrow the language of design.

In terms of levers for change, for me, the critical question to pose is how might designers engage with the making practices of the people with whom they are working, and recognize them not as something

Design for Social Innovation

to be taken up and made either "better," or even amplified through the terms of/or in the terms of design. Pointing to the question of reflexivity that Ahmed brought up and your points, Mariana, I would surface the question: What does it mean for designers to be one group of many, who do this kind of work? I think that there's a fundamental shift there that is important. And, back to Ahmed's points, let us remember that the colonial project was also a project of erasing differences. It was a systematic project that used constructions of, and imaginations of, difference, to order and produce violence.

Future-making work is about on-the-ground work in relationship with people. One of the important questions you should ask yourself as a designer is the following: are you being invited into this work? And, if so, what is the stance that you take, and what does it look like to be a participant in that work as opposed to imagining that you are coming to help people do their work?

Mariana: You're leading us to a place I was hoping we would end the discussion on—pointing us towards a direction of hope.

Fatou: In the work I do, a direction of hope is to witness that we are increasingly taking a multidisciplinary approach to understanding and communicating with affected communities, and positioning their voices and their needs at the center of our development and humanitarian system. It is certainly happening with this COVID response. But it remains a very new way for us; we have to be nuanced about the power dynamics at place and setting honest expectations. We are part of a large bureaucratic machinery and it is difficult to see change at an institutional level, yet I believe in its possibility.

My envisioning in any work I do, is one of fostering, strengthening, and snatching from the colonial project this idea of difference as threatening. We must do this in order to deepen the strengths that exist from the differences that we all bring to the table: whether it's from our disciplines, from our resources, and from the intersectionality of our identities. If we can begin to appreciate our difference, we will see the disbursement of power in places where we are creating and intervening. I would also like for us to rename and deepen some of these processes, so they're a little bit more political. In the humanitarian sector, instead of saying localization, why not call it decolonization? And why not champion calling it decolonization within a feminist framework? And then, lastly, being able to hold us accountable, and help us redefine how we measure accountability. The development sector is at a reckoning: we either adapt to the call for reformed ways of delivering aid or we will become obsolete.

This goes for governance and other sectors. People are demanding respect and dignity; this means a shift or a sharing of power. I find that hopeful. I need that necessary and needed.

Mariana: Ahmed and Shana, would you like to wrap us up by sharing what gives you hope?

Ahmed: Witnessing the recent uptake of a plurality of conceptions aimed at rethinking design, design practice, and its outcomes, represents one important source for a lot of hope for me. The global resurgence of designers who were historically at the margins of the field, and a real urgency—an imperative, almost, to seek and to find new ways of designing—also signals great hope.

The provocation that I would like to end with connects to the move towards the actual materialization and creation of deep difference. Surmounting many of the global challenges we face will depend on this kind of materialization and creation of different approaches, but also on the production of difference itself. What leaves me in a hopeful place is to see that we have a proliferation of epistemic difference and an ontological difference that is alive and well in current design discourse and practice.

Shana: As I was listening to Fatou and Ahmed describe hopefulness, I was actually thinking about students. The short answer I have is that what brings me hope right now are the students that I get to work with. They are phenomenal. They are asking good, strong, smart, thorough, thoughtful questions of themselves and their practices, and of the world. I feel very lucky to get to work with them.

1   Richard McKeon, "Power and the Language of Power," *Ethics* 68, no. 2 (January 1958): 98–115.
2   Arturo Escobar, *Designs for the Pluriverse: Radical Interdependence, Autonomy, and the Making of Worlds* (Durham, NC: Duke University Press, 2018).

Geographies of Power

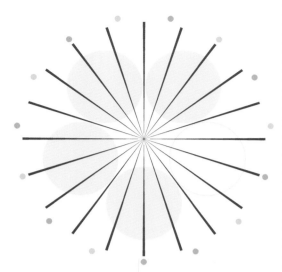

Edmonton Shift Lab
Collective 1.0

Confronting systemic racism against Aboriginal people, immigrants, and refugees by starting with housing

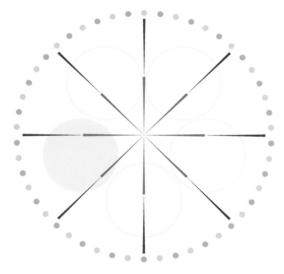

El Calendario del Mundo Wixárika
(Calendar of the Wixárika)

Crafting an artifact to help bridge between indigenous and Westernized cultures

Pink Dot
SG

Fostering understanding, love, and acceptance between all Singaporeans, regardless of sexual orientation

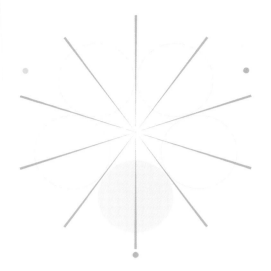

Equity by Design
Immersive Series

*Dismantling systemic oppression and
co-creating a future with equity for all*

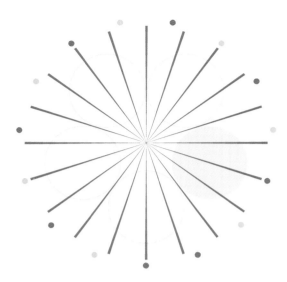

Digua
Community

*Repurposing unused spaces into
community innovation hubs*

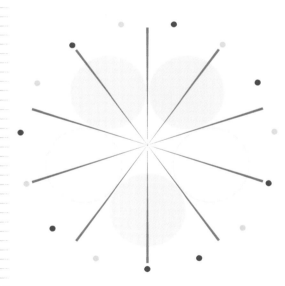

Paths to Inclusion
Vienna

*Advocating for people living with
disabilities through the co-design of
new services*

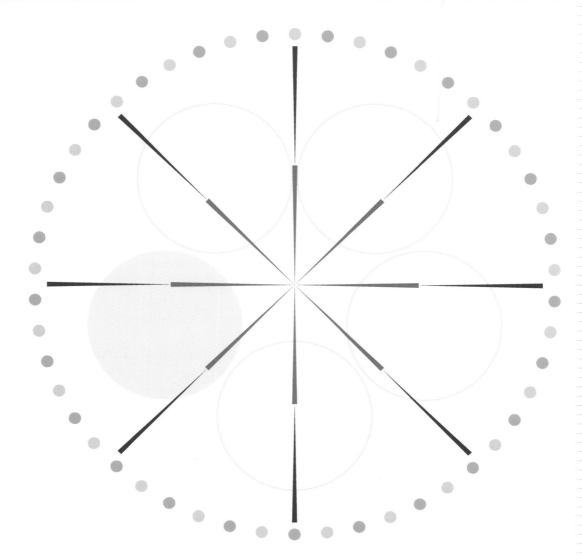

Duration
  June 2004–March 2006,
  December 2016

Location
  Guadalajara and San Miguel
  Huaixtita, Jalisco, México;
  Gainesville, Florida, USA

Categories
  Identity

Designer
  D4D Lab with University of
  Florida Graphic Design
  (BFA, Graphic Design, 2006
  students)

Partners
  Centro Educativo Tatuutsí
  Maxakwaxi

Key Contributors
  Centro Educativo Tatuutsí
  Maxakwaxi Community
  Sarah Berkin
  Maria Rogal
  Cassie McDaniel
  Avery Smith

Designer Organization Type
  ● Academia

Team Size
  ● 50+

Design Quotient
  ● 41–60%

Project Costs
  ▭▷ $1k–$25k

Source of Funding
  ▬ Government
  ▬ Foundation/Non-Profit/
    Endowment

Funding Mechanisms
  Grant

Impact Measurement Methods
  Qualitative: Observational
  Research

Mediums
  Physical: Calendar

Design for Social Innovation

El Calendario
del Mundo Wixárika
(Calendar of the Wixárika)

Crafting an artifact to help bridge indigenous and Westernized cultures

Westernized Mexicans generally know little about the Wixárika people or their cultural practices. Contemporary Wixáritari communities in the Sierra Madre Occidental mountain region continue to rely on natural signs to keep their own calendars that guide planting, harvesting, leadership rituals, and activities. As oral histories, they continue to be used throughout the year to call people together to give thanks for the harvest, prepare for the next planting, and other important rituals. For Wixáritari living, working, and studying in a Westernized Mexican culture, these individuals experience two times at once, and misunderstandings arise when the two times in which one is living, studying, or working do not conform.

A new cultural artifact for the community, a dual calendar that shares the Wixárika community of San Miguel Huaixtita's perspectives of time in relation to the Mexican (Western) calendar, was identified as a way to help bridge between these two perspectives. It was developed for Mexican and Wixárika youth, their teachers, and families, to foster a dialogue about perspectives and to teach youth to value Wixárika culture.

Corona Berkin, professor at the Universidad de Guadalajara, initiated the project by first seeking community consent and then recruiting Maria Rogal, professor at the University of Florida. They agreed to develop prototypes of a bi-cultural calendar with students in Rogal's graphic design course.

Rogal describes their process as "Horizontal in that participants sought to identify, address, and dismantle real and perceived hierarchies and political,

Corona Berkin demonstrates the prototype to community elders, teachers, and students at the Centro Educativo Tatuutsí Maxakwaxi in San Miguel Huaixtita as part of the co-design process

economic, cultural, and racial power structures so that everyone could engage openly and equitably, valuing what each person brings to the table. Dialogic in that the process was framed as an exchange of ideas, concepts, values, and beliefs. Co-designed so that it was activated through dialogue (observation, listening and conversation) where participants could explore cultures, values, stories, practices, tensions, etc. to generate new knowledge."

Corona Berkin served as the liaison between the designers and community stakeholders and worked with Rogal on an agile and inclusive project plan. Corona Berkin visited the University of Florida to launch the project with talks, brainstorming sessions, and iterative design sessions with 18 students. The teams proposed six different prototypes sent to México for review by Corona Berkin and Wixáritari leaders, who shared feedback and considerations for further iterations, and eventually one was selected to develop further.

Next, Rogal and the student designers, McDaniel and Smith, joined Corona Berkin in Guadalajara and San Miguel Huaixtita to take part in the important harvest ritual, experience daily life, and learn from the teachers and key stakeholders about Wixáritari beliefs, values, and sense of time. Informal and unstructured visits to homes, group meals, walks, and tours were all opportunities for learning in context to inform the designers and their work. While conducting fieldwork the designers engaged in numerous discussions and work sessions to adjust the proposed design so that it was culturally appropriate and responsible. The details of illustrations were finessed, color was made to be representative of

Design for Social Innovation

The internal panel of the calendar presents the year view as a whole, demonstrating the natural events and corresponding rituals that mark the passing of time

the colors seen in the community, and three languages were used on the calendar with the Indigenous language first.

The calendar presents the year in circular form, showing the continuity of months and seasons—central to the Wixárika conception of time—with written explanations in Wixárika, Spanish, and English. The calendar was designed to precisely connect Western time (days, months) with the Wixárika time, which is the time of nature. Corona Berkin added that the calendar allows people to "find an exact Western date and make the link to the natural time and understand what people in the Wixárika community may be doing. That is important for the Wixáritari to have less guessing when they have farming chores."

This concept was approved by Wixáritari partners for public dissemination of their beliefs, marking the first time that members of the San Miguel Huaixtita community authored their own story for public dissemination rather than be written about by outsiders.

Images: Maria Rogal

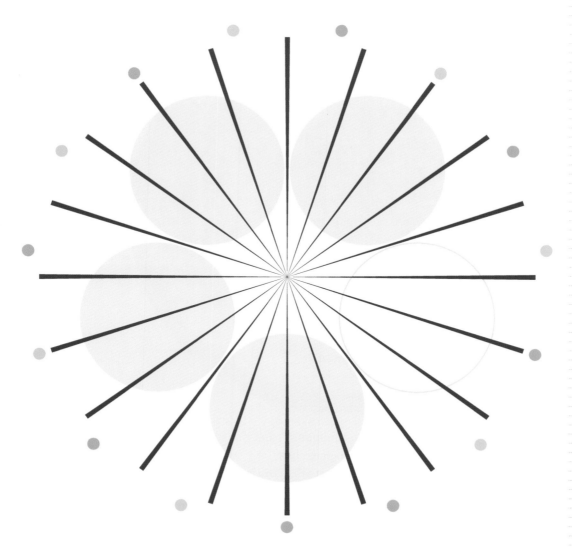

Duration
October 2016–ongoing

Location
Edmonton, Alberta, Canada

Categories
Identity

Designer
Edmonton Shift Lab

Partners
Edmonton Community
Foundation
Skills Society

Designer Organization Type
● Non-Profit

Team Size
● 11–20

Design Quotient
● 81–100%

Project Costs
▷ $100k–$500k

Source of Funding
■ Foundation/Non-Profit/
Endowment

Funding Mechanisms
Unspecified

Impact Measurement Methods
Qualitative: Observational
Research
Quantitative: Headcount/Time of
Participation, Verified Sharing
of Learning Experiences

Mediums
Digital: App
Experiential: Education
Organizational: Service
Physical: Information Guides

Design for Social Innovation

Edmonton Shift Lab
Collective 1.0

Confronting systemic racism against
Aboriginal people, immigrants, and refugees
by starting with housing

In 2015, the City of Edmonton identified the stark reality that, "Aboriginal people, immigrants and refugees [continue to] experience discrimination in workplaces, housing, services and facilities that exclude them from opportunities and put them at risk of poverty."[1] In response, the Edmonton Shift Lab, a collaboration between the Edmonton Community Foundation and Skills Society, a local disability rights non-profit, was established to "develop potential service, policy, system and community action prototypes that will help reduce racism as it contributes to poverty." The group operates as a collective.

Jodi Calahoo-Stonehouse, a Shift Lab steward, reflects on the Lab's first years of existence as being about "learning and exploring to see how Indigenous processes were applicable and compatible to social innovation processes. [They were] learning how to facilitate, observe, and engage in this field of study, to see the relationship and compatibility with Indigenous world views." By centering Indigenous practices and knowledge, the team acknowledged that they would work with marginalized members of their community on those communities' own terms. The Shift Lab has engaged Indigenous elders, Indigenous ways of knowing, and Indigenous practices since their inception and continue to look for ways to weave these together with human-centered design and social innovation in what they describe as a "triple helix" approach.

During their first six months of operations, the team adopted the frame of housing that would allow them to work on the intersection of racism and poverty with a more tangible area of focus. As their efforts continued, the group met regularly to share their knowledge, undertake research, and develop their ideas. This

**Shift Lab 1.0
collective
learning
prototyping
principles**

**Image:
Edmonton Shift
Lab**

resulted in three "prototype" project ideas that were tested through conversation with Shift Lab's extensive, multi-sector advisory group and community partners. One of them, a certification program for landlords whose practices "respect and promote diversity," is being piloted with a select group of landlords and tenants in 2021.

Now, in what they refer to as "Shift Lab 2.0," the team is currently piloting and testing (as of October 2020) four new anti-racism prototypes, which are an anti-racism box, a board game based on the Indigenous history of the Canadian prairies, a de-escalation guide to stopping racial harassment on the street, and an app designed to inculcate racial empathy amongst its users.

The Shift Lab is considering several metrics to measure efficacy and changes in behaviour. These include the adoption and implementation of prototypes by community partners, the number of landlords and tenants who enroll in the testing phase, changes in the percentage of (self-identified) racialized Edmontonians accessing services such as housing, and feedback from individual users

The ubiquity of racism presents challenges for the Lab, according to the team's own reflections, in that, even when successful in finding inventive ways to address a tangible expression of racism, like housing discrimination, there are still systemic structures, worldviews, and attitudes that remain hidden. An anonymous lab participant shared that they "did not explicitly think of access to safe and affordable housing as a key indicator of the intersection of racism and poverty [prior to engaging with Shift Lab]." That participant continued: "I never

thought about the ghettoization that occurs around social housing and affordable housing—that it is a class- and race-based segregation of people." Addressing the systemic nature of racism, in ways both visible and hidden, remains a consistent focus during the Lab's 2.0 phase.

"Look, we are not good at this. We are scared of tough conversations. We are afraid to feel vulnerable. It's hard to confront our own biases. It's emotional. It's about power. The Lab was a great start, but it's only a start."

Anonymous participant

I Quotations from Shift Lab Learning From Our First Year report, 2017 unless otherwise noted.

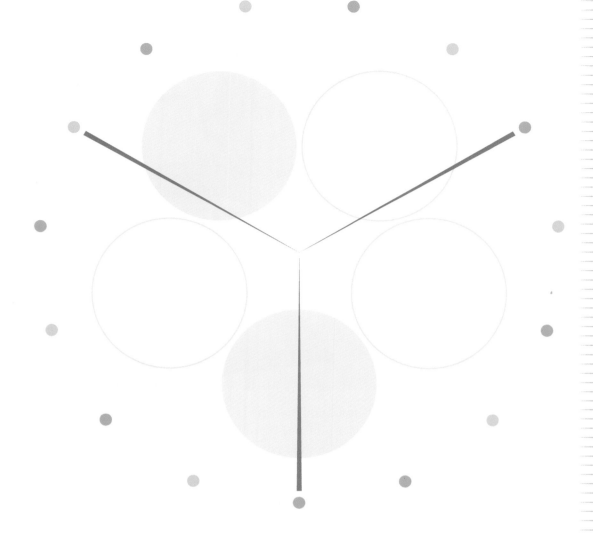

Duration
  2009—onwards

Location
  Singapore

Categories
  Humanitarian Affairs
  Identity (gender, culture, race)

Designer
  Pink Dot SG

Designer Organization Type
  ● Non-Profit

Team Size
  ● 11–20

Design Quotient
  ● 0–20%

Project Costs
  ▷ Undisclosed

Source of Funding
  ▬ Private Company

Funding Mechanisms
  Unspecified

Impact Measurement Methods
  Qualitative: Surveys
  Quantitative: Event Attendance,
  Web/Mobile Analytics, Project
  Replication/Citation by other
  Groups, Volume of Media
  Coverage

Mediums
  Digital: Network
  Experiential: Event

Design for Social Innovation

Pink Dot SG

Fostering understanding, love, and acceptance between all Singaporeans, regardless of sexual orientation

Section 377A of the Penal Code is a Singaporean law—inherited from British rule—which criminalizes sex between consenting adult men. Despite being repealed in other British colonies such as India, Botswana, and Hong Kong, this law still exists in Singapore. Though it is "not proactively enforced," as quoted by the prime minister in 2007, the LGBTQ+ community is still discriminated against in policies and legislation. Constitutional challenges to the law were unsuccessful in 2014 and 2019.

Pink Dot SG is a grassroots non-profit movement started by a group of individuals who believe that everyone deserves the freedom to love. Their name was inspired by the nickname given by the media, referring to the country as a "Little Red Dot" on a map. Pink is the color of Singaporeans' national identity card, that all citizens' carry, as well as the combined colors of the red and white national flag. The organization has held an annual Pink Dot Rally, Singapore's de facto Pride event, since 2009, and works to foster a more inclusive Singaporean society with access to equal rights for all, most importantly through the repeal of Section 377A.

Public protest in Singapore is restricted to a designated "free speech area" in Hong Lim Park. In 2008, the rules governing this park were relaxed, but activism was still not a significant part of Singaporeans political culture. Pink Dot was conscious that organizing in a way that relied on individuals to publicly out themselves as LGBTQ+ could lead to strained relationships with their families and friends, and may even threaten the livelihoods of people who outed themselves. In light of cultural norms, the Pink Dot team needed to design a strategy that was tailored to the psyche of Singaporeans to broach a potentially divisive

and controversial topic. While they were tempted by the idea of throwing a "loud and proud" Pride parade, the team chose to focus on rallying support amongst straight allies, with a call to come to the park dressed in pink to show support for the LGBTQ+ community. The brand they created needed to be accessible and non-threatening, "not an outright protest Pride march but instead focused on forming a human pink dot which represented acceptance and inclusivity that was not just for the LGBT community," in the words of Stephanie Ong, one of the lead designers involved.

The first year drew a crowd of 2,500 people from all walks of life: families, couples, friends, and communities showed up. Over the years it has expanded into a night-time and digital event with a wide variety of programming. Since 2009, an estimated 200,000 people have attended the physical Pink Dot Rally. To date, it is the largest and most public pro-LGBTQ+ movement in Singapore.

Six years into their organizing efforts, Pink Dot collaborated with Oogachaga, a Singaporean-led LGBTQ+ community organization, to submit a joint report to the *Universal Periodic Review* by the United Nations Human Rights Council in 2015. This report was supported by evidence collected, reported cases, and comprehensive community research that highlighted five key areas for improvement in the LGBTQ+ landscape of Singapore. The document helped define the practical trickle-down effects of law 377A and, in turn, shaped Pink Dot's initiatives by crystallizing the issues that they are fighting for and the change they

want to see from the government. Pink Dot SG has since submitted an updated report to the UPR in 2020.

In Pink Dot surveys run throughout the years, three main sentiments have been collected from attendees: "It is easier for me to come out now," "There is a deeper understanding of LGBTQ+ issues," and "Pink Dot is fostering inclusivity in Singapore." There have been 22 Pink Dot satellite events across ten international locations, and Pink Dot is regularly referenced and quoted in local and international media on LGBTQ+ matters.

Images: Pink Dot SG

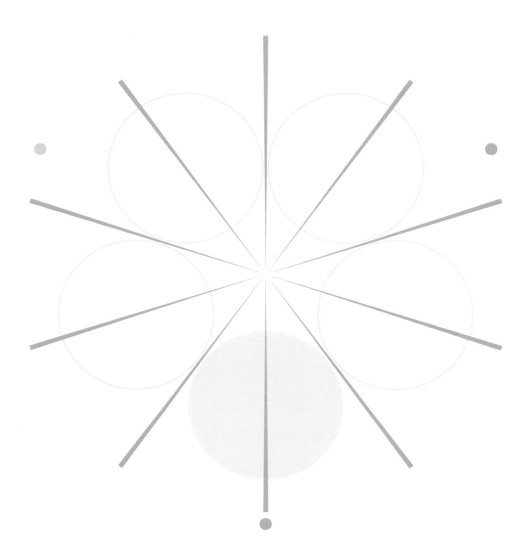

Duration
    June 5–7, 2019

Location
    New York City, USA

Categories
    Social Justice

Designer
    Creative Reaction Lab (CRXLAB)

Key Contributors
    Antionette D. Carroll
    Hilary Sedovic, LMSW

Designer Organization Type
    • Non-Profit

Team Size
    • 11–20

Design Quotient
    • 21–40%

Project Costs
    ▷ $25–$100k

Source of Funding
    ▬ Self-Funding

Funding Mechanisms
    Fee for Service
    Self-Funded

Impact Measurement Methods
    Qualitative: Stakeholder
        Interviews, Focus Groups,
        Surveys
    Quantitative: Surveys

Mediums
    Experiential: Workshops

Design for Social Innovation

Equity by Design
Immersive Series

Dismantling systemic oppression and co-creating a future with equity for all

In the words of Creative Reaction Lab founder Antionette D. Carroll, "systems of oppression, inequality, and inequity are by design, and therefore can be redesigned." But how is this possible when even the most well-known design methodologies and approaches come with their own biases? By rethinking the way design is practiced.

As a non-profit that provides leadership capacity building and education for Black and Latin youth and their allies, Creative Reaction Lab is developing new design methodologies and educational formats to build the capacity of people to do the work of redesigning systems of oppression and dismantling racial and health inequities. They refer to this as "Equity-Centered Community Design," which is a creative problem-solving process "based on equity, humility-building, integrating history and healing practices, addressing power dynamics, and co-creating with the community." The framework focuses on a community's culture and needs so that they can gain tools to dismantle systemic oppression and create a future with equity for all.

An example of this approach is provided by Creative Reaction Lab's Equity by Design Immersive Series in New York, conducted in June 2019. The purpose of the Immersive was to learn about Equity-Centered Community Design and to practice it using an issue relevant to the community. For these sessions, mass incarceration was the topic presented to the participants. During the learning engagement, Creative Reaction Lab's facilitators guided participants through interactive activities, dialogue, planning, and reflection about power, identity, social equity, and community design. Collectively, the group of 40 participants worked to nurture a space for unlearning and relearning. The Creative Reaction Lab

team incorporated history and healing while working to acknowledge, share, and dismantle power constructs and build humility.

Participants were a mix of community members, traditional designers, government employees, educators, and "Living Experts," the last of which represents an important constituency within Creative Reaction Lab's engagements. These individuals typically come from historically underinvested communities or populations who already experience significantly inequitable treatment, including erasure of their narratives and/or exploitation of their lives and stories. By ensuring that they are able to participate in sessions and receive fair compensation for doing so, CRXLAB's intention is to center the "significant value and wisdom of those experiencing mass incarceration day-to-day" compared to traditional design processes that tend to rely on "expert" opinions.

Learning engagements such as the Equity by Design Immersive in New York are a way to empower a community of participants, and they are also critical to Creative Reaction Lab's own process of learning and refinement by providing knowledge about which interventions are successful, when, and why. The engagement included multiple opportunities for participants to give feedback through methods including real-time anonymous comments; collective, public reflection on learnings each morning; and collaborative exercises including a group activity to create an "Equity Design Manifesto."

A post-Immersive survey collected data to verify the efficacy of the experience and to help Creative Reaction Lab refine their practices. Before the Im-

Design for Social Innovation

Participants conduct a word-mapping activity

Image: Indiana Kuffer

mersive, participants were asked how often they reflected on the influence of their personal identity and power. Afterwards, participants were asked the same question and reported a 50% increase in their own daily reflections on the influence of their personal identity and power. One participant noted, "the integration and focus on personal reflection is rare when thinking about [systemic] problems we are trying to solve, but so critical to doing truly meaningful work." Upwards of 94% of participants reported being "more likely" or "much more likely" to "explore and integrate the history and power dynamics of situations into the way they develop approaches to dismantle inequity."

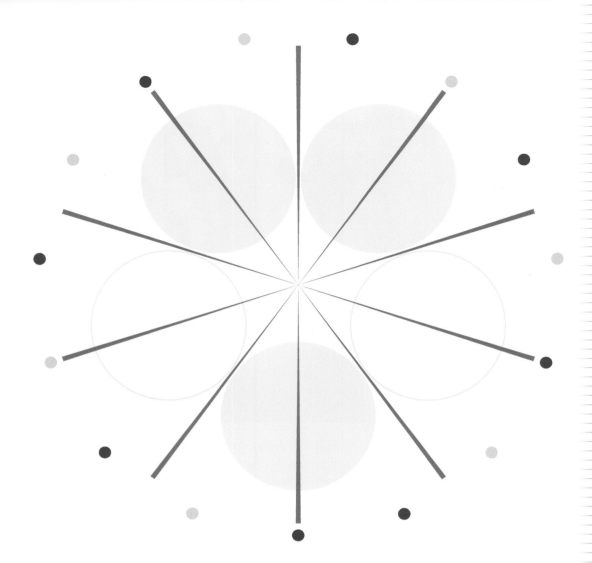

Duration
April 2016–October 2018

Location
Vienna, Austria

Categories
Inclusion

Designer
Wonderwerk Consulting

Partners
Fonds Soziales Wien (Vienna
Social Fund)
Dachverband der Wiener
Sozialeinrichtung

Designer Organization Type
● For-Profit

Team Size
● 11–20

Design Quotient
● 21–40%

Project Costs
▷ $25–$100k

Source of Funding
━ Government

Funding Mechanisms
Fee for Service

Impact Measurement Methods
Qualitative: Participant/Client/
User Feedback

Mediums
Digital: App
Experiential: Education, Event
Organizational: Service

Paths to Inclusion Vienna

Advocating for people living with disabilities through the co-design of new services

Like many cities, barriers to social participation still existed for individuals with disabilities in Vienna in 2016, despite the UN Convention on the Rights of Persons with Disabilities. Wonderwerk Consulting worked to address this by partnering with Fonds Soziales Wien (Vienna Social Fund), which supports 100,000 residents with disabilities annually, and Dachverband der Wiener Sozialeinrichtung, a networking platform that makes customized social services available to Viennese citizens. The goal of their collaboration, which they called Wiener Wege zur Inklusion (Paths to Inclusion Vienna), was to increase social inclusion by designing new services with and for people with disabilities in Vienna.

The team's research involved 220 participants in seven groups that consisted of people with disabilities, their families and assistants, and other stakeholders. Research approaches were selected that recognize the unique needs of this community, such as "shadowing" observations where the researcher follows someone going about their daily life and the use of prompts that help individuals talk about activities they are doing and would like to do. Additionally, in-depth interviews were conducted with 24 groups and 36 individuals to better understand the challenges.

Seven areas for intervention were identified during the research: enabling the use of public transport; eliminating violence; opportunities for people with and without disabilities to live together; new and diverse tasks in day-care facilities that educate and empower people with disabilities; creating new workplaces; counseling services; and relationships. Ideas were generated for each of these areas and evaluated by individuals living with disabilities who ranked ideas. The four top-ranking possibilities were prototyped: co-living, public transportation, violence, and daily structure.

The co-living prototype suggests that housing options should be made available that offer short-term contracts, which is important for people who have not been living by themselves. As some people with disabilities tend to live with their parents for a long time, they are often afraid to change their living situation. By having "trial contracts," individuals can try out living away from home in a more manageable way, giving them a more manageable pathway to independence. Partners oversee the shared apartments, deal with administrative issues, and provide a "living coach" who helps with individual daily issues as well as building a good community within the shared home.

To address public transit, the buddy app operates like a dating app that connects people who want a buddy with whom to ride public transport in confidence. Users are matched based on needs for assistance with buddies, which increases comfort and reduces the complications that an individual must navigate. An approach to reducing violence was prototyped by creating a course for peer-mediators in day-care and assisted living facilities. This empowers people living with disabilities to make peace and mediate between different interests and needs by themselves. After the first peer-mediation course ended, some of the participants are now working as peer mediators in day care facilities, working in conjunction with once-a-year events at day-care facilities that feature self-defense, psychotherapy, and theater to help people who have suffered structural violence overcome the trauma of these experiences.

Design for Social Innovation

A voting
exercise led to
the selection of
final concepts
to be prototyped

**Prototyping the
buddy app**

By Wonderwerk's own estimation, this was one of the largest service design projects in the public sector of German-speaking countries. At first it was difficult to motivate people to participate, but the number of stakeholders grew quickly and has resulted in a network that pays dividends beyond this discrete initiative. By bringing organizations together who were previously in competition with each other, Paths to Inclusion Vienna has strengthened the local ecosystem of care for people living with disabilities. Now Wonderwerk hopes to standardize and replicate the process in Austria's remaining eight states.

The transformation has not only been systemic, but also individual. Before the project, many individuals living with disabilities only talked through intermediary advocates (relatives, caretakers, assistants), but the project created an opportunity for people to practice speaking up and advocating for themselves. According to the former CEO of Fonds Soziales Wien, "In the current project, those affected were now able to help shape the development of new services. This is lived inclusion."

Images: Martin Habacher

Geographies of Power

81

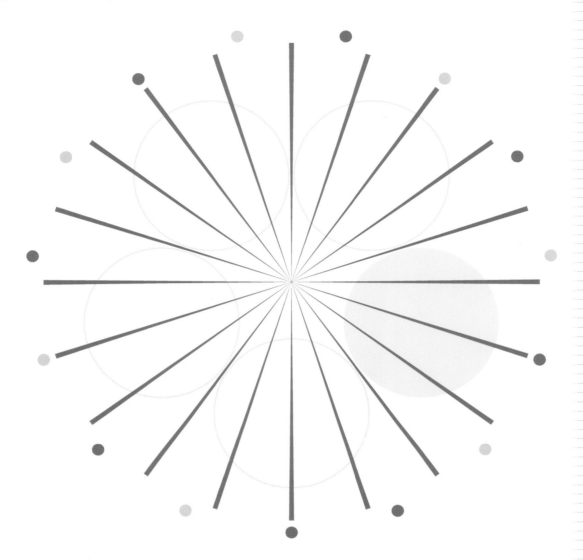

Duration
    2013–present

Location
    Beijing, China

Categories
    Environment
    Social Justice
    Policy

Designer
    Zhou Zishu (social designer
    and researcher), Wei Xingyu
    (graphic designer), Gao Qing,
    Lin Mucun (illustrator), Guo
    Xi, and Zhou Zishu (interior
    design)

Partners
    Community residents of Anyuan
    North Lane
    Student volunteers from Central
    Academy of Fine Arts

Designer Organization Type
    • Civil Society

Team Size
    • 11–20

Design Quotient
    • 41–60%

Project Costs
    ▷ $100k–$500k

Source of Funding
    ▬ Government

Funding Mechanisms
    Fee for Service
    Equity Investment

Impact Measurement Methods
    Qualitative: Awards Received
    Quantitative: Volume of Media
       Coverage, Quantity or Area of
       Spaces Created

Mediums
    Spatial: Interior Space

               Design for Social Innovation

Digua Community

Repurposing unused spaces into community innovation hubs

In 2012, Beijing's network of 17,000 bomb shelters housed over 100,000 people, including many marginalized migrant workers who arrive in the capital city with limited networks of opportunity. This leaves them socially isolated and vulnerable. Designer Zhou Zishu saw this as an opportunity to create a network of spaces that could build community for migrant workers while also providing places for them to acquire skills that could help secure better job opportunities. Starting in 2013, Zhou and his team set out to create exactly that with Digua Communities, named after the Chinese word for sweet potato which connects poetically to the agricultural roots of the workers these spaces are designed to serve.

For Zhou, Digua symbolizes the spirit of sharing, and that idea is carried through in the conceptualization of the Digua spaces. The network is based on the idea of the rhizome, where there's no center and edge, but an even field of connections. Key to meeting Zhou's goal of providing an easier pathway for migrant workers entering Beijing was the need to enhance trust, both within these communities and between cities and rural areas. The spaces foreground sharing activities as a way to accomplish this goal.

Within each Digua Community space, principles of environmental design and social research were used to help the local community build their own unique sharing economy that utilizes whatever skills, interests, and relationships are already present. Before each space is designed, Zhou's team organizes the community residents to vote on the kind of space they want. Since these "sweet potato" spaces are public spaces within the community, Zhou says "we need to listen to more people from different ages to achieve 'spatial justice.'" They have learned that movie theaters, libraries, self-study classrooms, and dance studios are all popular requests.

Unassuming entrance to Digua, inside a converted bunker

Their first space, Anyuanbeili, has seen 40,000–50,000 visitors per year since it opened in December 2015. It offers a children's play area, barber shop, library, 3-D printing room, cafe, exercise area, and meeting rooms, in addition to the open center area which is used freely by the public. Of special concern for the community was air quality, given Beijing's struggles to reduce particulate matter in the air, so Anyuanbeili uses a custom-designed air ventilation system to maintain healthy air despite being in a basement.

By building relationships within the community prior to and during the process of transforming the basement, Digua Communities ensure that community members see the space as a "platform" designed for them. One of the intentions of this approach is to foster a community of "pro-sumers," or consumers who are also producers, who share their own creations and skills with their neighbors while also benefiting from the skills of others. As one resident described, the Digua space "[makes] the community more human, the connection between the people more intimate."

A range of people from surrounding neighborhoods, including migrant workers, young entrepreneurs, local government and urban youth are regular users of the Digua Community spaces today. They have provided networking opportunities to all local residents to create meaningful social interactions, particularly those who do not usually have a broader social connection in a metropolis, who were the original focus of the project.

Digua Community has grown to a total of four spaces and counting: three underground spaces in Beijing, each with an area of 500–1,000 square meters, and one above-ground space in Chengdu that is 1,500 square meters. In addition to expanding to the network of spaces, the team is also developing a Digua app that facilitates the residents' use of each space and can be customized to each community. In 2016, The Digua project won the Design for Asia award and it was nominated for the Beazley Designs of the Year the by Design Museum of London in 2018.

Images: Digua Community

Geographies of Power

Uniquely designed spaces create a variety of experiences despite no access to natural light

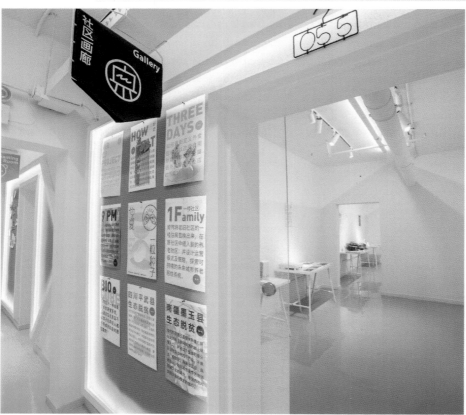

Design for Social Innovation

Digua's interior transformation is in stark contrast to the original context, seen here in the entrance

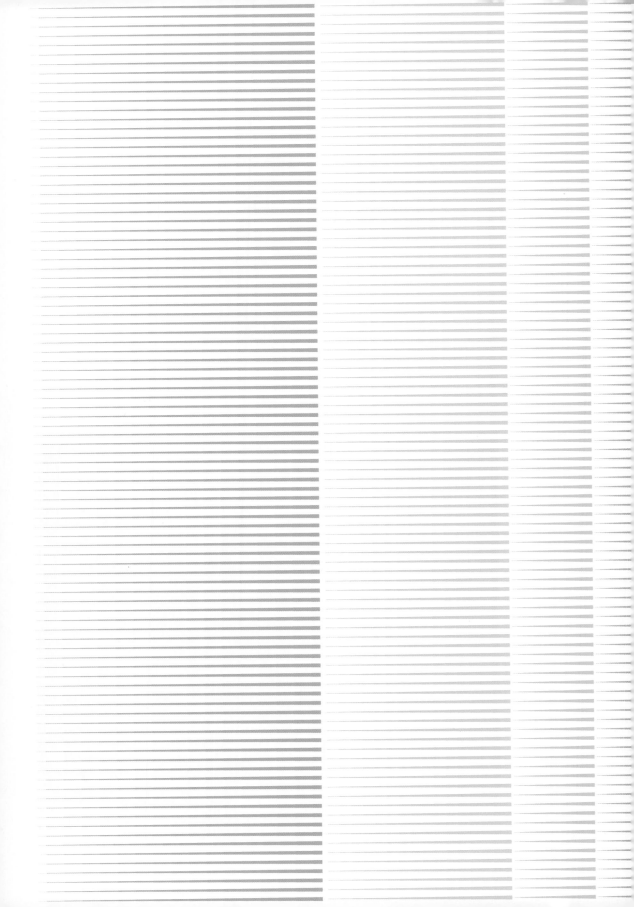

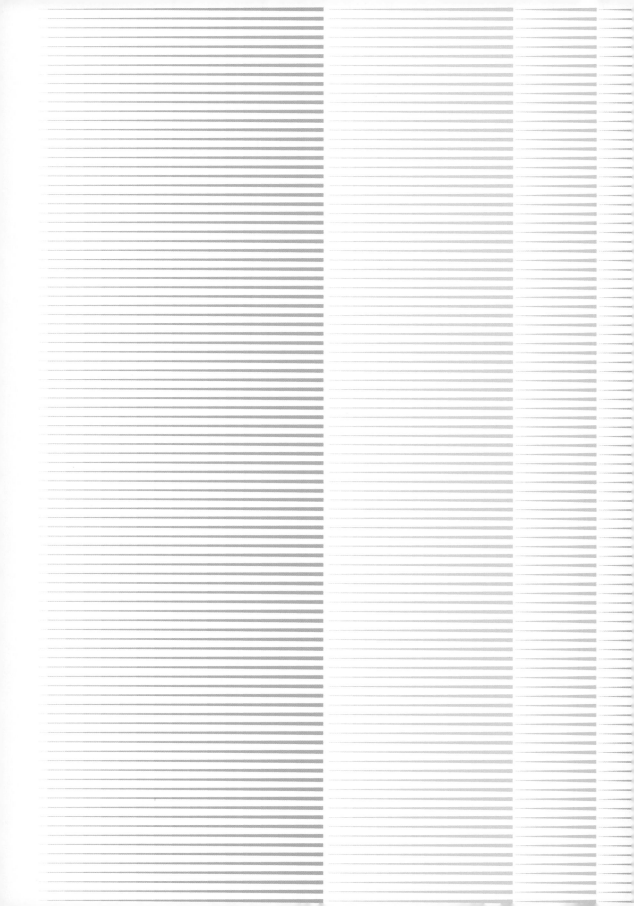

Trajectories of International Development

Ayah Younis, Sarah Fathallah, and Robert Fabricant, with Isabella Gady and Jenny Liu

From catalyzing refugee-driven innovation labs in Jordan to prototyping early childhood development programs in Lebanon, design is becoming an established practice in international development. We see signposts of its potential in geographies across the globe. However, a central question remains unanswered: can we confidently claim design has achieved meaningful impact in the sector? Despite significant investment from Western donors and prominent philanthropists, such as Melinda Gates, promoting the value of human-centered design (HCD) as a way to put beneficiaries at the center of the development process, many designers and experts would argue that design has not yet delivered on its promise.

Establishing "quality standards" for design's application in the context of international development demands a sophisticated appreciation of the unique limitations and factors that characterize the sector. Design teams who tackle international development projects must navigate fluid dynamics and many constraints: working with global teams and stakeholders with differing cultural perspectives, tight project resourcing, often lower access to technology, and last-mile delivery challenges to reach vulnerable communities around the world. Compared to the commercial world, where designers have clear measures of success, market-driven KPIs, and a solid understanding of the "customer," this is a space where what success looks like may be elusive and where the primary beneficiary of one's design solution may often be marginalized, powerless, and often hard to reach. The entrepreneurial culture of risk-taking that we celebrate in a commercial design context, and the tried-and-true techniques of design innovation, such as rapid prototyping and the start-up approach of "fail fast, succeed sooner," rarely align with the accountability logics and collective governance structures that underpin how the sector must operate to meet the systemic challenges of poverty alleviation, or humanitarian response.

Designers are making inroads despite many barriers. They are modeling new forms of collaboration and co-creation and facilitating stakeholder engagement with positive results. International development organizations are embracing design-led approaches and betting on a sustained commitment of both human resources and funding to try more and different types of solutions with design teams on their side. Design practitioners choosing to contribute to this field are taking hallmark methods such as HCD and adapting these with techniques from other fields such as ethnography, participatory action research, and insights from community organizing to expand on traditional design toolkits for iteration and problem-solving. This work is gradually shifting the mindset of development practitioners to be more user-focused, creating more empathetic and responsive teams. There is also a range of hybrid approaches that advocate for a more community-centered (vs. user-centered) design model that are emerging. In a sign of the field's progress, outcome evaluations and detailed measurement frameworks that link design interventions with other aspects of a project's goals are increasingly part and parcel of the build-out. The realization that feasibility, viability, and scalability criteria from the very beginning in the design process can increase the potential for success are considerations that are influencing how designers are approaching this work. As the field continues to grow, designers will need to expand on these efforts to continue proving design's merit for the sector.[1]

In this roundtable, our panel discusses some of the methods that are deployed, "wins," and ongoing challenges. Their insights represent an honest reflection on the humility and flexibility required to leverage design effectively amid the complexity of the sector.

The discussion took place at the beginning of May 2020 and was edited for clarity and length

Ayah Younis

I am a Jordanian designer, museum education specialist, and children's book writer. My career is focused on designing playful learning experiences for children 1 to 12 years old in Jordan and the Middle East. I started as a design engineer with an industrial design firm and then moved to the development sector, where I now apply design processes that are intuitively unknowing of best practices in the design field, to solve problems. When I learned about human-centered design, I realised what our intuition was seeking. Currently, I aspire to create an accessible design-facilitated environment that engages and enhances the lives of our local communities.

Sarah Fathallah

I am a Moroccan designer, researcher, and design educator who spent the last decade applying design to the social sector. My career first started in international development, specifically in the financial inclusion space. This was before I even knew what design was, or trained to become a designer. I always saw design as a collection of tools and processes that add to the range of approaches international development practitioners use to listen to, involve, or engage communities in the design and implementation of programs and services meant to serve them. I have since worked on a variety of engagements with governments, funders, and implementing organizations in over 20 countries and across several sectors within development.

Robert Fabricant

I transitioned to working in social impact full-time more than six years ago, as I did not see a model within the design industry for building a diverse practice that would tap into the creative potential of the communities that we seek to serve. It has been a profoundly challenging and humbling shift. I am extremely grateful to work with a talented and passionate team of designers in Dakar, Mumbai, London, Nairobi, and New York. Being part of the Dalberg Group has taught us how to apply design in increasingly strategic ways in development. It has also confirmed that too many well-intentioned, large-scale actors have lost touch with individual people and are ill-equipped to understand and adapt to the daily challenges they face in their lives.

Isabella: Design's presence in international development has been gaining traction. Let's start this roundtable with your insights and examples you may wish to share on how you see this unfolding. Are designers impacting the culture and practice of international development?

> **Ayah:** I'll speak of my experience with design both in local community-based organizations and international organizations. In the context of my prior work with The Children's Museum Jordan in Amman, I could see how much design we were doing without actually calling it "design." After I transitioned into my role at the Airbel Middle East Impact Lab at the International Rescue Committee [IRC], I began to notice gaps in practices between an international organization and a local organization. Many of the discussions that I was having with the IRC team included questions such as, "How can we bridge this gap?" At Airbel, when designing programs and designing interventions, we focus on identifying what people need and how we might be able to center our work around those needs. Local organizations do not always have the easiest access to many of the best practices international organizations have. It becomes our responsibility to find new ways to collaborate with these local NGOs, transfer knowledge, and build capacity together.

Isabella: Were there key learnings from your work in the Children's Museum that carried over into your current work in international development?

> **Ayah:** Working in a local organization, such as the Children's Museum, means mainly working with locals, listening to what they need, and setting up the right conditions for collaboration. There was a broad network of local talent that we leveraged in this way, and that's something that I am interested in bringing into my work at the IRC. I am now in the process of identifying how to engage with local creatives with my team. I realize they may not be designers by title, but I believe they are important contributors to the ecosystem we need to embrace. In the context of our international organizations, we are sometimes working not only in a bubble, but also in silos. That mode influences who we think of engaging with when it comes to collaboration—so often those individuals are not local. We must create a better balance between international experience and expertise and capitalizing on local talent to shape our projects. This is how we will sustain and scale, even after we are no longer working with a given local community.

Jenny: Sarah, let's pick up our initial question about design's evolution in international development with your perspective. You have worked in a variety of organizations—have you seen progress in design's uptake?

Sarah: I'll start off by acknowledging that if we were to define design as a process of creative problem exploration and problem solving, design has been far from the sole source of effective techniques for stakeholder engagement. Along with design, international development has adopted a variety of methods and approaches to explore and solve problems creatively. Methodologies such as participatory action research and community-based participatory research, which design has also embraced, started in the social sector first. Many of these tools have been around in the social sector for a long time; they have been informed by social movements and community-based practices and have proved effective in supporting stakeholder engagement. The new tools design brought us are certainly helping elevate and complement this other body of knowledge. We can attribute the interest in design and its visibility in the sector to funders and prominent actors in the philanthropy space. I am thinking of Melinda Gates, for example, who has been an important advocate for human-centered design's application in the field; her influential voice has made a difference I believe in the adoption of design by the sector. At this juncture, development practitioners are finding interesting ways to reconcile established methods with the new capabilities design brings to the table.

Jenny: So would you say that the overall narrative around development has changed due to design's contributions to the space?

Sarah: It's hard to say. I believe design's impact is often anecdotal actually; it's difficult to generalize what the impact really is at a sector level. There's the cynical view of, "Well, we were doing this before. You're just calling it something different and you're adding sticky notes to it." And then there's a more positive view, "Oh, this is a helpful process that formalizes the ways we were engaging with communities, doing research, and testing ideas before we implement them." Unquestionably though, development practitioners are becoming more fluent in the language of design. Again, whether that has actually truly impacted the practice—I don't know.

Robert: My sense is that design is a natural fit for the sector. The capacity of design to amplify how development practitioners conceive of the right ways to reach and engage communities, as well as drive broader creative problem-solving, is especially relevant. That said, I also believe design has not meaningfully impacted the sector yet. While concepts like "human-centered design" pop up with more frequency, I would argue that design itself is the least important piece of the narrative that is ongoing. It falls on us as designers, to be deliberate, humble, and supportive in how we bring additional creative skills and tools to the space and ensure they are perceived by our colleagues as well as a natural fit.

Another challenge we face for design's broader adoption in the sector, with the exception of a few influential cases, is that funders' priorities are not necessarily there. They'll talk about it, and recognize the importance of equity and participation, but they are often much more focused on a rather technocratic approach that tends to be framed in terms of "strategy." This is in contrast, and differs from the integration of design in the private sector. I came from a couple of decades of doing work in that other context. Within that world, the understanding of design as a user-centered approach, and the need to prototype ideas and iterate, has led to a meaningful shift in the mindset of leadership about why this matters. I am waiting to see what will happen in the development sector, where (again), the narrative is quite technical and generally driven by strategy and measurement and evaluation priorities.

Part of our goal bringing design to a firm like Dalberg—and the long game that we're trying to play—is that this place is a breeding ground for future leaders in the development space. Many employees are young when they join the firm. Some stay and become partners. Many move to other organizations and governments. Through their experiencing design first-hand, through our work my hope is that they will leave with a better understanding about what design can do for the sector. Outside this motivation of helping build the field, our team is doing a lot of community-based work that inspires us deeply. Sure, it is not easy to practice in this arena, since most decision-makers do not see this work as sufficiently strategic. This the journey we're on, and I think we're still in the early stages.

> **Isabella:** Robert, please unpack your statement about design not yet having achieved a meaningful impact in international development.

Robert: Oh, OK, give me the "easy" question. I certainly see a meaningful shift in the narrative about design influencing effective co-creation practices in the sector. Currently, there's a gap: the sector lacks mechanisms for communities to participate in shaping the very programs and interventions meant to contribute to their livelihoods. While I believe there is increasing recognition of this gap and attempts to design programs differently, there is also a great measure of lip service that continues to be paid to co-creation and similar forms of participatory engagement. I'll give you an example: recently, we worked with a couple of big funders to embed a co-creation framework across a portfolio of national-scale programs that targeted youth in multiple countries. It wasn't something we initiated. In another example, this approach was part of the funder's entire strategy. Yet, when we later explored digital platforms, they were like, "I don't think we need to do user research." So, yes, there are some best practices out there, but a bit of the disconnect remains.

On a positive note, funders are starting to recognize the importance of adopting more agile prototyping-first methods in order to implement effective programs. They know designers can help them master these approaches. Our team often engages in this kind of training. Our clients face constant barriers when trying to engage stakeholders and shift behavior when they work from a typical top-down logic; as we know, these strategies don't create the flexibility for co-creation. This is clearly a pain point for many partners we work with. It's equally important not just to ask, "Are you engaging people?" but "Are you engaging people in a quality way to produce a quality experience?" Doing this well is by far the hardest. One could argue that the international development sector has lived for too long with suboptimal outputs. The quality of those outputs has too often been low given time and resource constraints, with the outcomes showing these deficits. In sum, when it comes to meaningful community engagement and the role of design in it, I believe it remains challenging to influence the narrative from our side. Besides, quality is also a very foreign concept to most people I talk to. Identifying and articulating design's worth from an evidence-based perspective is still a work in progress.

> **Sarah:** Jumping off on Robert's point on design quality, part of the dissonance is that design, as applied in the commercial sector, works with a market-driven logic and competitive-driven model. In that capitalistic model, you have several agencies providing services, each competing on their value-add in terms of what they bring to the table to different clients. The assumption is that competition increases quality. You cannot apply that mindset to international development and the social sector in the same way. The typology of funding we have to operate with and the timelines are different. We are often contending with short to midterm project-based financing, which doesn't allow for long-term impact thinking when designing interventions. While the design community seems to have a more substantial interest in working in these spaces, we haven't rethought what it means to get to higher-quality design practice standards. We are far from operating with the collective and reciprocal mindset needed to succeed in the social sector, rather than with a competitive, scarcity-based model. An hypothesis of mine is that the competitive model, where different professionals and agencies have a "secret sauce" that isn't shared with others, prevents the sharing of best practices around the work that we do, and hinders us from improving our standards of work through collaboration. The dissonance that I am referring to lies with the fact that we just took a model that thrived within the private sector and applied it in the

social sector. The irony is that here's a sector where we should all be striving to provide the best-quality services to tackle the complex problems at hand, even if that means acknowledging that someone else is better placed to do the work.

Jenny: Ayah, Robert, from your experiences, do you each see learning mechanisms sufficiently integrated into the day-to-day practice of designers working in international development?

Ayah: One of the challenges we face with the design process, regardless of what we name it, is connected to the fact we're always racing against time. Even if the funder or donor champions design, time and capacity are always in short supply. As Robert points out, we must ask ourselves, "Are we doing enough co-creation across our teams, the community, and with other designers in the field?" In my opinion, we are not there yet.

"One of the challenges we face with the design process, regardless of what we name it, is connected to the fact we're always racing against time. Even if the funder or donor champions design, time and capacity are always in short supply."

Back to your question on learning, it also matters that we learn how to work better with internal colleagues and make the effort to involve them more and get them to understand the value of our processes. Our task as designers in the sector carries the responsibility to be reflective and articulate about our roles in these processes. It's not just about creating a solution. It's not just the end-user that we're working for/with. Creating meaningful interventions depends on it.

Robert: Let me touch on a couple of the points that Ayah and Sarah made. One of the reasons I love doing this work is connected to the fact I get to take a much longer timeline than I did working with private sector clients. Also, it is a fundamentally less competitive space that is much more open and where I find myself in active dialogue with many designers and peers. At this stage in my trajectory, I find this generous dynamic incredibly gratifying. Let me exemplify this point. Not too long ago, we helped launch a joint health initiative—Design for Health[2]—which was funded by some of the biggest donors in the US healthcare space and brought together a wide community of stakeholders. In that project, I witnessed the power in the sharing and learning we are discussing. But, even if we come together, we are such a tiny community when we compare ourselves to the scale of the issues that would benefit from design. It comes back to Sarah's point: it is imperative that we put our heads together to share best practices and leverage the lessons and insights about what we are good at doing now so that we can start scaling this work through different forms of outreach. In a research project at Dalberg on financial health amongst the aging US population, we experimented with this approach working with community-based organizations in Memphis. At first our partners were completely confused by the approach we were taking. But, as we progressed through the project together, their question became: "Why haven't we had these tools before? Why aren't other folks we're working with helping us do this?"

> **Isabella:** Affordances of time and the perceived value of design seem to be recurring dimensions in our discussion. Sarah, I would like to ask you to reflect on your work at the Mahali Lab,[3] and in particular its mission to build design-thinking capabilities within local communities.

Sarah: Since we have been discussing co-creation, it might help to interrogate a bit more what we mean by the term. MIT D-Lab's framework on participatory design[4] offers an orientation I quite like. Participatory design in this context serves as an umbrella term for any design process that at some point or another involves individuals and communities that are potentially impacted, affected, or served by its outcome(s). The framework sets out three prongs: design for, design with and design by. "Design for" is what we would typically consider to be design thinking or human-centered design, where community members are involved at sporadic moments. "Design with" refers to what we might call co-design in the Scandinavian "cooperative design" late 1960s and '70s sense of the term. Finally, there's "design by," and MIT D-Lab refers to it as creative capacity building, i.e., the community's capacity to effectively lead the process of design. In this case, designers or design professionals are only bringing their skills to the table to elevate existing creativity or capacity and the community itself leads.

Mahali Lab adheres to the "design by" framing. Over a project that took over a year to unfold with Syrian refugees, we explored with them at the driver's seat the many complex problems related to long-term displacement. They were in charge of guiding the exploration of what problems should be prioritized. Our role as designers in this project at the IRC became more that of capacity building and guidance rather than of execution of the work. Learning what skills are necessary for people to thrive in a design process without putting an emphasis solely on formal educational or academic training has been a significant dimension of our work. For example, how do we promote facilitation, inquiry, and creative problem-solving as skills? How might we create the conditions that enable community members to lead and make connections with the right resources as part of our work?

"How do we promote facilitation, inquiry, and creative problem-solving as skills? How might we create the conditions that enable community members to lead and make connections with the right resources as part of our work?"

Jenny: As you each know, designers often find themselves in the position of balancing a great variety of stakeholders: donors, implementing organizations and the beneficiaries of the services and programs that are being designed. Can you touch on some of the issues related to this balancing act?

Ayah: The IRC takes its responsibility as an international organization to educate funders and donors very seriously by scanning for the community's needs at large and then turning them into thematic focus areas. For example, early childhood development wasn't a high priority in the humanitarian aid field, despite studies that proved how important it is to work with children in the early stages of their development in a post-conflict context. Through our design work, we built a strong case that convinced funders to invest in early childhood development in one of my current projects. Design methodologies can identify the community's actual needs and bring together attention and action to addressing these needs.

Isabella: That's a great story of a win. Robert has already brought up the often political character of this work. What would you say are some of these strategies to avoid the donor's agenda taking over the agenda of an implementing organization? How can we ensure that the beneficiaries' needs remain at the center?

Robert: It is important to recognize our role beyond the effectiveness of some of the design methods we are deploying in the sector. For example, in the Collective Action Toolkit,[5] we turned what we first thought was

Design for Social Innovation

a co-creative process into a leadership training program that had much higher value for communities we worked with. In user-centered design, we do research to understand stakeholders who are decision makers. However, the problem we keep on running into is that when people hear user-centered design they say, "Oh, user-centered design. I only need you to understand my end-users," when it's actually, "No, you also should use this process to understand why someone in a government ministry is making a decision, or why someone in your own organization who might be doing measurement and evaluation is making decisions." Part of the learning curve for us at Dalberg Design is helping stakeholders understand this kind of systems capacity-building design can also be unleashed through direct community engagement. Figuring out how to translate community engagement insights into useful data points for strategic decision-making becomes crucial. The Human Account[6] is an example where we took what we learned during research in the form of rich stories and robust data, and then worked to structure this body of insights for use across different initiatives with stakeholders as varied as Safaricom and Lagos Business School. I believe that in design we are not strong enough in this area of harnessing our data; it is a learning curve we're in. We invest a lot of time on the ground, but our research is often not set up for ease of replication and it can be challenging to build on prior learnings.

> **Sarah:** First, I'd like to comment on the skills and creative capacity-building piece from a critical theory view. I've been reading Sasha Costanza-Chock's book *Design Justice*. The argument made, which I wholeheartedly agree with, is that no matter how inclusive, participatory, or democratic design processes are, by and large, they remain extractive to communities. The benefits of engaging with communities through a design process essentially end up in the hands and minds of the professional designers or design institutions involved in a project. I believe that capacity building might be one way to make that interaction less extractive. Compensation and creating local jobs within communities are also important to invest in. Transferring the responsibility of leading and managing international consultants' processes to local teams can also make a difference. Bottom line: our involvement with communities is extractive by default. When designing our engagements, we should keep asking how to make our processes less extractive front and center. A second point I'd like to make relates to legacies of financing in international development that also hark back in the US to neoliberalism historical trends of the '60s and '70s. This time saw the proliferation of philanthropy elites, and the expansion of the non-profit and social sectors aided by an outpouring of tax-exemptions investments. In this sense, much of the social sector is built on the goodwill and the agenda

building of philanthropists, charities, and foundations, and the power dynamics there are complex and should not be underestimated.

Ayah: That makes me think of a research paper I worked on a few years ago which investigated how foreign funding had influenced children's literature in Jordan since the beginning of the Syrian war. I agree, at times funders come with a very specific agenda. They have a particular idea about the kind of influence they want to see through their work.

Robert: Let me jump in here and complement Sarah's perspective on how power and money flow within the sector. We see it all the time and feel uncomfortable, given many of our clients. However, many of our partner organizations and funders would like to see themselves as addressing what they will call a market failure. They want to encourage more entrepreneurial approaches. Some of the most exciting work we're currently engaged in and where we see real traction is with social enterprises or entrepreneurial activities that are pretty localized and driven by grassroots capacities and needs. Social enterprises tend to be quite agile and can positively influence how larger institutions implement programs. In contrast, government projects can involve a very long cycle of slow institutional change. I wish we could map pathways between the two; we need them both working together more effectively, because government agencies are rarely where many solutions start, even if they're in the best position to institutionalize work. There are many opportunities to increase capacity and grow and strengthen some of the entrepreneurial efforts we see unfolding. Design can play an influential role here.

Jenny and Isabella: Any final thoughts?

Sarah: I'm always craving conversations among practitioners who work in or around design in the social sector. Many of these conversations are tackling thorny issues, and there are a few I'd like to highlight. The first one touches on the unintended consequences of design in the sector. IBM defined design as "the intention behind an outcome." The Creative Reaction Lab, headed by Antionette Carroll, offers a definition of design as "the intention and unintentional impact behind an outcome." As we put designs out in the world, do we absolve ourselves from the responsibility of any kind of misuse or abuse of the work produced? How do we anticipate, mitigate, and hold ourselves responsible for the unintentional harm we might cause? Second, let's be more aware about the privilege and power dynamics we cannot avoid; George Aye from the Greater Good Studio speaks eloquently about this critical awareness we must own. Finally, I believe we should engage in more substantive discussions about trauma; there is important trauma-informed research to be leveraged in this sector. We work with vulnerable communities who have experienced a lot of trauma and have an opportunity to leverage principles that promote healing in our prototyping, co-creation, and facilitation processes.

Ayah: I'd like to emphasize the importance of having a stronger hand in modeling the design culture we want to see within our organizations. There's a saying that one hand doesn't clap. We need to create this enabling environment for our work because, ultimately, it's not about us. For example, Jordan ranks amongst the top five countries globally when it comes to water scarcity. Since I was young, they ran water conservation campaigns. And we still have the same problem today. There is something not working well there. As Robert asked earlier, how are we creating meaningful interventions that are advancing the well-being of our communities? It's not just the method or solution that we should be concerned with; it's also the system we are working within/around that we must engage with.

Robert: I have a couple of final points. The first is patience about the learning curve we are on. I think this is a great rich community to be a part of. I am inspired by almost everybody I meet who is doing this kind of work. The second is about being fundamentally user-centered about this whole effort, beyond just our potential beneficiaries but also with our non-design partners. Who are we trying to reach? Have we brought them sufficiently into our processes? Are there enough non-designers involved in our efforts? Are we doing enough to spell out our methods and be inclusive of others so they can have more of an understanding of the value of our work? I believe that expanding on the multidisciplinarity of perspectives and voices that weigh in on this work is fundamental. Failing to do so, I fear, would mean we are just speaking to ourselves as designers. Bringing others along will make all of the difference as we continue on the journey of building design capacity for the sector.

1   Jocelyn Wyatt, Tim Brown, and Shauna Carey, "The Next Chapter in Design for Social Innovation," *Stanford Social Innovation Review (SSIR)* 19 (1) (January 1, 2021): 40–47.

2   "Design for Health," accessed April 9, 2021, www.designforhealth.org/.

3   Mahali Lab is a case study included in this book (p110).

4   "Innovation Practice | MIT D-Lab," accessed April 9, 2021, https://d-lab.mit.edu/innovation-practice/.

5   frog, "Collective Action Toolkit 2019," n.d., https://info2.frogdesign.com/en/collective-action-toolkit.

6   The Human Account is a case study included in this book (p120).

Trajectories of International Development

Mahali Lab

Enabling Syrians and Jordanians affected by the refugee crisis to identify and solve problems in their communities

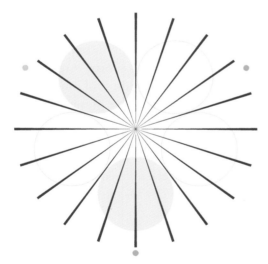

Beyond Bias

Removing the implicit barriers that limit the education of youth about contraceptives

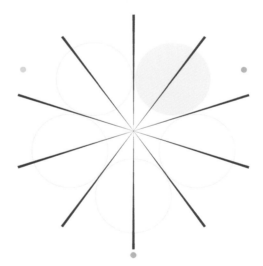

Nawe Nuze Innovation Hub

Institutionalizing innovation methods and management within an international NGO

Design for Social Innovation

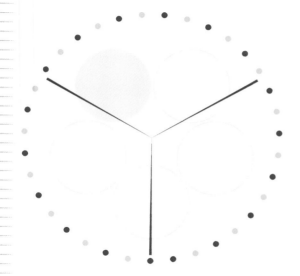

The Human Account

Transforming how financial service providers understand, invest in, design for, and engage the billions who are underserved

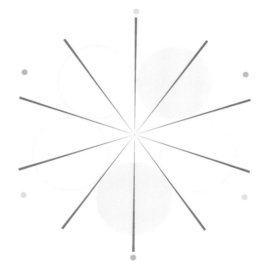

Yala Food Market

Prototyping solutions for food systems in Thailand by integrating a local and global approach

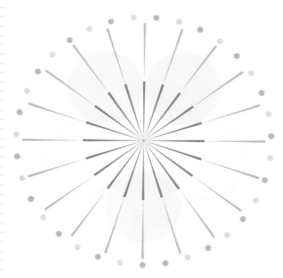

Redesigning U-Report

Helping youth connect on their own terms with international development

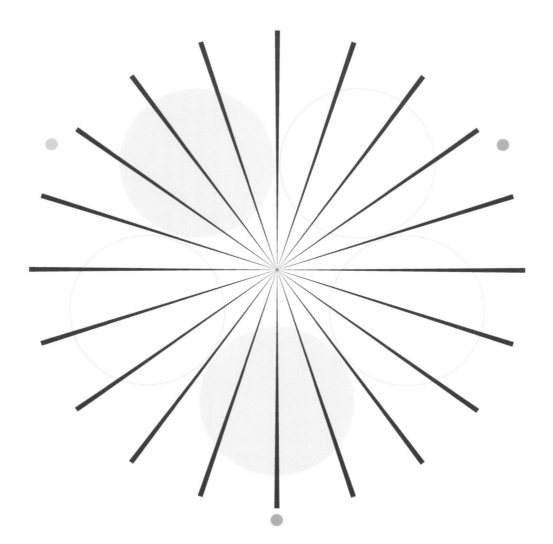

Duration
2016–2019 (design), 2019–2021
(implementation)

Location
Pakistan, Tanzania, Burkina
Faso

Categories
Health and Wellness

Designer
YLabs

Partners
Pathfinder International
Camber Collective
RAND Corporation
Bill & Melinda Gates Foundation

Key Contributors
Theo Gibbs
Jordan Levine
Caroline Wong
Andrea Lacorrazza
Rebecca Hope

Designer Organization Type
• Non-Profit

Team Size
• 2–4

Design Quotient
• 61–80%

Project Costs
▱ $100k–$500k

Source of Funding
▰ Foundation/Non-Profit/
Endowment

Funding Mechanisms
Grant

Impact Measurement Methods
Qualitative: Stakeholder
Interviews, Focus Groups,
Mystery Client Visits,
Participant/Client/User
Feedback
Quantitative: Randomized
Controlled Trial, Surveys

Mediums
Spatial: Exhibition
Experiential: Workshop

Design for Social Innovation

Beyond Bias

Removing the implicit barriers that limit the education of youth about contraceptives

Of the estimated 38 million sexually active young people ages 15–19 in the Global South who don't want a child in the next two years, roughly 60% have an unmet need for contraception and contraceptive usage among youth is low. There are many contributing factors that prevent young people from even stepping foot in a healthcare clinic to explore their contraceptive options, including community stigma, spousal or parental opposition, and misconceptions about negative side effects. In many contexts, community healthcare providers can act as gatekeepers to selling or prescribing contraception to young people. YLabs, a global design and research organization working to improve health and economic opportunity for young people, found that providers might judge a client as being too young to be sexually active and refuse to provide contraceptive options. These biases are often unconscious and implicit and are heavily influenced by the societal norms of the providers' communities. As one provider reflected, "We are also mothers, sisters, and aunties—this is where we fail as providers."

Working with a small consortium of partners, YLabs' challenge was to design a scalable health service model that would reduce the bias of healthcare providers against young people in Burkina Faso, Pakistan, and Tanzania. The goal was for all youth clients between the ages of 15 and 24 to receive unbiased, comprehensive contraceptive counseling and services, regardless of age, marital status, or parity. To approach the challenge, the team worked with both private and public sector health facilities and co-designed solutions with healthcare providers, government officials, health managers, and young people themselves.

To overcome the challenges of this work, the team combined multiple qualitative and quantitative research approaches to develop and evaluate this program. First, a quantitative survey of 811 providers in three countries was conducted to identify six psychographic segments of healthcare providers. Next, YLabs conducted qualitative design research with 373 young people, providers, and community members. This included training young people to conduct "mystery client" visits (similar to the mystery shopper technique) to gather direct information about providers' actual treatment of clients. To the best of the team's knowledge, this was the first project of its kind to rigorously characterize provider bias across multiple countries and systematically test solution approaches.

Two providers test the service design model during live prototyping

The team prototyped in two phases with 214 providers and youth. During the first phase, "rough" prototyping, ten different early concepts were tested with providers and young people in a simulated clinic setting using rapid testing methods like paper prototyping. During the second phase, "live" prototyping, three refined concepts were tested in real clinic settings over a three-month period. To know if their live prototypes were working, the team developed a framework identifying six principles of unbiased care and an accompanying client survey to assess providers' performance on each principle. Client feedback data during live prototyping was collected from each of the 29 participating clinics using a custom-built, self-administered audio-visual survey application to protect client privacy and accommodate different literacy levels. Nearly 40% of youth clients responded to the survey (n=3,215).

The final design developed as a result of prototyping, client feedback, and the input of a technical expert review panel tasked with ensuring that the proposed design leveraged existing evidence from public health literature. The resulting Beyond Bias intervention is a three-pillared program that supports healthcare providers to activate self-awareness of their own biases, apply unbiased practices in their daily work, and receive public recognition when they achieve improvements in services to youth clients. While the overall strategy is consistent across all three countries in order to increase scalability, the program is adapted for each context based on the segment mix in that country. For example, one pillar of the intervention involves engaging providers in a peer learning community on

Healthcare providers earn certificates and symbols of achievement as a part of the Reward pillar of the Beyond Bias program

WhatsApp. In Tanzania, the WhatsApp content and discussion prompts were more focused on correcting hormonal method misconceptions and addressing HIV risk concerns, which were the primary drivers of biased treatment for the provider segments in that country. In Pakistan, which had a very different mix of segments, the WhatsApp content focused on addressing providers' fears related to long-acting reversible contraceptives and creating space for discussion about social norms.

Across the three countries, the attitudes and knowledge of healthcare providers improved during the three-month live prototyping phase. For example, 82% of the providers who previously believed that hormonal birth control methods were harmful to adolescents' bodies reported that they no longer held this medically inaccurate belief after participating in the prototype program (n=88). As one provider in Burkina Faso described, "Before, when a young girl came for a contraceptive method, we said, 'No, you are young and you should not use an implant.' But now, with the training received through [the program], she is free to choose the method that she wants." In September 2019, Pathfinder International began full-scale implementation of the designed intervention in 227 facilities across the three countries. A 12-month mixed-methods randomized controlled trial is currently underway to evaluate the project's impact on provider behavior and attitudes. The results of the evaluation will inform the global health sector's approach to the critical and persistent issue of provider bias in reproductive healthcare provision.

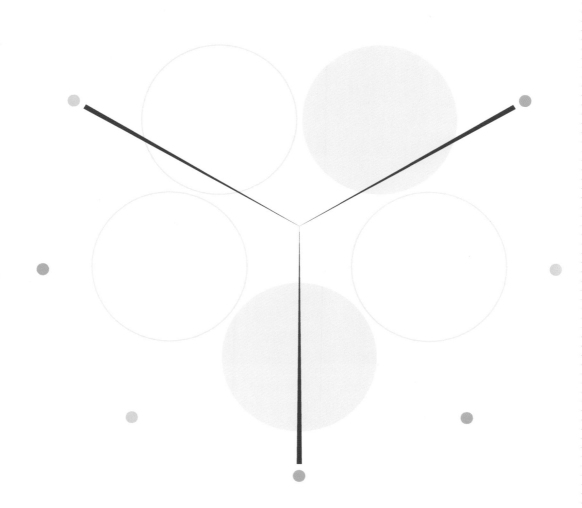

Duration
September 2017–April 2019

Location
Jordan (Amman, Irbid, and
Mafraq)

Categories
Humanitarian Affairs

Designer
Airbel Impact Lab

Partners
International Rescue Committee
(IRC)
Shamal Start

Designer Organization Type
• Non-Profit

Team Size
• 8–10

Design Quotient
• 21–40%

Project Costs
▷ Undisclosed

Source of Funding
▬ Foundation/Non-Profit/
Endowment

Funding Mechanisms
Grant

Impact Measurement Methods
Qualitative: Assessment
of Change to Internal
Organizational Practices

Mediums
Experiential: Training,
Workshops
Organizational: Service

Mahali Lab

Enabling Syrians and Jordanians affected by the refugee crisis to identify and solve problems in their communities

In 2017, as the Syrian crisis was entering its sixth year, the work of the humanitarian community in Jordan was moving away from an emergency response model, crucial in the first years of refugee displacement, to encouraging self-reliance and improving the lives of the 655,000 refugees in a now protracted situation. The Mahali Lab at the International Rescue Committee was created in response to this situation with the goal of uncovering "the articulated and unarticulated challenges and needs that occupy the time, efforts, and mental energy of Syrian refugees and their host communities," and work with the communities to address those challenges. Mahali Lab's participation model put community members in charge of the design process so that they were not just giving input or generating ideas, but co-creating from beginning to end. As they describe, "those who are affected by a problem are best positioned to solve it."

The Lab was part community consultation and part incubator. Syrian refugees and vulnerable Jordanians were asked to help to identify problems and then entrepreneurial individuals and teams were supported in developing solutions to those problems. It started by conducting a series of open-ended community consultations to understand the challenges faced by Syrian refugees and their host communities. These discussions acknowledged the obvious issues as well as making room to surface those issues which were going unspoken. Six challenges were identified that represented experiences heard across locations, genders, and age groups, and these were opened to the community for feedback through in-person and social media voting to narrow it down.

Three emerged as the highest priority. First, people struggled to access enough income to meet a dignified standard of living. Second, people were not

Participants sharing their perspectives on how familiar but difficult problems may be solved

accessing services they had the right to. Third, children were not learning. Underpinning all of these was a general sense that people did not feel in control over their future.

These challenges were turned into prompts for a series of three ten-week design sprints that included 15 teams, with the Lab providing workspace, financial support, and access to full-time mentors and experts (designers and researchers) to help with the process of moving from challenge to actionable response. Proposed solutions were evaluated on criteria like financial feasibility, market demand, team experience and commitment, and scalability, and the strongest candidates received incubation services from partner accelerator Shamal Start.

One team is working with local hospitals to create a blood bank to ensure that Syrians living in Jordan, who aren't allowed to donate blood, can get blood transfusions when needed. Other teams' ideas include a card deck for deaf children and playground equipment to foster early childhood development. The Lab is currently exploring different pathways for these ideas, including identifying NGOs or other social sector actors within Jordan that can potentially pilot those solutions as part of their programming.

The larger shift represented by Mahali Lab is from providing services for refugees to creating enabling environments where they can thrive despite the challenging conditions they are dealing with. For those who are displaced from Syria to Jordan, 93% of whom are living below the poverty line, Mahali Lab shows that one's circumstances are not synonymous with one's identity. While the world tends to see refugees as people in need, refugees are also needed as the ones who are best positioned to develop resourceful responses to the desires and demands of their communities.

Design for Social Innovation

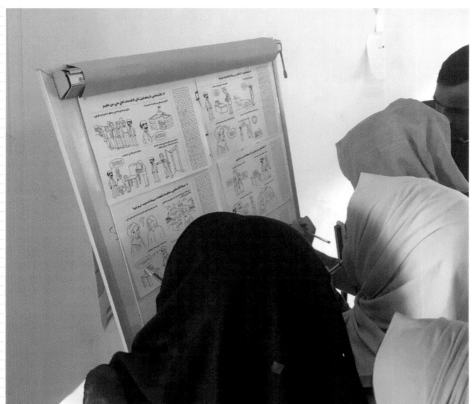

Mahali Lab volunteer and community activist leads a voting exercise with community members to determine the most promising ideas

During one of the design sprints, multiple ideas to solve the challenge of income and livelihoods were generated, tested, and ranked

Children were also invited to give their opinions of the ideas under consideration

"When I saw the Facebook ad… I thought if I was a part of Mahali, I might be able to better help make the NGOs understand the problems refugees face and to be a voice for my community… My favorite part about being a part of the Lab has been that my personality has changed. I've become more confident and I feel like I have more ways to express my feelings and articulate myself to people. I've learned not to be shy when I'm expressing my thoughts, and how to ask for things."

Hiba, community innovator

Design for Social Innovation

Innovators
use design
research tools
with Syrians
with disabilities
to understand
their greatest
barriers in the
labor market

**Images: Mahali Lab, Airbel Impact Lab, and
International Rescue Committee**

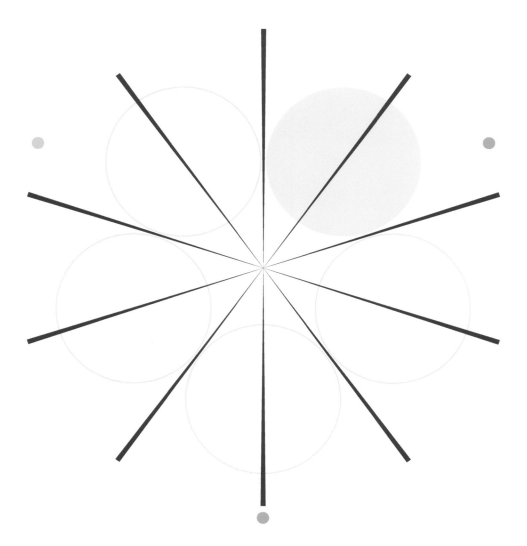

Duration
January–August 2019

Location
Bujumbura, Burundi

Categories
Social Justice

Designer
CARE USA Innovation Team and
CARE Burundi Task Force

Partners
CARE Burundi

Key Contributors
Tim Bishop
Grace Hsieh
Dana Tzagaegbe
Dane Wetschler
Ninon Ndayikengurukiye

Designer Organization Type
• Non-Profit

Team Size
• 2–4

Design Quotient
• 81–100%

Project Costs
$25–$100k

Source of Funding
Foundation/Non-Profit/
Endowment

Funding Mechanisms
Fee for Service

Impact Measurement Methods
Qualitative: Adoption by the
Organization and/or Other
Organizations, Participant/
Client/User Feedback
Quantitative: Number of Projects
Initiated, Financial Viability,
Including Funding/Revenue
Generated, Growth in Product/
service adoption or usage

Mediums
Organizational: Innovation Lab

Design for Social Innovation

Nawe Nuze Innovation Hub

Institutionalizing innovation methods and management within an international NGO

In 2016, CARE International, a large humanitarian and international development NGO that operates in over 90 countries, conducted a global survey of over 5,000 of staff across the organization and learned that 86% of staff had or knew about an innovative idea, but only 13% of them knew the support systems or resources within CARE to test, iterate, and bring those ideas to life. As with other major international NGOs, CARE faces several hurdles to innovation, among them being the disproportionate decision-making and strategy-setting power that lies across the hierarchy of the organization and an organizational culture that struggles to embrace exploration and experimentation.

Program design at CARE often follows donor-issued requests for proposals, leaving community members peripherally engaged in the process. This model represents a barrier to innovation by distancing the organization from opportunities for more diverse insights. CARE Burundi realized that to make greater progress on the challenges facing their country, they would need to change the way they designed programs. "Social challenges such as gender-based violence, malnutrition, youth unemployment, and lack of governance are huge problems in Burundi," said Afurika Juvenal, the Country Director for CARE in Burundi, "They are too complex for old methods and demand new approaches."

To enhance its ability to respond to such complex challenges, CARE Burundi leadership launched the Nawe Nuze Innovation Hub in 2018 as a center for facilitating civil society, communities, the private sector, and government to co-design solutions, policies, and programs that address injustices faced by women and youth. CARE Burundi enlisted the support of CARE USA's Innovation Team to provide strategic advice as they activated the Hub.

The team's goal was to help position CARE Burundi as an "ecosystem catalyst" for innovation on a variety of social challenges in Burundi, meaning

CARE Burundi would be convenor and connector rather than sole or primary actor. To do so, they built the capacity of staff to deploy new methods, mindsets, and processes that would allow for greater participation among community members and other key stakeholders to contribute to the program design process. New management systems and accountability mechanisms were established to institutionalize these new ways of working among staff and stakeholders. Success would be measured by CARE Burundi's ability to effectively engage multiple external stakeholders to co-design, secure resources for, and launch new programs that generate impact.

In their first visit to Burundi, the CARE USA Innovation Team learned that staff lacked clear incentives, time, support, and concrete tools and methods to operationalize progress on bringing new ideas to life. In response, the team introduced an innovation strategy, management framework, and set of new methods for program design. This included: standardized "activity canvas" templates designed for staff to use in capturing new ideas; training exercises showing staff how to move from idea generation, to a validation plan, to test prototypes of the ideas; and a blueprint for senior management on how to manage, evaluate, and "green-light" new initiatives pursued by staff by viewing them as a portfolio.

CARE USA provided three months of coaching as CARE Burundi built their internal capacity and made a second visit to Burundi to help troubleshoot and evolve the new way of working. Due to emerging adaptation challenges escalated by CARE Burundi leadership, the Innovation Team worked with eight project design teams from CARE Burundi to uncover additional opportunities for refinement. This helped uncover additional roadblocks, such as time-starved team members, the need to more closely track return on investment, and uncertainty on how to approach a portfolio-based way of making decisions.

As a result of taking the leap to adopt this new way of working, CARE Burundi has been able to secure funding to support programs that were designed and validated under this new approach with institutional donors such as the Norwegian Agency for Development Cooperation and the European Union. Examples include a youth-centered social innovation and entrepreneurship program that has scaled to three regions in the country; a national storytelling competition and campaign to spread strategies for ending gender-based violence; and the country's first Policy Design Lab, which works to advance gender justice in the country. As an added bonus, the Hub space generates revenue through event rentals, lodging, and other business services, which collectively offset operating costs.

CARE's work on the Nawe Nuze Innovation Hub, and the Hub's accomplishments to date, demonstrates the importance of establishing management systems, operational frameworks, and building a common culture to ensure the long-term success of design practices within NGOs.

Awards ceremony for a hackathon created to expand access to entrepreneurship among women and youth

Image: CARE Burundi

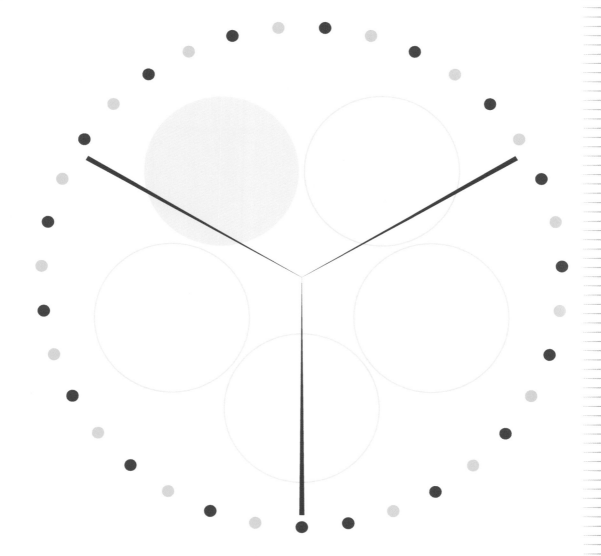

Duration
May 2017–present

Location
Nigeria, Kenya, Tanzania,
Pakistan, India, Myanmar

Categories
International Development
Economic
Policy
Financial Health and Inclusion

Designer
Dalberg Design

Partners
Rockefeller Philanthropy
Advisors
Bill & Melinda Gates Foundation
Lagos Business School

Ashoka University's Center for
Social & Behavior Change
Karandaaz

Key Contributors
Robert Fabricant
Prerak Mehta
Michael Mori
Stephen Morrison
Priti Rao

Designer Organization Type
• For-Profit

Team Size
• 21–49

Design Quotient
• 21–40%

Project Costs
▷ Undisclosed

Source of Funding
▬ Foundation/Non-Profit/
Endowment

Funding Mechanisms
Unspecified

Impact Measurement Methods
Qualitative: Observed Impact on
Policy
Quantitative: Web/Mobile
Analytics, Project Replication/
Citation by Other Groups,
Participants/Stakeholders
trained

Mediums
Digital: Website

The Human Account

Transforming how financial service providers understand, invest in, design for, and engage the billions who are underserved

Nearly 3 billion people around the world lack access to affordable, high-quality financial services for needs like a line of credit to start a small business or insurance against emergencies. Despite the years of concerted efforts in the financial sector to sign up unbanked people for accounts, cheap digital bank accounts have not been widely adopted and have had little impact on people's lives.

To address this, Dalberg Design—a global organization that taps into the creative potential of people, local communities, and organizations to co-design solutions supporting their needs and aspirations for a better life—partnered with Rockefeller Philanthropy Advisors, Bill & Melinda Gates Foundation, Lagos Business School, Ashoka University's Center for Social & Behavior Change, and Karandaaz. Together they created The Human Account, an open-source public information resource aimed at enabling better design of products and policies to help people live a healthier financial life.

The team's goal was to better understand the contexts, preferences, needs, and aspirations of customers in emerging markets, and to support the creation of products and services that meet those needs. Better understanding of the needs and contexts of individuals will lead to better financial services, policies, regulation, and development work.

Dalberg developed a three-dimensional research framework to reveal the contextual, behavioral, and psychological dimensions of customers' financial lives, including aspects of their identity and circumstances, what they do to manage their households and their lives, and why they chose particular financial strategies. This framework enabled the collection of 5.5 million demographic, behavioral and psychological data points across all six countries in the study.

Still from a documentary video produced by the team showing a farmer in Limuru, Kenya check his bookkeeping

Image: Ben McIntire, cinematographer and Danny Abel, director

From that massive data collection effort, the team developed market segmentations. For each country, the market segmentation describes four to six indicative groups per country based on characteristics of an individual's financial life and behaviors. In total, 34 data-based, nationally representative customer segments were identified, all informed by contextual, behavioral, and psychometric data and research establishing critical factors that underpin financial health.

Dalberg also created 78 in-depth qualitative user profiles, and six national datasets representing 11,500 respondents across the six countries, to help users of The Human Account understand the financial lives of 1.98 billion people. Throughout the process, the team applied multiple research and analysis disciplines including human-centered design, cognitive psychology, behavioral science, and large-scale survey-based market research. This included cluster, principal components, regression, and descriptive statistical analysis to identify areas within which to apply more focus through contextual, behavioral, and psychological models. Combined, this allowed the team to interpret findings and describe the segments in rich detail. We then developed mini-surveys for each country to enable providers to quickly identify each segment within their customer base.

The defining characteristics of each segment are presented through profiles of individuals who represent them. These real-life accounts, represented in compelling first-person short documentary videos, add the human element which is sometimes missing from such a wide study. They are meant to highlight the incredible creativity, resilience, and resourcefulness with which individuals nav-

Design for Social Innovation

igate their financial lives. The team was able to generate a more realistic and actionable understanding of people's financial lives at scale, by combining the depth of qualitative research with the numerical rigor of quantitative analysis. Since its launch, The Human Account has been adopted by a wide variety of partners, from the India Post to Safaricom to Lagos Business School, to inform product innovation, go-to-market strategies, and government policy.

Khin Mar Aye (left) participates in a household financial mapping activity with researcher Tnang Pan in Shan State, Myanmar

Image: David Hollo

Khin Mar Aye, a farmer in Shan State, manages the bookkeeping for her household

Images (left and facing page bottom): Ben McIntire, cinematographer and Danny Abel, director; *The Human Account—Khin Mar Aye*, short documentary video

Dalberg Design's James Maina (left) conducts human-centered design research with Marion, a farmer and local retail entrepreneur in Limuru, Kenya

Image: Stephen Morrison

Sein Tun, a security guard and farmer in Shan State, walks to his sugar cane farm

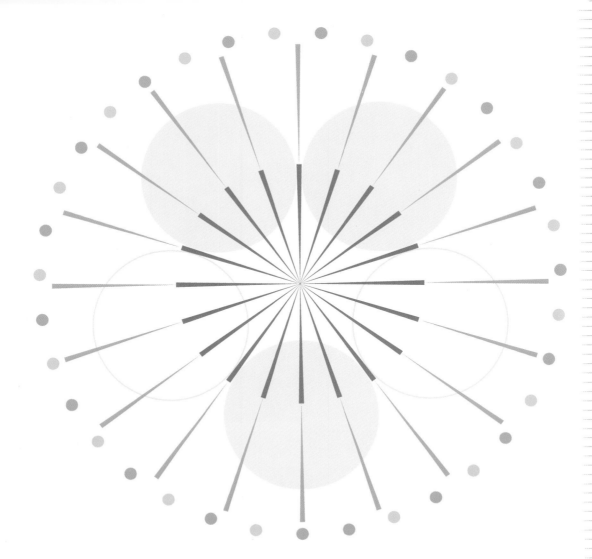

Duration
   November 2018 — October 2019

Location
   Started in Uganda, now in 72
      countries

Categories
   Policy

Designer
   UNICEF Office of Innovation

Partners
   Over 40 country-specific steering
      committees comprised of
      members of government,
      NGOs, and young people
   350-plus partnerships with
      government, NGOs, youth
      organizations, private sector
   Global steering committee

Key Contributors
   Tanya Accone
   Jonathan Newberry
   James Powell
   Hira Hafeez-Ur-Rehman
   Christopher Brooks

Designer Organization Type
   • Non-Profit

Team Size
   • 21–49

Design Quotient
   • 0–20%

Project Costs
   ▷—— $100k–$500k

Source of Funding
   ►—— Private Company
   ►—— Self-Funding

Funding Mechanisms
   Self-Funded
   Grant

Impact Measurement Methods
   Qualitative: Stakeholder
      Interviews
   Quantitative: Growth in Product/
      Service Adoption or Usage

Mediums
   Digital: App, Website, Social
      Media Communications, SMS,
      Chatbot
   Experiential: Training, Education
   Organizational: Service

Redesigning U-Report

Helping youth connect on their own terms with international development

Too many of the most vulnerable children and young people around the world are still excluded from the development processes designed to improve their lives—recipients of aid rather than the shapers of their own development. In response to this challenge, the Innovation Office of UNICEF developed a way to communicate directly with children and young people called U-Report, launching the platform through their Uganda office in 2011.

U-Report sends SMS polls and informational alerts to its participants, collecting real-time responses, and subsequently publishes gathered data. Issues polled include health, education, water, sanitation and hygiene, youth unemployment, HIV/AIDS, and disease outbreaks. Two-way communication on these topics helps create effective "citizen reporters" who are empowered to speak out on issues that matter to them, while also providing a way for leaders to receive and be informed by real-time data from often-excluded constituencies.

In Nigeria, U-Report provides life-saving information and one-on-one counseling services to assist child protection and monitor disease outbreaks. In Italy, U-Report On The Move focuses on the care, protection, and social inclusion of young migrants and refugees. In Mozambique, U-Report has provided information on issues like HIV/AIDS prevention, sexual and reproductive health, early marriage, or violence against children daily. A community of counselors from UNICEF Mozambique partner organization Associação Coalizão responded to over 300,000 individual questions on the platform in 2018.

In the process of scaling U-Report (as of 2020, U-Report is active in 72 countries), the team found that the product required a redesign to reduce the complexity of the app for users and make it easier for UNICEF to synthesize useful feedback from user messages. Initial feedback reported that the product was difficult to use, with results often displayed incorrectly due to aging technology.

Deloitte conducted an independent evaluation in 2018, and found that, "There is an opportunity that is not being seized to more meaningfully and strategically integrate U-Report as a platform to inform program priorities, design and implementation across all programs. This is the case at both the global level and at the country level." In that sense, redesigning the product was an opportunity to correct existing issues while realizing broader opportunities to leverage the platform as a decision-making aid in larger investments.

During the redesign process, UNICEF's Office of Innovation internal design team worked with U-Report users and partners to pinpoint the biggest struggles, to amplify the areas of most excitement, and to fully understand these various perspectives. Input fed in through design research including interviews, journey mapping, and co-creative exercises in Côte d'Ivoire, France, Brazil, Ukraine, and Tanzania. Redesign ideas were tested through a cycle of iterative prototyping that put the rethought product back in users' hands, enabling the team to hear directly from key stakeholders and youth reporters. Feedback was quantified with surveys and measurable written feedback before finalizing the new version of the product.

The redesigned product clarified the user experience to "build for simplicity and focus on the results and stories," according to U-Report, both individually and in the aggregate. The research process, largely about listening to users, also identified important technical upgrades such as making the site fully mobile-friendly for the smartphone era after learning that young people were

"almost never visiting the platform via a desktop computer." In addition to SMS, they have now expanded to include other digital messaging options.

Since its inception in Uganda, U-Report has matured into a critical feedback loop for UNICEF's global work that includes partnerships with over 400 government and civil society organizations. According to the UNICEF Office of Innovation, U-Report continues to expand at a rate of one new U-Reporter sign-up every 15 seconds. In the wake of the COVID-19 pandemic, a U-Report information chatbot was implemented as part of the emergency response, with over 20 million young people and communities engaged on COVID-19 through the tool as of June 2020.

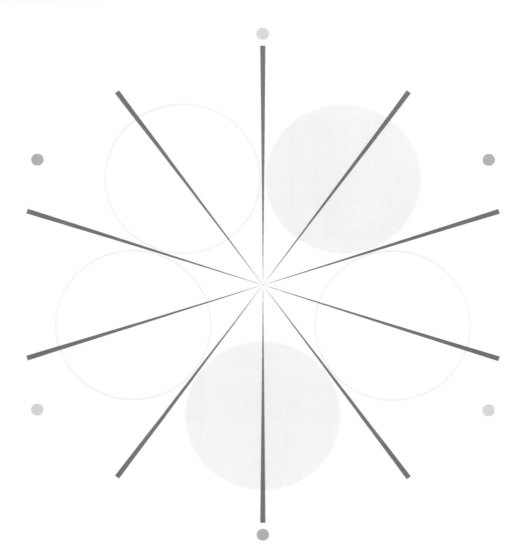

Duration
August 2019–present

Location
Yala, Yala Province, Thailand

Categories
International Development
Health and Wellness

Designer
Agirre Lehendakaria Center

Partners
UNDP-Asia Regional Hub
Danish Design Centre

Key Contributors
Tanya Accone
Jonathan Newberry
James Powell
Hira Hafeez-Ur-Rehman
Christopher Brooks

Designer Organization Type
● Academia

Team Size
● 5–7

Design Quotient
● 21–40%

Project Costs
▭▷ $25k–$100k

Source of Funding
▬▬ Government

Funding Mechanisms
Fee for Service

Impact Measurement Methods
Qualitative: Participant/Client/
User Feedback
Quantitative: Number of Projects
Initiated, Jobs Created,
Financial Viability, Including
Funding/Revenue Generated

Mediums
Experiential: Training
Organizational: Business,
Services

Yala Food Market

Prototyping solutions for food systems in Thailand by integrating a local and global approach

The UN's development agency, the United Nations Development Programme (UNDP), has taken on an agenda of organizational reform as part of its current strategic plan to help countries achieve the 2030 Sustainable Goals Agenda. The plan aligns with the overall UN reform agenda[1] and sets out a vision for the evolution of UNDP that responds to a changing development landscape by focusing on innovation and integrated, multi-stakeholder partnerships at the country level. As part of this ongoing transformation initiative, UNDP worked with the Danish Design Centre to reimagine their organization for the 21st century by moving toward a "platform way of working," where UNDP does not own projects from beginning to end, but instead acts as an enabler and connector of a constellation of initiatives.

One such effort is the collaboration between UNDP and the Agirre Lehendakaria Center, launched in August 2019, to reinvent local food systems and food markets in southern Thailand for the future, considering challenges such as climate change and violent conflicts. Shortly after launch, however, the COVID-19 pandemic disrupted supply chains worldwide and created new challenges specific to food production and consumption.

Echoing UNDP's "platform" approach, the core principles of this initiative are to develop a portfolio of mutually reinforcing design solutions that operate as elements of a long-term socio-economic transformation strategy as opposed to a linear, piecemeal approach.[2] UNDP and Agirre Lehendakaria Center brought together a variety of stakeholders including public institutions, and corporate and community representatives, to develop a mix of projects, pilots, and prototypes aimed at reinventing the post-COVID food market of Yala.

Fish being sold at a food market

To forecast the rapidly emerging changes in the context of COVID-19, digital listening sessions and ethnographic research were used to understand perceptions and behavior changes. This allowed the team to assess the impact of the pandemic on local food businesses and communities, many of whom operate outside the formal economy.

Informed by this research, the team co-created solutions with local stakeholders such as restaurant owners, food suppliers, entrepreneurs, and artists. They also drew on a global network by bringing Imago Food Innovation Lab, a group based in the Basque region which is also renowned for its inventive food culture. This effort resulted in 50 potential initiatives to support the local food industry.[3]

The team then turned their attention to Yala, a town of 60,000 people, and its food market, as an experimental space where their initiatives could be tested and nurtured. The relevant concepts included the physical and digital redesign of Yala food market, a system of digital traceability for all products offered in the market, a new training program for young local chefs, and the international commercialization of Southern Thailand's traditional fermentation techniques.

To measure impact, the initiative has incorporated a developmental evaluation process. Quantitative indicators include the number of new businesses generated as part of the portfolio, number and quality of employment opportunities, new training programs, amount of investment attracted, etc. To gauge qualitative impact, a narrative-based approach called Most Significant Change is

Design for Social Innovation

National Art award winner Jehabdulloh Jehsorhoh explains his piece, *The Beautiful Flower Hidden in Pattani,* during a listening field visit at the Pattani ArtSpace

Images: Agirre Lehendakaria Center

being utilized. This has been embedded through an evaluation matrix that Agirre Lehendakaria Center co-created with the Advanced Consortium on Cooperation, Conflict, and Complexity at Columbia University.

The project operated at two scales. By focusing on the local issues of Yala food market, this initiative addressed the challenge of strengthening the local food system and illuminated possibilities for other interconnected challenges, like providing employment opportunities for vulnerable groups such as migrant workers, promoting local products and traditions, and tackling environmental issues. At a larger scale, and as one of UNDP's first platform-based projects, this initiative is also a learning opportunity for UNDP as a global organization. It provides a feedback loop from which to test and advance the platform way of working that was developed in collaboration with the Danish Design Centre.

1   Executive Board of the United Nations Development Programme, the United Nations Population Fund, and the United Nations Office for Project Services, "UNDP Strategic Plan, 2018-2021," 2017, https://undocs.org/DP/2017/38.

2   Regional Innovation Centre UNDP Asia-Pacific, "New Peacebuilding and Socio-Economic Development Approaches in Asia," Medium, October 22, 2019, https://undp-ric.medium.com/new-peacebuilding-and-socio-economic-development-approaches-in-asia-a31e715567d8.

3   Regional Innovation Centre UNDP Asia-Pacific, "Post Covid-19 Local Food Systems- and Related Systemic Responses to the New World," Medium, May 22, 2020, https://undp-ric.medium.com/post-covid-19-local-food-systems-and-related-systemic-responses-to-the-new-world-153ae1de2702.

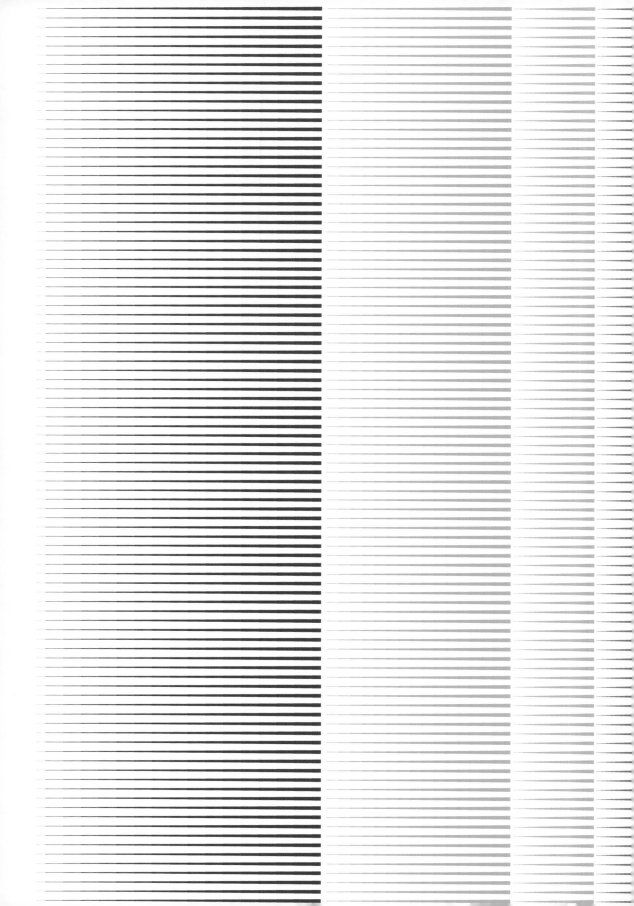

Organizing the Work

Alexandra Fiorillo, Christian Bason, and Tessy Britton, with Bryan Boyer

Imagine being a curiously minded European in the year 1660 who spends their days doing chemistry experiments. Your drive to understand the natural world would compel you to conduct one experiment after another, gaining knowledge in tiny increments and likely with great frustration at the failures and dead-ends along the way. Meanwhile, some of your peers would have been concerned with more grandiose efforts like converting tin into gold. In Europe in 1660, there was no difference between the serious chemist and the fanciful alchemist. You would not have been able to call yourself a "chemist" because that word was not coined until 1661, when Robert Boyle published *The Sceptical Chymist*. Can you imagine the frustration of knowing that your work is different, yet not having widely understood words to express that difference? Can you imagine how clunky it would be to resort to sentences or even entire paragraphs of explication to separate yourself from alchemy, rather than having a beautifully succinct term like "chemistry"?

New things in the world require new words to describe them, and usually those new descriptions balloon in complexity before they become clear and simple. "Design for social innovation" is finally a simplifier, even though, it must be said, it is not a perfect label and not all of the individuals in this book would even identify with the term themselves. At their most benign, labels are a way to begin relating to others, but we cannot let them become lifeless definitions. Luckily, "design for social innovation" points us toward a lively bundle of mindsets, methods, and conversations more than an ossified practice. As you follow this discussion with Alex Fiorillo, Christian Bason, and Tessy Britton, what's striking is that they're not fixated on the intricacies of being designers but are instead describing new ways of being humans who work together to care for others.

As a group of editors, we published a prior volume titled *LEAP Dialogues: Career Pathways in Design for Social Innovation*[1] in 2016 that highlighted the personal experience of more than 80 designers. Though inspiring, that research was also a reality check. All of the individuals in that book had to fight tooth and nail to carve out the very possibility of a career in design for social innovation. Today it's easier to find individuals who are following their own path as professionals, but at the organizational level there are still fewer strong case studies of clear and sustained design for social innovation teams or operations. Design labs come and go. Startups shut down. Pilot projects fly off into the sunset.

If it's still hard to build and sustain an organization to do the work of design for social innovation day in, day out, that is because the world is still waking up to the ways in which it has to change to make the most of these new practices. We're between alchemy and chemistry, if you will. This discussion is about the gaps between the largely transactional, top-down structures of industrial society and the more nimble, relational approaches favored by many in the design community.

What's promising about the trajectory of the organizations led and built by our roundtable practitioners, and others like them, is that they show us how it is possible to do the work of design for social innovation on a sustainable basis, without relying on the polite simplifiers of industrial society like "for-profit" and "not-for-profit." When misfits band together to organize their work, it's just a little bit easier to span the gaps between the world we have and the world we want.

Alex Fiorillo

I am the Founder of GRID Impact, a global social enterprise research and design collective. We use participatory research and collaborative design practices to help create equitable and inclusive systems and programs in the global social impact space. I am a behavioral designer currently based in Colorado in the USA.

Christian Bason

I'm based in Copenhagen, Denmark, where I lead the Danish Design Centre [DDC] as CEO. We're an independent, non-profit foundation working to advance the value of design as a driver of sustainable change for Denmark and the world.

Tessy Britton

I am chief executive of Participatory City Foundation, an initiative that is building a large urban network of widespread practical participation, the kind of participation that works with the fabric of daily life.

The discussion took place in May 2020 and was edited for clarity and length

Bryan: What is the number one challenge to the longevity of your organizations?

Tessy: With Participatory City, we've set ourselves up as a five-year R&D project and we're fully funded to do that. The aim is that we can measure the impact of people and place, and also to start to untangle some of those "systems balance sheets," and to make a business case for sustaining the platform long-term.

The plan was always to build it, test it, and to make a case for it becoming part of the system. We see this as very much the same system or a new, revised version of a public library or other public spaces [that are funded through those traditional channels]. That idea is quite ambitious, and we're still at the early stages in terms of how we understand the impacts that are created. We've still got the challenge of quantifying the impact.

We could easily close down after five years as an organization, but what we want to live on is the approach which we're testing in new iterations in other places. We have two different sets of ambitions for the project.

The distributed nature of it is part of what's making it challenging to quantify the impacts. We also know that different funders have different interests. The state is interested in cost savings to the public purse, but there are other funders and foundations who are actually more interested in what kind of neighborhood we're building, and looking at their future focus. It's not a binary picture. It's quite nuanced because the potential is that this platform might be sustained through multiple means over the long term. It's complicated, or at least it feels complicated.

"The bigger picture is whether you are perceived by decision makers to be a relevant and worthwhile investment. We are still discussing with key stakeholders what it takes to be seen as relevant."

Christian: The first thing I jotted down, which I've also addressed in some of my writing around innovation teams,[2] is about being perceived as a legitimate player or relevant player. Ultimately, for us the need is to be seen as an investment in relevant societal outcomes, rather than as a cost or as something a bit frivolous in a time of crisis. Currently our longevity is dependent on government backing in the sense that the government both provides quite substantial core funding and also provides some program funds that are more time-limited. It's about 30% of our funding that's straight from our main government backer in the Ministry of Business, so our long-term sustainability as an organization also depends on a quite broad range of other funding sources. [These other sources have to come from] robust and longer-term relationships with our funders. It's everything from the European Union's Horizons programme, to major Danish foundations, and corporate partners. We need these to develop meaningfully over time so there is a deepening and longer-term relationship there. There are multiple things here, but it all boils down to, are we perceived as a worthwhile investment? Are we then good at building relationships that make us resilient when it comes to external shocks like the one we're seeing right now?

Bryan: How long have you been at DDC?

Christian: When I came in, five and a half years ago, the perception was that this was an outfit that was very close to closing or not being relevant anymore. Now, we've gotten to a safer place. The next question is, being legitimate is about making an actual impact and being able to document it and demonstrate impact. We can pursue the perfect impact assessment, or outcome measurements, or key performance indicators and evidence, and so on—which is important—but ultimately, for the decision makers who determine whether you exist or not, or whether you have funding or not, it's much more nuanced than that.

The bigger picture is whether you are perceived by decision makers to be a relevant and worthwhile investment. We are still discussing with key stakeholders what it takes to be seen as relevant. But also, how do we position ourselves in the world, so to speak? How do we place ourselves and how do we differentiate ourselves from any other activities, any other actors that are playing roles in the ecosystems we are part of? It becomes a much more complex discussion, but it comes back to the question of perception. I know it can sound superficial, and maybe even cynical, but in my experience, perceptions are actually quite critical.

Bryan: That's a really key point, because as much as the design community has mobilized around the question of documenting our impacts and being as quantitative as possible, numbers are not everything. My partner works in the venture capital world and of course they pay very close attention to numbers, but the decisions are not

Design for Social Innovation

made on numbers alone. There's a broader question here about the "cultures of decision making," which I've written about previously. Different professional or sectoral cultures have their own forms of evidence, rituals, and lingo that they need to perceive things through to construct an idea of legitimacy.

Christian: Where we want to get is having the design perspective or also the digital perspective as a partner in the conversation rather than something exotic that is on the sidelines. It can't be that "when the adults are discussing policies" and so on, it's [just] the economists and the lawyers. The question becomes, how do you get invited [to the table], and how does [design] increasingly seem like a natural way of working? There have been major strides being made the last five to ten years in terms of placing this broad field of design closer to policy making and decision making, and the same with the social sectors, but I don't know that we're quite there yet.

Alex: My response is a little different. Longevity is not an ambition for our organization. We're a collective structure, so we're a member organization. "Member" is not really the right term, but we don't have a better English word for it. Everyone that works through and with GRID Impact is an independent designer, researcher, behaviorist, ethnographer, or whatever the discipline might be.

When working on GRID Impact projects, we have a specific methodology, and approach, and a brand, and a way of engaging with our partners, but everyone including myself are encouraged and expected to also work in our more traditional disciplines. A lot of our members are not necessarily social impact designers or social impact researchers all the time. They might come from Silicon Valley, or from academia, for instance. The model that we've created is one of ultimate flexibility and adaptability. Our lines are very porous. We have a set team, but the team members come and go, depending on the current work and engagements of GRID.

GRID was really founded to run two experiments. One is, can you really take the academic rigor of the behavioral sciences, the cognitive sciences, and integrate that seamlessly into a participatory design process? The other experiment was that we wanted to play around with organizational structures, and what it means to be a 21st-century organization. We have always been a fully remote organization and we will always be a fully remote organization. Before the roundtable, one of the reasons I was joking about quarantine not being so terrible [for us] is that we've always worked remotely anyway. What we really care about is democratizing rigorous research and design functions within organizations around the world dedicated to social impact or social innovation. Our goal is to "level up" skills. Sometimes that means that we're doing just capacity building for organizations, and that's great. We do a lot of teaching and training of trainers.

But, for example, I want to share a decision we made in the last two years. We used to do a lot of work in Kenya. There is no need for us to be in Kenya anymore, despite us having Kenyan team members. We feel like there are Kenyan-owned and Kenyan-led behavioral and design organizations that can do a lot of work in Kenya. Great! There's not yet a behavioral or a design firm in Niger, though, so we'll focus on markets where perhaps there is still a void for our capabilities.

For us, longevity isn't so much our ambition, and we've designed the organization such that we don't take any core funding. We try and keep our expenses really low. Obviously, being a fully remote organization helps in that. But we really try and just focus on depth and breadth rather than massive scale. I've worked at a number of non-profits in the past where you get caught up in the donor funding cycles, and you start hiring to staff projects, and then you need to fundraise to pay the new staff.

Bryan: How does your lean organizational model affect the conversations that you have with a client like the Inter-American Development Bank. How do they perceive you next to a more traditional team with formal offices and such?

Alex: We still come as a team, we still come with a brand, we still come with a process and a methodology. Though, we're definitely seen as smaller and more nimble. We have 48 members in the collective, not a staff of 400. It's not that we have zero overhead—there's some, of course. We still have a finance and administrative need. We still have some operations costs. We're kind of like the small, scrappy, nimble adaptable team, but we still take ourselves and our work very seriously. I don't know that our clients necessarily experience us differently, but I think the GRID Impact collective members do experience it differently.

If you talk to our members, there's a reason that they've opted into this structure, this lifestyle. We definitely have far fewer junior members, because this is more of an irregular, project-dependent, client-dependent work experience. It usually takes someone who's more mid-career or later in their career to be able to find other types of consulting and project work outside of GRID, so we don't have a lot of younger, early-career members in the collective. That is one way that our clients might experience us differently. We don't have a lot of research assistants, design assistants, or client associates. They get a smaller team, but everyone brings ten to twenty years of experience, not three to five.

Bryan: Tessy, your model is also non-traditional, in that you are making a diffuse set of small investments across a neighborhood. Are there challenges getting funders to understand and buy into your model?

Tessy: It was very hard to put together. It was really hard work, and that doesn't surprise you! It is worth mentioning that we don't do grants at all. We're trying to set up an ecosystem, not of hundreds of organizations, but actually a non-organization ecosystem. We're working toward a living, breathing, dynamic set of activities and networks where people come in and out, and projects die out or replicate or grow, but the ecosystem as a whole [is what's important]. It's not a static ecosystem, so the people and groups who are part of our project are always changing.

What has helped us get funded in this case is that the borough we're working in is the poorest in London and it had probably one of the smallest third sectors in the whole country. Because of this, we had a set of foundations who were desperately wanting to support residents but couldn't follow their traditional vehicles of making investments because those groups were not strong enough or just didn't exist in the neighborhood. They just weren't getting the applications from what would normally be small charities or community groups. If they hadn't been in that situation, it would have been even harder for us to secure funding.

This speaks to what Christian was saying. You can do all the number crunching, but we have to be more hard-headed about our own work than anybody else. We have to share our value, but a lot of the challenge we have is communicating and actually grabbing people's imagination. We're still really in lots of ways in the very early stage of showing the value of design. By us having a design team in place, in an area where the traditional system has faltered or just isn't performing at the level that it should, we're showing the potential of embedding design capacity as part of the soft infrastructure of the neighborhood. The Council should be employing designers on their team, not just people who've gone and done a degree in policy. But that happens so seldomly.

Alex: Sometimes, as a non-traditional organization, foundations and large NGOs have expectations of things we can do that we actually can't do. When a huge RFP [request for proposal] comes up and one of the big global health organizations writes and says, "Hey, we want GRID to be the partner on behavioral research and design. Can you, in 24 hours, put together these 50 pages of RFP documents?" My response is like, "Probably not." We don't have a business development team sitting on call ready to do that! Foundations sometimes ask for a product or output at a speed or at a volume that a collective has a much harder time meeting.

Bryan: Or reporting, for that matter.

Alex: We usually build reporting into our projects, so that's easier for us. But it's those one-off requests that we don't have [as much bandwidth for], because our team isn't billing for those deliverables that are outside of the current contract. They're not getting paid a set salary every single month, so billable time is important to us. Reporting, especially around impact metrics and whatnot are built into our projects, but additional requests that we would love to answer are more difficult for us to meet. We have to find workarounds for that.

Bryan: All of you are organized as non-profit and/or are a small organization in the grand scheme of things. Is there room for traditional, for-profit firms to work in this space?

"There is a place for two opportunities. One is not ignoring that profit-seeking enterprises are also part of creating good social outcomes. If you want to lift an area from poverty… it's about jobs."

Christian: So, on the one side, you could say, we at DDC have been framed or also framed ourselves for quite a long time as mainly existing for what might be called economic development. So how do you stimulate innovation and growth in the private sector, and bring designers and design capabilities and skills into other parts of the business community that haven't tried it before? Ultimately, our role has been framed as improving competitiveness for Denmark through design. That's still relevant but these days, and it's not new to me, but I think it's still new in terms of bringing it into our organizational context, the bigger game is not about competitiveness.

That's an old-fashioned model. What we're looking at [now] is how to create societal impact across a number of different measures. As you do so, how do you activate all of society's resources to ultimately make positive, sustainable change? The business sector is clearly a key part of that. Also, for-profit design consultancies and agencies are, or could be, part of that.

What we see more and more is to put societal missions at the heart of our strategy so that we work to create impact. That could be social and environmental change; sometimes the impact is more clearly related to economic development. We try to understand the kind of system we need to activate. We look at how the private sector can be activated, perhaps as a contracted partner with government, and then also academia and civil society. All of these need to work together to get important things done.

We also see a space opening up in impact investing. Investors with large amounts of money that may be institutional investors or high-net-worth individuals want to make an impact while also getting some kind of investment return. The return could be maybe the same, or maybe even higher than they otherwise would get.

There is a place for two opportunities. One is not ignoring that profit-seeking enterprises are also part of creating good social outcomes. If you want to lift an area from poverty, ultimately it's about jobs. Right now we're working with a foundation on youth that have been in foster care, and how can we design better transitions for them into adult life. The foundation explicitly asked us to work with them because we know how to work with private businesses, and private businesses are probably relevant for those kids' futures as well. Then, on the question of advisory or consultancy services being for-profit, one shouldn't really care whether a consultancy is for-profit or not-for-profit. The question is whether it's any good.

We are very sensitive to not being seen as someone who's cannibalizing or pushing out for-profit design agencies. But there are absolutely projects where we would say, we don't think anybody else could do it as well as we can [at DDC]. We also quite often bring in design consultancies as partners, so we would fund their participation and their roles in the project. Which we're also doing on the youth project I already mentioned.

There's a bigger question at stake when all of us at this roundtable are doing this kind of work, and Tessy already mentioned it, which is the question of capability. Building capability in a system where you leave the system and the actors you work with better off than when you met them. This is relevant because some for-profits would say, "Well, as long as we make money, we don't care [what changes]." Whereas, you can also be a for-profit and say, "We have a business model where we invest in our clients or invest in our partners, and even though we can pull a profit out of this, our main purpose is actually to create a larger impact." So we're back to train the trainers and capacity building!

I've seen not-for-profits act in an extremely profit-hungry, capitalist, cut-throat way, and I've seen for-profits and design consultancies in Denmark being extremely altruistic and sharing, and being open and going another mile for something that's just worthwhile doing even though it doesn't pay anything. We have to be careful about putting organizations in these pockets of for-profit and not-for-profit, but surely we [at DDC] are a not-for-profit. For us, that means we have independence. There's legitimacy. Nobody should be able to question whether we are in the game for making an impact, or if we are in it for [making money].

> **Bryan:** Are there other ways to think about the nature of the organizations in this space? Are there other terminologies that are relevant?

Alex: We call ourselves a social enterprise. We are technically a for-profit entity, but we have ways of reinvesting our profits into our work and into our team through dividends or finders' fees, for instance. "Fees" is a weird word, but we try and incentivize collective members to bring projects and clients in, so there are benefits that are given back to the collective members when they do that. My ambition for 2020 was to bring all of the collective members together for a physical professional development retreat. That is not happening this year! I was clapping and double-clicking everything Christian was saying, because I do think that this binary non-profit, for-profit, doesn't mean the same thing that it meant 30 years ago.

We care about lean, we care about efficiency, and we care about impact, of course. We felt when we started that a for-profit entity was the easiest way for us to achieve those goals. We do not have a board, and I have worked for a number of non-profits that had a board that was amazing and helpful in a lot of ways. I've also worked for some non-profits, one in particular I can think of from years ago, where we had a board but it was not a particularly effective or helpful board. It depends on the people and the leadership. It depends on who is making the decisions and who is running the work. But I don't think it really matters what the entity is anymore. We like fee for service, we like service contracts with foundations [as opposed to grants]. We feel like [this is more] clear and direct, because then there are clear metrics that we are trying to attain. Again, I don't want to have to also feed a beast.

> **Christian:** That also raises the question of what you say "no" to. Or what are the values guiding your choices? Alexandra, you were giv-

ing an example of new organizational models, new ways of organizing work, organizing engaged talents, that form teams in ways that can really be impactful. This is very high on our agenda as well right now. We are somewhat traditional in our organization, but we also have a culture that is quite nimble and ready to change; for instance, our team was really, really quick to pivot to digital and working remotely when the crisis hit. We don't want to lose that. We've tried to find the things we've learned in the crisis that we can keep and that we want to bring into the next [iteration of our] organization.

Bryan: That touches on something that came up in *LEAP Dialogues*, a book that my co-editors and I worked on a few years ago and was a predecessor to this one, in a way. There are a lot of individuals who are doing design for social innovation and have been doing it for years. Most of them feel lonely in different ways. I'm kind of struck by, on the one hand, the appealing side of being a nimble network of flexible people who you only bring in when you need them. Then, at the same time, trying to reconcile that, frankly, it can be hard to find a community of practitioner peers if you don't happen to live in a hotbed of this work like London, New York, etc.

Alex: The reason we started the collective was because of that loneliness you just touched on, Bryan. When I left my previous organization, I had a particular client at the World Bank who wanted to continue doing behavioral research and design. I could have done it alone, but guess what? I am not great at all things. I am good at something specific. I knew that there were bigger impacts I could have and bigger projects that I could engage with using my specific skill set, but I am not great at everything. That's why we work as a collective.

I'm a generalist in some senses, but I also am a specialist. I believe that the sum is much greater than the individual parts, and all projects, all engagements really, always benefit from interdisciplinary teams. There are some amazing Slack workspaces that have emerged in the last few years that I think are giving individual freelance, independent designers and researchers amazing communities to leverage. The Design Gigs For Good group on Slack, for example, has such incredible connections and synergies being made that did not exist five years ago, for sure.

Bryan: Another function of organizations is to provide a baseline of trust. You're supposed to be able to trust your co-workers, at least to a certain extent! How does trust factor into the collaboration amongst folks who are not co-workers but neighbors, or even more tenuously connected?

Tessy, in your projects have you found ways to build between strangers in an accelerated fashion? Or do you even need to?

Alex: We're taking notes, Tessy, because I want your answers!

Tessy: Trust is one of the most important considerations, but I'm not quite sure how to answer your question. If I can backtrack slightly on your previous question about organizational models, we found it quite heavy that we had to become a registered charity in order to receive our funding. The result is that we have one foothold in the existing system, and another one in [a different world]. Sometimes we have to remind our team that we're really not a charitable foundation, we're actually a design and innovation team. Those labels are really unhelpful sometimes.

"It's part of our job as designers to create a bit more fluidity around structures like for-profit and not-for-profit, which feel quite static."

Also drawing back to the idea of for-profits, it is part of our job as designers to weave things together in new ways. We're working with IKEA at the moment and there's no doubt that they're a for-profit, but they also pay close attention to environmental impacts, and so do we. It's part of our job as designers to create a bit more fluidity around structures like for-profit and not-for-profit, which feel quite static. Now back to the trust question!

Some of my team are asking, "If we're working with an organization that's selling stuff, how does that affect us?" What's really important in terms of trust is that anyone who comes into contact with our team knows that we only have one thing that's important to us: them. One of the things which really stood out when we did the in-depth interviews last year was how many people come into our shop spaces[3] and subsequently tell us that they have never had a conversation where they walk into a space, and people ask them questions about themselves, apart from the typical commercial inquiries like "What you need," or "What can I help you with?" Our team asks questions like, "What do you like? What are your talents? What do you dream about? What does your family aspire to?" One of the key ways of building trust is never letting any shred of doubt ever creep in that you care about anything other than the people in front of you.

Design for Social Innovation

Alex: It's about the opposite of transactional relationships, right? Design and anything social-impact-related is so relational. Some of the topics we work on are so complicated and difficult. We've worked on delaying the first pregnancy of child brides, for instance. If that's not the most relational thing I've ever had to work on, I don't know what it is.

If you're just in a contractual, transactional relationship with a fellow designer or researcher, there is no way that project will succeed. I hate even talking about our work as project-based, because even that sounds so transactional. But what I'm hearing Tessy describe is that trust is the foundation and it's built through relations and relationships. We [at GRID Impact] spend a lot of time hanging out with each other. It's virtual, but we make time for a lot of non-project-related experiences in order to build relationships among our team. We're working with only 50 people, not the hundreds or thousands that Tessy's working with, so it's easier, but it's always relational and not transactional.

Tessy: Even as citizens, people are used to being instrumentalized because in nearly every other kind of participation work that we know of, people are seen as units of resource in one form or another. Either as volunteers, or voters, or campaigners, and so on. I think that that feels very different to how our team communicates with people. It's very easy to adopt that top-down instrumentalization of people, but people see through it straight away. In the UK we had our Big Society [policy initiative] ten years ago, and people can see right through it.

Christian: One of our related challenges has been framing the work we're doing with small and medium-sized enterprises, so-called "SMEs." But actually, small and medium-sized enterprises are people! It's owners who founded their business. It's families. It's small teams. Who is it that we work with, and that we bring design to? How does it matter to them personally? What are they trying to achieve? What kind of dream are they pursuing that we are contributing to?

This is a space that is, in a sense, transactional because it's got to do with business, but you shouldn't underestimate the amount of emotional investment and meaningfulness [that a small business has] to someone's life. Even though what the company produces may seem quite simple.

All of us in this discussion work with a systems change, which is by definition wider in scale than the individual. The question is, how do you work with trust when it comes to systems change? How are you seen as an actor who is meddling with or intervening in a broader context? That's maybe back to my first remark, which was about legitimacy. In what way are you a legitimate actor that has a role to play [in changing the system]? How do you join a conversation? We increasingly want to be an actor in some of the difficult areas that society is facing, like climate change, but we are not born into the climate change conversation. We're coming from a design perspective and we're coming from a systems change perspective. So how do you become a valued, legitimate, trusted conversation partner with that entire ecosystem and not seen as someone who's trying to join a party coming quite late, not having the right dress code, asking for the wrong drinks, and vomiting on the floor?

We can enter a field such as climate change and establish ourselves with all humility as a relevant conversation partner. When that happens, it is usually coming from a relational approach and being honest about our intentions. Which is, we're just here to help, and we bring new capabilities in terms of design for societal innovation.

Isabella Gady: When it comes to design for social innovation, is it even possible to do this work, ultimately, as an outside partner or is it a necessity for designers to be embedded within institutions and systems?

> **Christian:** We would love to find better ways of helping institutions and organizations attract, recruit, retain great designers that are able to function inside. We've come to realize that we cannot just activate or bring in the [traditional] Danish design community into some of these institutional contexts. Designers also need a new set of skills to be successful there. That's going to be quite a big provocation to the [traditional design] industry.

Alex: What comes up for me hearing Isabella's question is that I don't think it's a limitation of the fee-for-service model, per se. It's more about an organization's capacity to do really good scoping and contracting. If it's a big, wicked, hairy problem, like the effort to delay the first pregnancy of recently married child brides that I mentioned earlier, that's not a three-month project! We can't just go in, do some research, design some things, and then we solved a challenge that has existed for hundreds of years and is embedded in culture and society.

We need to do a much better job of having a long-term partnership with our implementing partner and embedding into their team. One of the lessons that we have learned the hard way is that we now refuse to work with organizations that see us as an external vendor. Yes, there's still a contract and deliverables and there are still metrics that we are trying to attain, but we require full embedding into their team. Depending on the project, it could be the marketing team, the research team, or the adolescent sexual reproductive health team, but we become part of it.

We also require secondment of several of their team members onto our team, so that we are also building capacity through experience and integral working relationships. If any design company says that they can go in and solve a particular problem in three months, I call "BS" on them! That is not how it happens. Is it a two-year relationship? Definitely, maybe it's even longer. It depends on the problem that you're trying to solve.

We really want to be involved throughout implementation, and that is not for every partner. Christian was talking earlier about what you say "no" to. We say "no" to projects that are proposed to us where either there isn't capacity building built into the scope or we can't be involved in implementation.

We did some amazing work several years ago in Kenya, early on in the life of GRID Impact. We were so excited about the possibilities, and then a third party entity ran the randomized control trial to measure the impact of the things that our team designed. For a variety of reasons, the implementation was completely botched, and we weren't allowed to be involved in it. A lot of our amazing work went down the tubes, unfortunately. Now it's like, "Nope." We're going to be right there, working with you. We'd like to be there coaching, supporting, embedded, and working with you. Not every design firm requires that or pushes for that, or even knows how to do that. Our collective is made up of a band of misfits including impact evaluators, researchers, and designers, so that's where the multidisciplinary team becomes critical... but that's a whole 'nother conversation!

1   LEAP was the name of a conference hosted in 2013 at ArtCenter College of Design which brought together hundreds of practitioners and educators from across the US.

2   Christian Bason, *Leading Public Sector Innovation: Co-Creating for a Better Society* (Boston, Mass.; New York: Policy Press, 2010).

3   Participatory City operates storefront spaces as local project incubators. For more, see the case study on page 180.

Organizing
the Work

Design Harvests

*Promoting Circular Economy
Principles to Strengthen the Rural
Areas Around Shanghai*

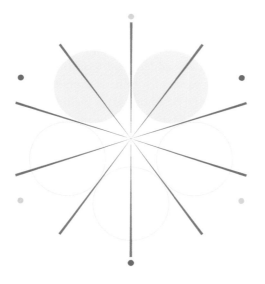

Involved

*Increasing youth voice in
national policy design*

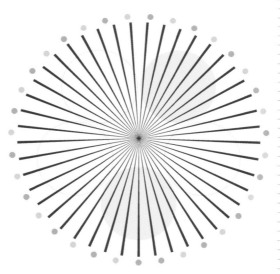

Community Housing
Start-Up Process

*Facilitating Communal Living with
Structured Collaboration*

Design for Social Innovation

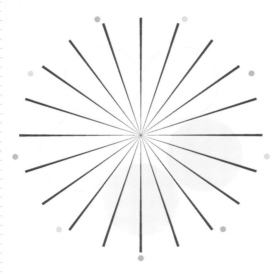

Boxing Future Health

Cultivating a discussion about the future of health through tangible scenarios and co-creation

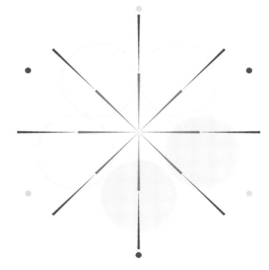

Thüringer Church Hostels

Breathing new life into old churches and rural communities

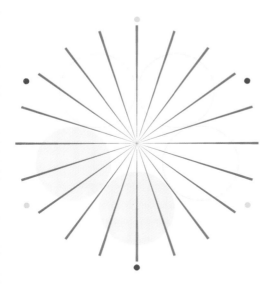

Financial Literacy for Ecuadorian Microentrepreneurs

Educating microentrepreneurs through a "less is more" learning approach

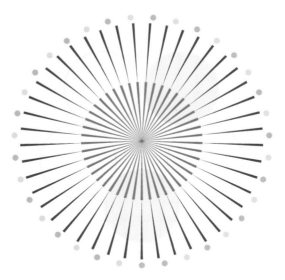

Every One
Every Day

Building participatory infrastructure for local residents to shape their neighborhoods

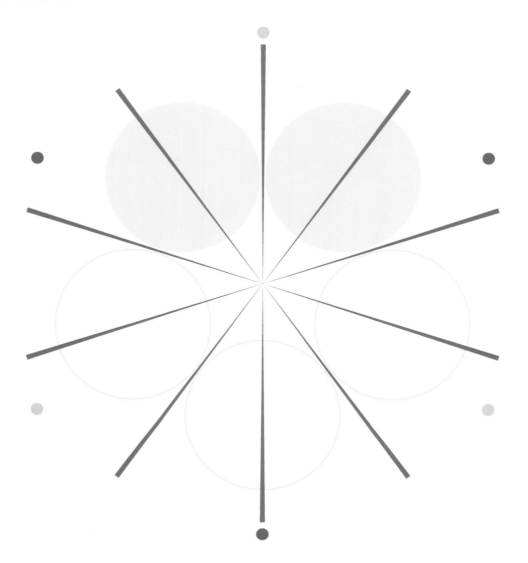

Duration
Late 2018–spring 2019

Location
London and Peterborough, UK

Categories
Policy
Education

Designer
Policy Lab (UK Government)

Partners
Youth Team in the Department of
Digital, Culture, Media & Sport
British Youth Council
The Mix

Key Contributors
Sanjan Sabherwal
Nina Cutler
Alice Weavers
Anne Spaa
Laurenz Reichl

Designer Organization Type
● Government

Team Size
● 5–7

Design Quotient
● 61–80%

Project Costs
▭ $25k–$100k

Source of Funding
▬ Government

Funding Mechanisms
Fee for Service

Impact Measurement Methods
Qualitative: Observed Impact on
Policy, Awards Received
Quantitative: Web-Mobile
Analytics

Mediums
Digital: Social Media
Communications
Organizational: Service

Involved

Increasing youth voice in national policy design

Article 12 of the UN Convention on the Rights of the Child recognizes that young people have a right for their voices to be heard. Giving youths a voice in their communities has been shown to increase feelings of belonging, civic responsibility and connection to government, particularly for young people who are part of underserved communities.[1]

In 2018, Policy Lab supported the Office for Civil Society (located within the Department for Digital, Culture, Media & Sport) to develop and test a new digital service that would enable large numbers of young people to play a role in consulting and program design across government. Policy Lab partnered with the British Youth Council, which was responsible for running a Youth Steering Group, focusing on youth ages 25 and younger. Policy Lab also partnered with The Mix: an online charity that serves as the first point of contact for any young person seeking help or information on any subject—wherever and whenever they need it. The Mix supported Policy Lab in testing prototypes with young people.

The project sought to design a new service that would integrate into the existing consultation process, wherein government solicits input from the people on policy changes. By applying user-centered design approaches, Policy Lab hoped to enable policy makers to widen their reach during public engagements, ensuring more meaningful and accessible participation. A third objective was to educate young people on how government works.

In order to inform the design of a consultation service that would be used both by young people and policy officials, the team conducted "timeline interviews" with policy makers, where participants were asked to map their process as a series of sequential steps. This helped Policy Lab map the process that officials go through, including their lived experiences making use of digital consultation tools, and their appetite to hear from young people. To understand the other side

of this experience, Policy Lab ran research on youth forums to understand the perspectives of young people on civic engagement. Finally, the team mapped the existing consultation process and examples of digital tools meant to enable civic participation, which could be learned from.

Policy Lab then planned and facilitated two co-design sessions with a diverse group of young people. In the first session, the group spent half a day reviewing insights from the research to identify possible opportunities and challenges to consider. They co-developed design principles to address the needs of both young people and policy makers before starting the idea generation process and creating prototypes. After the first session, the team up-skilled participants to run their own user testing, and placed prototypes on youth forums for feedback. Policy Lab tested solutions with policy makers, and The Mix tested prototypes with tech experts. All of the research findings were then presented back to participants in a second co-creation session for further reflection and iteration.

After considering budgetary constraints and user research, the project team decided to further develop a service that asks accessible government consultation questions to 13- to 25-year-olds via Instagram stories. Participants took ownership of the project, pitching it to two government ministers and receiving funding for a year-long pilot.

The final output was a digital engagement tool called Involved, funded by the Department for Digital, Culture, Media & Sport and managed by the British Youth Council. Involved develops online content, delivered via Instagram Stories and overseen by members of the Youth Steering Group, that acts as a bridge between policy teams and young people. The Involved project team supports policy teams by framing questions with language that is accessible and engaging to young people in the target age bracket. From there, feedback is sent to the government, and youth are guided to official consultation pages. Involved is able to increase its reach over traditional consultation processes by producing content that youth are interested in engaging with. In its first month of activity, the service reached over 1,000 followers.

The co-creation and testing process uncovered significant cost efficiencies. While the team's initial intention would have been to develop a stand-alone webpage, using Instagram Stories instead allowed budget monies that would have been spent on web development to instead be redirected to marketing that helped get the word out. The fact that young people participated in the process and continue to run the service means that time has been saved on government staffing as well. Furthermore, Involved has created an opportunity for young people to learn more about the policy-making process by interacting with policy makers more directly. According to Harley Taylor of the Youth Steering Group, "Young people are passionate about seeing social change in their communities and must be able to participate in the decision making of government. Involved will serve as an important opportunity to gauge young people's views on the hot topics within government."

Baroness Barran, a Minister for Civil Society, described the project's promise by sharing that, "Young people often feel like it is hard to get their voices heard. Involved will give them an easy way to contribute their views on issues that matter to them, helping our decisions as Ministers to reflect these better." The project won the Cabinet Office's Innovator Award in 2019 in recognition of its participatory approach. Recently, the department for Health and Social Care has used Involved to understand more about young people's experience of COVID-19, and the service is also promoting the #YoungandBlack campaign led by UK Youth, the Diana Award, and My Life My Say.

1   Jennifer L. O'Donoghue, Benjamin Kirshner, and Milbrey McLaughlin, "Introduction: Moving Youth Participation Forward," *New Directions for Youth Development* 96 (2002): 15–26.

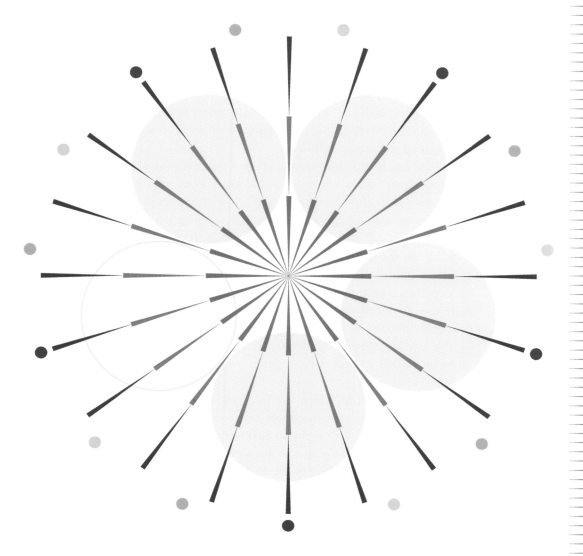

Duration
2007–present

Location
Xianqiao Village, Chongming
Island, Shanghai, China (1.0),
ZhangYan Village, QingPu
District, Shanghai, China (2.0)

Categories
Social Justice
Economic

Designer
Studio TEKTAO & College of
Design and Innovation, Tongji
University

Partners
TEKTAO
DESIS Network

Key Contributors
Professor Yongqi Lou
Professor Aldo Cibic

Designer Organization Type
● For-Profit
● Academia

Team Size
● 11–20

Design Quotient
● 61–80%

Project Costs
➤ $100k–$500k

Source of Funding
➤ Government
➤ Private Company
➤ Foundation/Non-Profit/
Endowment

Funding Mechanisms
Fee for Service

Impact Measurement Methods
Quantitative: Academic
Publications, Volume of Media
Coverage, Financial Viability,
Including Funding/Revenue
Generated

Mediums
Digital: Website
Experiential: Education, Event
Organizational: Service, Non-
Profit
Spatial: Exhibition, Repurposed
Buildings

Design Harvests

Promoting circular economy principles to strengthen the rural areas around Shanghai

Although cities and villages represent two different ways of living, they are co-dependent, so while urbanization continues in China, it is more important than ever to identify opportunities for common prosperity and more sustainable development. This was the focus of Yongqi Lou, Dean of Tongji University College of Design and Innovation, when he founded Design Harvests in 2007. It's a design-driven, community-based project to create new symbiotic relationships between rural and urban areas by creating an interlinked network of social entrepreneurial efforts.

Design Harvests began at Xianqiao Village on the rural island of Chongming, an agricultural center known as the "rice bowl" of greater Shanghai. Counterintuitively, Xianqiao Village was selected because it was not very special. It is inconveniently located, reachable only by ferry, and does not have any particularly special resources except for one important element: the people of Xianqiao were open to working with the Design Harvests team to find a new rural way of doing things. Design Harvests took an "acupunctural" approach to make a series of small interventions that are intended to catalyze broader, bottom-up, sustainable development.

Examples of the acupuncture points include Design Harvests Farm, for which the team rented a piece of land in Xianqiao Village to test different ideas of creative agriculture. Through this effort, local health foods can be found at markets on the island, in metropolitan Shanghai, and online through a subscription service. Design Harvests Greenhouse is designed to attract urban residents by providing in-depth rural educational experiences with exhibitions, cuisine, and event hosting.

**Pathways
cutting through
one of the
area's rice fields**

An Artist Residency Program was jointly initiated by Design Harvests and the Shanghai International Cultural Association in 2016. An abandoned pig shed in the village was renovated into a gallery, studio and dormitory for the artists, providing more ways to attract people to the region so that they can be exposed to the local developments. To make that easier, Design Harvests Hospitality is a set of three houses in Xianqiao Village that have been renovated by the team into multifunctional spaces and that provide tourists and workers with accommodation, catering, public life, and communication. These individual efforts are connected by the Design Harvests digital platform and communications.

As an effort lasting more than a decade, the team have conducted extensive ethnographic research to get to know the local context and community. Co-creation workshops with local communities, business partners, NGOs, and individuals from other backgrounds have been a primary tool to develop interventions including those described above. The team has also connected local challenges with insights from global communities through Tongji University's international network, including over 20 universities and organizations such as Politecnico di Milano, Aalto University, Willem de Kooning Academy, Design School of Basel, IDEO, Nokia, and Philips.

In 2019, Design Harvests launched a "2.0" version of itself, now operating as an independent company. Design Harvests 2.0 covers the whole 2 square kilometer areas of ZhangYan village in the QingPu district northeast of central Shanghai. Through building a community of innovation and entrepreneurship based on circular economy principles, Design Harvests 2.0 is integrating agriculture, industry, and commerce to become a test bed for next-generation rural economic models. It promotes the design-driven model of rural revitalization for the whole Yangtze River Delta.

**Design Harvests
2.0 Festival
in ZhangYan
Village**

**Design Harvests
2.0 exhibition
curated by John
Thackara**

Organizing the Work

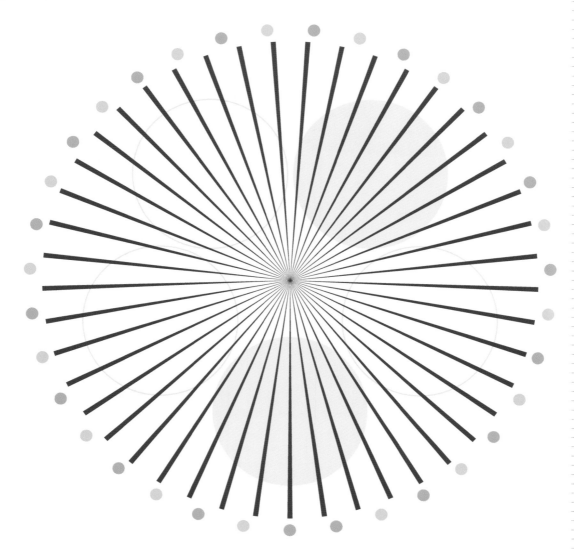

Duration
  2014–present

Location
  Milan, Italy

Categories
  Policy

Designer
  Fondazione Housing Sociale

Partners
  National Bank of Italy

Key Contributors
  Luciana Pacucci
  Roberta Conditi

Designer Organization Type
  ● Non-Profit

Team Size
  ● 21–49

Design Quotient
  ● 0–20%

Project Costs
  ▭ $1MM+

Source of Funding
  ▬ Foundation/Non-Profit/
  Endowment

Funding Mechanisms
  Fee for Service

Impact Measurement Methods
  Qualitative: Stakeholder
    Interviews, Focus Groups
  Quantitative: Surveys

Mediums
  Experiential: Training
  Organizational: Policies

Community Housing Start-Up Process

Facilitating communal living with structured collaboration

The 2008 global financial crisis strained families around the world, including those in Italy, where it became difficult even for previously stable "average" families to continue paying for a caregiver or finding a suitably sized apartment. In 2013, Fondazione Housing Sociale (FHS)—a non-profit that works to improve the public and social interest by developing innovative and sustainable approaches to structure, finance, build, and manage social housing initiatives—received national funding for Social and Affordable Housing (SAH). In SAH arrangements, residents share spaces and services with their neighbors—allowing them to perform daily tasks without having all of the required resources in their own homes.

For all of its benefits, this lifestyle takes some adjustment and FHS received an investment to prototype a collaborative "Community Start-Up Process" as a one-year process to help people make the most of their new housing. FHS has a history of collaborating with the design school at Politecnico di Milano, and in general has a high level of fluency with design, so they were able to develop the Community Start-Up Process in house, drawing on service design and co-design methodologies.

Giordana Ferri, who is executive director of FHS and co-director of the Social and Collaborative Housing Masters program at the Politecnico di Milano, adds nuance to the collaborative nature of this process by nothing that, "Of course, we are always telling our projects' residents that we hold no expectations regarding their activities; rather, what we offer them is a different way of inhabiting their neighborhood that each individual can choose to follow or not. We assume that sharing does not automatically mean collaboration, and that collaboration is possible only when sharing products/services also produces relational benefits."

The Community Start-Up Process lasts for one year and includes four phases, beginning about six months before the arrival of the first residents and ending after the building has opened.

The first phase of the Community Start-Up Process involves selecting candidates who will be a good fit for the housing opportunity. After selection, they then enter the "warm-up" phase, where they are assigned to an apartment, get to know their peers, and to start experiencing the advantages of working together as a group. This involves dealing with issues that are the most urgent for the future tenants, like moving furnishings into the new house.

Next is the "planning" phase, which includes a series of workshop activities that focus on helping residents effectively use all of the communal spaces. Participants draw up self-governing rules and are trained in developing collaborative activities that can be carried out in their shared spaces.

The activities that have been designed and prototyped during the "planning" phase, are put into practice for the final phase of roughly four months. Included in the activities of this stage is the creation of a constitution for the tenants' association.

This model is underway in six housing projects and will be used over the next two years in an additional ten projects. To date, approximately 1,200 households have utilized the Community Start-Up Process and FHS is actively working on or planning housing initiatives that will touch an additional 3,200 households by 2025.

Common spaces and communal activities such as this concert in the garden are the outcomes of the Community Start-Up Process

In FHS's estimation, this model has been crucial in starting collaborative housing across Italy. As each Community Start-Up Process progresses, FHS monitors the social value of the project, with a goal of understanding "how the community strengthens." To do this, they collect intangible or relational data that is often overlooked during evaluative processes focused exclusively on things that can be easily measured. Input comes from residents as well as local stakeholders, such as the local religious leaders, managers of the local schools, retailers, and representatives from local voluntary organizations.

This assessment helps FHS learn how to improve their investments on a forward-looking basis, as well as to make a stronger case to public institutions whose support could extend the work. As a member of the FHS team put it, "Our ultimate objective is to make it possible to repeat an experience that... put[s] into place tools which will allow spreading the model." The ultimate goal is to enable individuals to build their own neighborhoods through available tools, spaces, trust, and collaboration.

Images: Fondazione Housing Sociale

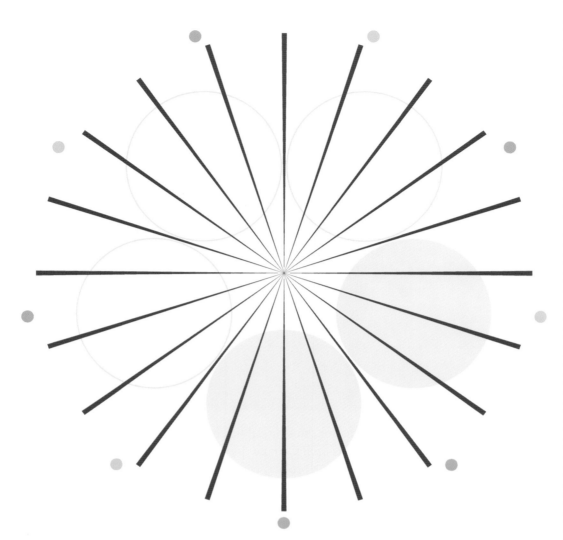

Duration
April 2016–June 2018

Location
Denmark

Categories
Health and Wellness
Policy
Education
Economic

Designer
Danish Design Centre

Partners
Fokstrot Public Futures
University Hospital of Denmark
  Rigshospitalet
New North Zealand Hospital
Industry Association
  Medicoindustrien
Aalborg University
University College Copenhagen

Key Contributors
Christian Bason
Sara Gry Striegler

Designer Organization Type
Non-Profit

Team Size
8–10

Design Quotient
41–60%

Project Costs
$100k–$500k

Source of Funding
Multiple Sources

Funding Mechanisms
Fee for Service

Impact Measurement Methods
Quantitative: Surveys, Web/
  Mobile Analytics, Event
  Attendance

Mediums
Spatial: Exhibition
Experiential: Workshop

Boxing Future Health

Cultivating a discussion about the future of health through tangible scenarios and co-creation

Boxing Future Health is dedicated to imagining healthcare challenges in 2050 amid changes in demographics, social structures, and the composition of healthcare as an industry and a social goal. Led by the Danish Design Centre, which is the leading organization in Denmark that works with business and government stakeholders on the role of design in innovation in development, this project addressed a societal tendency to fixate on healthcare issues that are discrete and infamous, such as cancer. On the other hand, less high-profile, more introspective discussions about the nature of care itself, health, and illness are harder to initiate.

As the Danish Design Centre's largest design experiment to date, this project was co-created with over 100 experts and professionals with backgrounds ranging from technologists to doctors, and including priests, designers, and scientists. Collectively they hope to spark a transformation of the healthcare sector.

Boxing Future Health took a long view. Using 2050 as the timeline, the team developed four scenarios that bring to life "possible futures" complete with business models, collaboration modalities, and governance concepts. These were designed to provoke and inspire public and private actors across the healthcare landscape to radically rethink their work by engaging in uncomfortable discussions about how things could be done radically differently.

To prime these conversations, the team first conducted research on trends and tendencies based on analyses from groups like the World Health Organization and Organisation for Economic Co-operation and Development (OECD). Experts from across the field of health also contributed opinions and data to help identify certainties and uncertainties, trends and tendencies.

This was synthesized into four distinct visions of health in the year 2050 mapped onto a 2x2 matrix, responding to axes representing spectra from individual to collective, and from biomedical health to whole life-focused health. Each of the four scenarios were presented as sensory experiences in the form of small exhibitions. How could that scenario look, feel, smell, or taste? Visitors to these scenario exhibitions could also listen to fictionalized citizens from each alternative future providing their perspectives on living in that world.

By combining design and scenario planning, the Boxing Future Health team sought to create a rich and immersive environment within which far-ranging conversations about the future of healthcare could be cracked open. The methodology itself also had an impact on participants. As Jannicke Schumann-Olsen, innovation director at the Scandinavian insurance company Tryg Forsikring put it, "Boxing Future Health was a real kick-start to our work with future scenarios for healthcare services. It has been invaluable for us to get such a compact introduction to such a grand theme, and in such a pedagogical and engaging way. This has... made our own process more tangible and solid."

By the Danish Design Centre's measure, upwards of 4,000 people have visited the Boxing Future Health immersive experience to date and at least 32 companies have utilized a digital version of the content in their own strategic planning efforts, demonstrating that a combination of design and scenario planning represents a captivating way to make the unknown future a little more approachable.

Installations give the explorers the opportunity to engage all of their senses

The immersive nature of the scenarios world gives visitors a chance to engage more viscerally with the content

Images: Courtesy Danish Design Centre

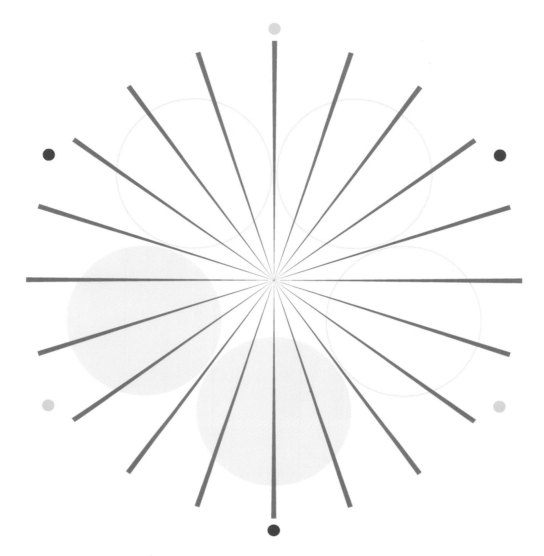

Duration
  2015–2017

Location
  Quito and Guayaquil, Ecuador

Categories
  Economic

Designer
  GRID Impact

Partners
  Banco Pichincha
  Inter-American Development
    Bank

Key Contributors
  Alexandra Fiorillo

Designer Organization Type
  ● For-Profit

Team Size
  ● 5–7

Design Quotient
  ● 41–60%

Project Costs
  ▷ $100k–$500k

Source of Funding
  ▬ Government

Funding Mechanisms
  Fee for Service

Impact Measurement Methods
  Quantitative: Randomized
    Controlled Trial

Mediums
  Experiential: Education
  Physical: Journals, Posters

Design for Social Innovation

Financial Literacy for Ecuadorian Microentrepreneurs

Educating microentrepreneurs through a "less is more" learning approach

"It is so hard to keep track of everything," explained an Ecuadorian micro-entrepreneur interviewed during this project. "The business is busy and my life is busy. How can I track every single sale? It's not possible. I need a simpler system." Captured in this quotation is the crux of the challenge when it comes to financial literacy. Microentrepreneurs, who make up the vast majority of firms in Latin America and the Caribbean according to OECD,[1] are often mentally overtaxed by the pressing needs and associated "microdecisions" that dominate their day-to-day activities. Adding more work and learning on top of their already busy lifestyle often proves too onerous.

GRID Impact, a global design collective, addresses issues like this by combining behavioral science and design methodologies. In Ecuador they partnered with Banco Pichincha del Ecuador and the Inter-American Development Bank to develop an approach to business training that is simplified but still enables improvements on the financial literacy and financial health of local microentrepreneurs.

Previous efforts relied on classroom training to build financial literacy. Recognizing the challenge of "cognitive scarcity," which says that individuals only have so much time and attention, GRID's experience told them that they would need to be inventive while creating ways for individuals to increase their knowledge, skills, and attitudes toward finance without dedicating too much time to the effort. Instead of formal lesson plans, the GRID team designed a system of financial heuristics or "rules of thumb" that could easily be followed during a busy workday.

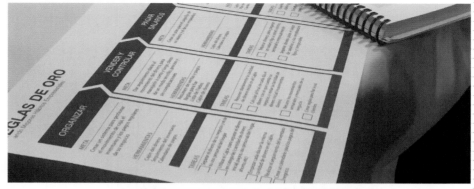

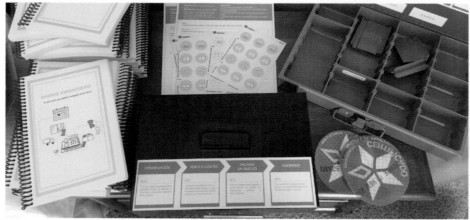

Through in-depth interviews, GRID was able to identify behaviors that correlated with the successful business practice among microentrepreneurs in Quito and Guayaquil. Analysis of existing business practices and data enabled the GRID team to develop several profiles of existing businesses in both cities, which were then cross-checked with quantitative data and insights provided by Banco Pichincha and Inter-American Development Bank. Once findings were validated, they were codified into a series of heuristics and packaged for dissemination.

For the pilot, entrepreneurs were introduced to the new heuristics-based program through one four-hour in-person workshop and then invited to participate in a 30-day challenge to apply the practices they learned in their business. To support them, participants took home a set of materials that would support their new practices and behaviors. This included a cash box to help them organize their cash, a journal with worksheets they could use to plan for savings or keep track of customers, and visuals to remind them of the heuristics they selected to practice in their business. Participants were visited every two weeks by an officer from Banco Pichincha, who helped reinforce the practices and check on the entrepreneurs' progress.

After completing an eight-month research and design process, the Inter-American Development Bank ran a randomized controlled trial (RCT) with 2,408 microentrepreneurs located in Pichincha and Guayas. The experiment tested the heuristics-based program against a control group and a traditional finan-

Interviewing a microentrepreneur in Quito, Ecuador

Images: GRID Impact

cial education program, which was much more time- and effort-intensive, with approximately 800 participants per group.

Results indicated that entrepreneurs who participated in the heuristics-based training increased their sales by 7% and profits by 8% on average, compared to the entrepreneurs, who did not receive any training. The results were better for women, due to their higher adoption of the heuristics practices compared to men in the RCT. GRID hypothesizes that "since women might be more cognitively taxed than men (due to social norms), awareness about cognitive load could be key for improving gender mainstreaming efforts." Designing with a sharp awareness of the personal context of microentrepreneurs and an acknowledgment of the cognitive scarcity of these individuals demonstrates that "less is more" can create a meaningful impact.

1 "Latin America and the Caribbean 2019: Policies for Competitive SMEs in the Pacific Alliance and Participating South American Countries," OECD, accessed April 4, 2021, www.oecd.org/publications/latin-america-and-the-caribbean-2019-d9e1e5f0-en.htm.

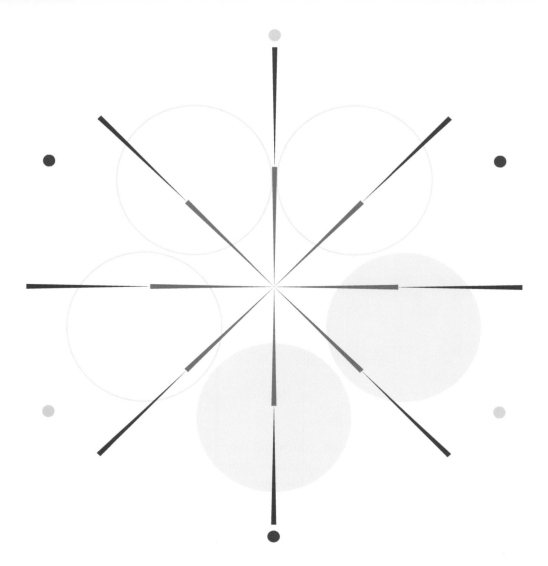

Duration
  2017–present

Location
  Neustadt am Rennsteig, Free
    State of Thuringia, Germany

Categories
  Social Justice

Designer
  studioetcetera, Berlin

Partners
  Local parish and associations
    aiming to reinforce community
    life

Key Contributors
  Horst Brettel
  Elke Bergt
  Hannes Langguth
  Cosima Speckhardt
  Ulrike Rothe

Designer Organization Type
  • For-Profit

Team Size
  • 5–7

Design Quotient
  • 81–100%

Project Costs
  ▷ $1k–$25k

Source of Funding
  Government
  Foundation/Non-Profit/
    Endowment

Funding Mechanisms
  Unspecified

Impact Measurement Methods
  Quantitative: Growth in Product/
    Service Adoption or Usage

Mediums
  Experiential: Event
  Spatial: Repurposed Buildings

Thüringer Church Hostels

Breathing new life into old churches and rural communities

Churches in Germany have seen a significant loss in size of their congregations since the Second World War, with 40% of the population abandoning church membership in that time period.[1] Currently, the Evangelical Church in Central Germany claims less than 4% of Protestant Christians as members, but has about 2,000 churches, half of which are older than 500 years. How could they be put to use?

If disused churches were converted into hostels that welcome visitors for overnight experiences in the evening, and serve as community spaces for activities including cinema nights, open choir practices, or communal meals during the day, what broader changes might this kick-start? Berlin-based architecture and urban and regional planning studio studioetcetera won a Europe-wide competition with their concept of "Herrbergskirchen" ("church hostels" in English). The studio specializes in community-based design projects that can be built upon by others, and that is exactly what they proposed for the future of Germany's underused churches. Beyond the local impacts, the design team envisioned a network of spaces that would strengthen regional tourism and provide social and cultural opportunities to mountain communities throughout the Thuringian Forest region.

After being commissioned, studioetcetera conducted a spatial and contextual analysis of the region, including several on-site visits and interviews with local parishes aiming to identify the current challenges, needs, and potentials of church halls and their local communities. The team's design approach included participatory methods such as idea workshops and collective mapping practices. Collaboration with local carpenters, tailors, and smitheries, as well as the use of local building materials including wood from the local forests, were core to studioetcetera's desire to create a regional circular economy.

Views of Her(r)-
bergskirche,
Neustadt am
Rennsteig

Images:
René Zieger

By offering such a new and experimental form of regional tourism approach, the number of overnight guests in the local church hall has steadily increased from an initial 80 guests in 2017 to more than 350 guests in 2019. Visitors are mainly younger people who had not visited the region before, but were attracted by the possibility of having a special experience away from the city. The architectural design of the new accommodations is based on sensitive and minimal intervention practices. By highlighting existing fractures and material traces, old and new materials are brought together to retain the history of the site, while reframing it as more accessible to younger generations.

Social and cultural events sparked by the creative reuse of church halls have also enhanced everyday life and exchange within local communities in rural Thuringia. Church halls are now used for a variety of new uses: regular open practices with local choir, large dinners that are regularly organized by local communities, cinema nights, concerts; and artist-in-residency programs and exhibitions. While these spaces are no longer churches, they provide a similar function in a more secular context. As a resident put it, "I increasingly feel a stronger belonging to other people within our community" after the Herrbergskirchen renovation.

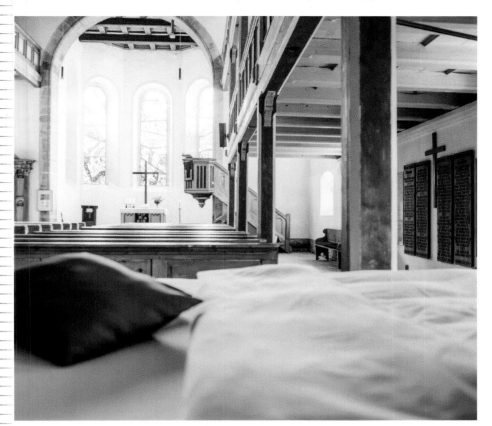

Organizing the Work

*"To collaborate with all these young people
from Berlin, Leipzig, and Vienna during
the design and development process has
been a wonderful experience for me."*

Horst, local parish, June 2019

1   Evangelische Kirche in Deutschland EKD, "Gezählt 2020. Zahlen Und Fakten Zum Kirchlichen
Leben.," July 2020, www.ekd.de/ekd_de/ds_doc/Gezaehlt_zahlen_und_fakten_2020.pdf.

Preparation for communal meal

Images: studio etcetera

Cinema night

Organizing the Work

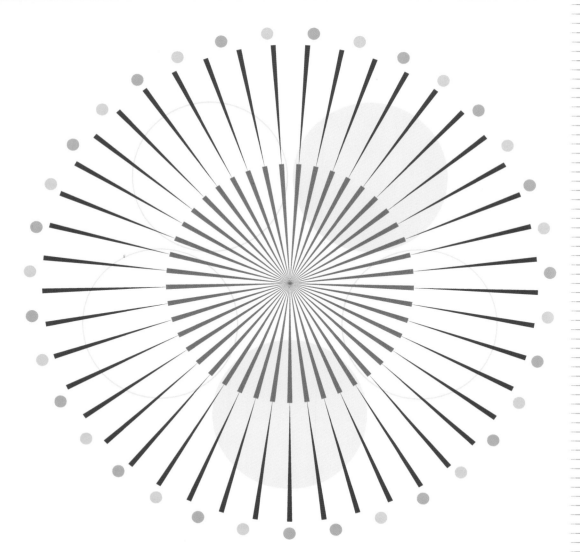

Duration
Aug 2017–July 2022

Location
London, UK, neighborhoods of Barking and Dagenham

Categories
Health and Wellness

Designer
Participatory City Foundation

Partners
Board consisting of five core funders, including the local council

Designer Organization Type
● Non-Profit

Team Size
● 21–49

Design Quotient
● 41–60%

Project Costs
▷ $1MM+

Source of Funding
━ Government
━ Foundation/Non-Profit/ Endowment

Funding Mechanisms
Grant

Impact Measurement Methods
Qualitative: Stakeholder Interviews, Team Reflections
Quantitative: Surveys, Headcount/Time of Participation, Event Attendance, Number of Projects Initiated

Mediums
Experiential: Event
Organizational: Non-profit

Design for Social Innovation

Every One Every Day

Building participatory infrastructure for local residents to shape their neighborhoods

Building on careful study of successful models of participatory culture and co-design on smaller scales across the world, Every One Every Day is testing a deceptively simple hypothesis in a borough of London. What if every one of the 220,000 residents participated in activities of mutual aid, every single day? The project is funded for five years with the aim of delivering lasting change in the Barking and Dagenham neighborhoods, while also validating the feasibility, potential, and impact of this unique approach to inclusive social infrastructures.

As a way to bring people into dialogue with one another, the Every One Every Day project focuses on "common denominator" activities that make up the fabric of everyday life, including things like community-organized summer camps, family cooking sessions, new retail shops for home-produced goods, and co-working. Driving this is a focus on individual agency, which Participatory City Foundation has demonstrated is a result of practical participation. Foregrounding these approachable activities over more "abstract" collective engagements such as planning and meeting was a careful design choice by the team at Participatory City Foundation, who are stewarding the work.

That playful and almost effortless nature of the activities that comprise Every One Every Day hides the careful effort of the team, who act as system stewards. Their extensive annual reports, each 100-plus pages, reveal the depth of planning and thinking that enables these diverse activities to succeed, not just as one-offs but as a constellation of interlinked efforts.

As the participation ecosystem grows in Barking and Dagenham, currently working with more than 6,000 people across 160 projects, the team is increasingly able to measure the impacts of this different form of neighborhood participation. They've tracked an array of "public metrics," such as the number of children who are participating in activities (up more than five times between years one and two)

and the total number of hours of different neighborhood activities (up three times in the same timespan).

Every One Every Day builds upon seven previous years of research carried out by Participatory City Foundation into peer-to-peer participation models in neighborhoods across the world. The research used a mix of qualitative and quantitative evaluation to identify what worked and why, and is documented on their website.

Participatory City Foundation does not dictate a set of activities, but is instead designed as an infrastructure to amplify whatever it is that the neighborhood is already interested in. That infrastructure includes storefront and maker spaces, materials and equipment loans, event organizing, and arranging of necessary items like insurance and health and safety considerations. By lowering many practical barriers to engagement often faced by community members in order to engage, their model allows them to focus on what's important—each other. To date, the project has tracked some 34,000 hours of time that neighbors have spent together participating in activities.

Every One Every Day currently operates five local spaces around the neighborhood, four of which are designated as neighborhood "shops" (project incubators) and one of which is a makerspace warehouse that allows for small-scale manufacturing. This makerspace also offers product prototyping, skills development, and business development opportunities.

　　　　　　　　　　　　　　Design for Social Innovation

Every One Every Day models a unique funding arrangement in which all funders have pooled their contributions and adopted the same measurements and outcomes. Five years in, £7.2 million has been raised for this platform approach, which allows the prototype to run now with a clear focus on delivering rather than further fundraising.

Having begun as a research project learning from the world, now the world is paying attention to Participatory City Foundation. The McConnell Foundation in Canada plans to trial the approach in Montreal, Toronto, and Halifax.

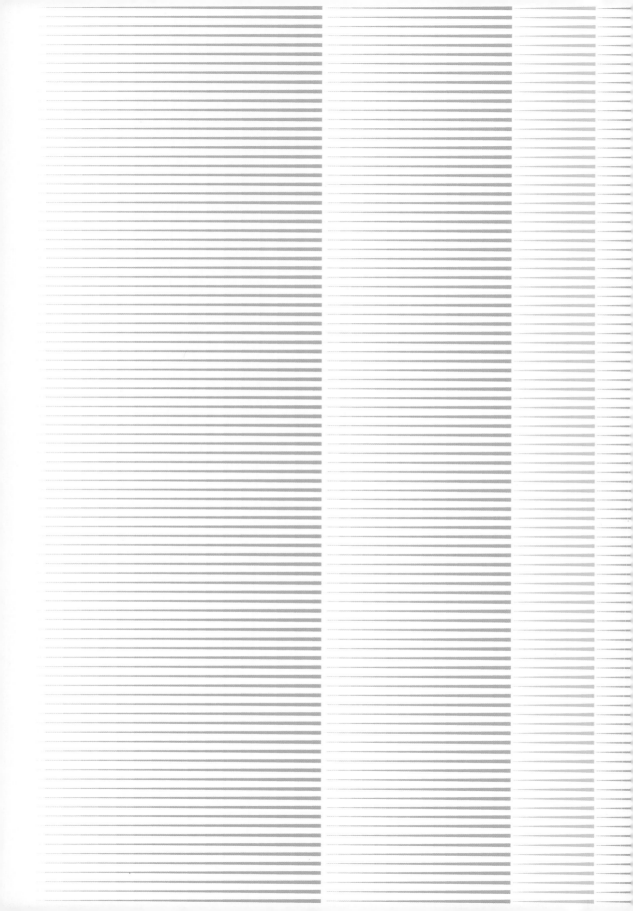

Navigating Partnerships

Nandana Chakraborty, Vivek Chondagar, Jesper Christiansen, and Fumiko Ichikawa, with Jennifer May

Design for social innovation occurs at intersections throughout this book: of sectors, disciplines, organizations, and people. None of the 45 cases in this book—indeed, none of the nearly 200 projects that we reviewed during the research for this project—feature designers working in a vacuum. Each case describes some form of collaboration through formal and informal partnerships with universities, governments, NGOs, non-profits, community organizations, advisory boards, committees, and subject matter experts. On average, the cases in this book list three partners; Redesigning U-Report touts over 380. "Partner" is a word that is open for interpretation, with some cases listing only organizations, while others, such as Beegin, City of Rain, and Digua Community, list end-users or a group of end-users.

Partners are integral to the work of design for social innovation because of the necessary elements they bring to any project: subject matter expertise, networks, resources, and funding. Partners forge connections and help liaise with their contacts, assist teams while navigating questions of infrastructure, policy and process, and often hold the key to channels of implementation or distribution. However, for all that they bring, they also add layers of complexity to the work. For instance, a change in personnel or policy can lead to shifting expectations or new priorities emerging in the middle of a project. Where partnerships are transactional, change can be troubling. Where teams have managed to build relationships, the inevitable surprises that emerge during social innovation work are easier to navigate due to the strength of the team as a whole.

The participants in this roundtable have different models of practice. Nandana Chakraborty and Vivek Chondagar work in the corporate social responsibility initiative of one of India's largest technology consulting firms. Jesper Christiansen crosses international borders with his non-profit, consulting with governments and organizations around the globe. Fumiko Ichikawa focuses on individuals, communities, and cities in Japan at a "think and do tank" that she co-founded. All of their work is dependent on an ability to build and maintain strong partnerships with broad coalitions of organizations and people.

Using concrete examples, we explore the ups and downs, ins and outs of working in partnership. What are the scale and scope of partnerships that work well? How do designers set expectations initially, and then balance those expectations among many different stakeholders and shifting circumstances?

This discussion took place over two sessions in July 2020 and was edited for clarity and length

Nandana Chakraborty

I've been working in the social innovation and impact space for eight years now; a combination of both my academic and professional experience. In my academic days, I had the opportunity to work with the government in the maternal and child health-care sector, and when I joined Tata Consultancy Services (TCS) as a part of Digital Impact Square, the opportunity expanded to other areas as well.

Vivek Chondagar

I've been in the social innovation space for more than five and a half years. My educational background includes a degree in psychology design and engineering. My first two years were spent on individual client and consultant-based projects. For the last three years I've been in the social innovation center, run by Tata Consultancy Services, which is currently one of the largest IT industries in the country. Their corporate social responsibility initiative encourages the next generation to come to us right out of college, and to work with us to address social challenges with a focus on rural India and urban goods.

Jesper Christiansen

I have a Ph.D. in social anthropology and started my career in public innovation practice at MindLab in Denmark. MindLab was the Danish government's innovation unit, working across ministries with the mandate to reshape policy practices and to create organizational cultures around human-centered design. I was drawn from a research standpoint to this work and curious to discover what's behind design and innovation in government when we go a little bit beyond just the methods and the flashy stories of innovation. I was interested in what innovation meant when socially produced. I've recently been working with States of Change, which is a non-profit global innovation learning initiative trying to build the field of public innovation through a network approach.

Fumiko Ichikawa

I'm co-founder and managing director of a company called Re:public, which was started seven years ago. Prior to that, together with my co-founder, we were working for an ad agency, and simultaneously teaching innovation at i.school at the University of Tokyo, which was started in 2009 to focus on human-centered innovation. They brought together professionals outside of the university to teach practice-based design and innovation. We were working with students along with corporate partners and creating an ecosystem of new business and transformative projects. Then the 2011 earthquake and tsunami struck northern Japan and changed everything. That's when we decided to start Re:public.

Jennifer: Can you all explain the role of partnerships in your current work?

Vivek: The current focus of Digital Impact Square centers on rural India. Predominantly, we work with seven different teams representing transportation, mobility, agriculture, healthcare, education, housing, and the environment. Our current slate of projects is geared towards education, healthcare, and agriculture; we focus on getting the right kind of partner in our work. Before each new year, we conduct challenge sourcing, where we speak with government agencies, private organizations, and non-governmental organizations that have a social interest in a particular team's focus. If we take agriculture as an example, we will be talking to government agencies working in the agricultural sector. For another challenge, we connected with Tata Consultancy Services because we needed their input as an IT company about the emergent challenges they see in that ecosystem. With each new cycle, we work with partners to identify and validate the problem. And, once we identify the challenges to be addressed, those partners help us connect further. Many of our team members have just graduated from college. Their focus is to address a social challenge that will positively impact society, but they don't know who to talk to. They just don't have the resources yet. Our partner ecosystem allows them to research, experiment, and validate their findings during the six-month or year period they are with us. Partners also help us connect to new partners and widen the circle. For example, I work with the agricultural sector, and Nandana works with the healthcare and education sectors. When I pick up an agricultural challenge, I go to a farmers' producers organization (FPO); they function as a collective that has a great capacity to open up other partnerships for our projects. Some FPOs can have as many as 8,000 farmers that we can access; they are instrumental in connecting us with agricultural universities around the country and students who want to get involved.

Nandana: In the case of our work on healthcare partnerships, we are intentionally slow to form alliances. We work to understand the vision of the potential partner first, and their area of expertise. Getting this understanding at the start is an integral step. We've learned that a partnership will often fail because there were mismatched expectations between the two parties. For us, the first step is always about understanding a partner's expertise, what they do, what we do, and then identifying how we can work together.

Jesper: My involvement in public development has been using bottom-up approaches, which means placing a heavy focus on partnering, whether with citizens directly, looking at co-creating outcomes across sectors, or collaborating around building organizational capacities. Our work at States of Change aims to create a culture change in government, whether it's partnering with other governments to transform themselves or partnering with organizations to support the government in their learning journey. Making government work for people is the focal point and the goal at the same time. We usually take a fairly pragmatic angle as to how we intervene in people's lives and ask, "Are we legitimately doing that?" Then there's the question of what "legitimate" looks like. Coming from an anthropological background, I find it very curious how little we know about people's lives concerning effective interventions in policy. Embracing people's own experiences as vantage points and building trust needs to be at the center of this work on partnerships.

Fumiko: I would describe Re:public as a think and do tank. The primary reason for our partnerships draws on the ecosystem concept Vivek was referring to earlier: it is about understanding what it means to be in that ecosystem.

Not that we were able to do this successfully at the beginning of our work. As professionals, we thought we would be able to show up in a community and make a difference. Working in rural Japan, where we were unfamiliar with industries such as fisheries, taught us how wrong we were to make this assumption. Our work after the 2011 earthquake in Japan provided us with the opportunity to involve communities and build partnerships driven by local interests. We learned the value of facilitating partnerships with government entities. We become a bridge of sorts as part of the larger ecosystem. The difficulty is that visions are not always shared between sectors or companies or between governments and schools. Everyone keeps to themselves, especially in smaller places where they might not find value in a larger ecosystem. Our approach is to focus our work creating these spaces for connection. We don't believe change can happen in silos or simply via bottom-up or top-down approaches. We need both. We need the collective.

Jennifer: What are the scale and scope of your partnerships? What kind of stakeholders are you all working with?

Jesper: In States of Change, one example that comes to mind is a partnership with the Canadian government to support a cross-departmental network for systems transformation challenges. On the one hand, it was a straightforward, professional development task: equipping people to deal differently with the problems they're facing in their daily work tasks by leveraging the cross-cutting resources we were putting together for them. On the other hand, the initiative had an additional dimension that was much more complex: it engaged a Canadian government council with 15 departments with distinct mandates and goals. The initiative's multi-stakeholder nature was an opportunity to create institutional change in the Canadian government across departments and outside organizations.

"Partnering is not something we talk about when we are putting together project briefs; it's just how we operate in those capacity-building efforts. It's the starting point."

I believe that everything we do around partnerships can be broken down into a contractual relationship; someone invests in a learning journey, but that journey relies on multiple partners supporting the endeavor because our primary goal is to build innovation capacity and showcase how working with diversity of approaches can influence strategically prioritized challenges. This entails embedding this capacity and process with the people responsible for creating the impact. If you don't do this, it becomes a fringe, temporary activity, and you don't get to effect the change you set up to do.

A couple of years ago, we worked with the Colombian government, partnering with the Department of National Planning to build their innovation strategy for the new national development plan. We quickly realized that Colombia's all 33 regions had to be part of this national development plan's mindset for it to succeed. In these planning processes, the traditional approach has been: we write content, we tell people what to do, and they will do it—which in essence is not a partnership, but more of a command and control logic. Partnering is not something we talk about when we are putting together project briefs; it's just how we operate in those capacity-building efforts. It's the starting point.

> **Nandana:** Our projects typically cover a period of 12 to 18 months. Once that's over, and they have a good outcome and model, they will be developed further in the incubation center, but in the interim, they will provide mentorship to other projects starting up. When we partner, we have to always begin with a trial engagement to manage expectations about moving forward and subsequent phases. For example, when we started working in healthcare in 2018, we selected a challenge connected to autism. We had never attempted a challenge of this kind because it's very expert-driven, and it needs a lot of medical expertise to inform it. We made it happen by follow-

Design for Social Innovation

ing the systematic process that characterizes our work: we begin by evaluating what capacities we will need to shape a relevant innovation; and then we will follow several steps to assess its potential for getting converted into a startup. Our internal assessment protocols are critical. By the time we are ready to set up a partnership, we are equipped with the right questions to be intentional with our goals and shape clear communication channels and a collective vision with our partners to make the challenge successful. And yet, despite all of this rigor, the journey is not always smooth.

Fumiko: While our operations' scale is not India's in terms of its demographics, many of our projects are touching considerable numbers of people. In city governments, our smaller projects typically touch 300,000 people at the prefectural level; this is a scale we can be very productive in.

Getting a partnership going is so hard, isn't it? At the start of our projects, we work hard to set clear expectations, and we allow some time, typically three months, for iteration and flexibility around these goals. We also make sure that there is support for the project locally, within the government. We include them as key stakeholders. Their participation tends to make our projects viable and vital. There's usually skepticism at the beginning that we have to overcome. But the good news is that, when we get a few government officials on board, it becomes much easier to move ahead and scale.

Jesper: We have been most successful when people brought a discovery approach to their projects, so when expectations change, they are more flexible about that change. For example, in the Canadian case, they had a set of assumptions around what the future role of public servants would look like and had specific ideas about how to organize the project while recognizing they might be proved wrong. That humility from the get-go and saying, "Well, what we need is not someone who promises that this will work, but someone who can help us steward and support this process," factored in the project's success.

Vivek: Considering that we are a corporate social responsibility (CSR) initiative of a large IT corporation, we don't have any set expectations and no client-based requirement from the community. It's just the vision of two parties coming together to make the community stronger. Here is a good example. In a village 60 kilometers away, there are 150 farmers. The challenge is to connect them with a larger ecosystem of farmers, producers, and organizations and the extensive supply chains that exist. Integrating those small-town farmers into the large ecosystem would greatly benefit them when it comes to selling their goods into the market. Trust is the biggest problem that we face. At first, communities are not going to trust you because they've never seen you. They come with their own social biases. So we usually follow B2B2C (business to business to consumer) structure, where we always talk first to the larger organization, who has familiarity with the local area. When we embark on the journey, we first have to build trust with the organization, foundation, or department. Initially, when we first talk about it, we have a series of meetings and workshops where we work together to figure out ways of reaching the end consumer or end-users, which will bring efficiency to the ecosystem. We encourage our teams at every step of the way to have full creative sessions. The organization is also involved in deciding the next course of action to reach the initial expectations. That process will differ depending on accessibility. We first want to come together to validate assumptions and potential ways forward. Within the first six months of projects like this one, we typically will have multiple conversations with the organization, 10 to 15 on average, and approximately 40 to 50 interactions with our end-users.

So, back to your question about shifting expectations in a project, my answer is that, when strong bonds form, expectation shifts are easier to manage.

> **Jennifer:** To expand on the concept of trustworthiness we have been discussing, can you share how you introduce the value of design methodologies and translate what you do with partners unfamiliar with these processes and their potential relevance to their work?

Fumiko: We look for framing that everyone can understand and relate to and for opportunities to identify a common vision with our partners.

"While the design part may seem less evident... when you're focused on creating a business model, it's crucial. The value of design in this stage is a message we need to get across better when we engage with multidisciplinary cross-functional teams in these partnerships."

> **Jesper:** We have extended lead times into partnerships, between six and eighteen months, maybe even longer. We use this time to talk about our work, what we are trying to do, what it looks like, how

we make sense of each other's context and expertise and point of view, etc. It's very informal, it's not a structured workshop process, and usually, at least in pre-COVID times, it included face-to-face interaction. With the Canadian project, before its start, I spent two days at a conference with the main stakeholders openly discussing how we each were processing the brief from our perspectives. In this part of the world, we face the critique that many designers are still too naive or uninformed about the complex social issues at hand in these projects. There's a lot of domain expertise in the sector that designers must learn about to engage with this work. Some designers seem to go in with the mentality of selling design rather than embedding design into the process, and it ends up becoming a strange negotiation with partners.

Nandana: As we know, partners' sensitivity and design maturity fall in a broad spectrum. Many of our partners are in bureaucratic structures governed by top-down decision making; our design principles feel foreign to them. We've seen that the human-centered design approach is very successful. Typically, there is a lot of buy-in at the beginning and ideation stage of a project and as we engage in problem-solving and converting ideas into a minimum viable prototype for testing. Our partners and organizations are excited—you've identified the problem, we're ready to move forward. Then, as implementation nears, the focus often shifts. It goes from the design-centered approach to a more technical and business-centered one, and suddenly no one is talking about the value of design and innovation anymore. I realize that while the design part may seem less evident during the stage of the project when you're focused on creating a business model, it's crucial. The value of design in this stage is a message we need to get across better when we engage with multidisciplinary cross-functional teams in these partnerships.

"We find that [partners] might not... refer to our projects as 'about social innovation, or transformation.'... [These] terms do not necessarily connote real value or earn buy-in for many partners operating outside design. We respect this, and... we allow people to experience, digest, and spread the value they find in our work in their own

words within their communities."

Jennifer: Fumiko, you work with city governments, but you're really serving the communities of those cities. Vivek, you were talking about working with farmers, but you really are doing this business-to-business-to-consumer model where you have an intermediary to the communities. And Jesper, in your example about Canada, it seems like you have really dual end-users, one the end-users of the actual project, and the other the government itself in terms of moving to a new way of working. I'm wondering, how do you all balance the needs of your partners (who might also be funders) with really making sure that solutions are serving your end-users?

Fumiko: That's a difficult question. Let me get in there! I think almost every process has that kind of struggle. In our case, we've made the conscious decision not to become too big. We receive more requests than we can take on, which aligns expectations from the beginning. Often, when we talk about incubating ideas and building collectives, people get confused—is this about technology, or is this a flashy new startup? We reassure them that's not the intention, and that they will have a more unique and rewarding type of entrepreneurial solution at the end of our engagement together. Our Bike is Life project is an interesting example. It looks like a regular mountain bike, but we were able to bridge the product and service function of the design in this case. The entrepreneur not only produced nice and easy-to-ride bikes in terms of their formal design, but they also provided bike tours to local cities that were not known centers of popular tourism. The project became a catalyst for reinventing the city and its experience for visitors. Creating that connection between the role of product design and service design was part of the conversation and innovation offered. Of course, the solution ended up serving many stakeholders: the local government with tourism, the entrepreneur with an acclaimed new product and service, and tourists and residents. We call this approach "Power of 10," meaning that as long as we engage key stakeholders within a specific industry and engage the right people, we know that they will become champions of the project. They will find a way to speak a common language and help the project arrive at outcomes that operate and amplify at multiple levels. We often see that, once such projects get adopted by communities, they scale and sustain. Community partners will often use their own vernacular instead of ours. We find that they might not use the terms "human-centered design" or refer to our projects as "about social innovation, or transformation." None of these keywords are in the vocabulary used; these terms do not necessarily connote real value or earn buy-in for many partners operating outside design. We respect this, and as we move through our partnership process, we allow people to experience, digest, and spread the value they find in our work in their own words within their communities.

Design for Social Innovation

Vivek: What usually happens is the funder for the project is TCS. We usually don't have any other external funding coming from any of the partners. So, there is no financial interest between partners at any point in time. We also don't expect any kind of equity from the innovations that are coming out of our innovation center. When a project becomes sustainable, that validates the reason for the investment, right? Sometimes we have to separate our partners' intentions, i.e., what they wish to do and what actually may be acceptable for the end-user. In other instances, we may need to negotiate competing agendas, and ensure that they will not impact negatively the outcomes of the project. We usually have two to three co-creation workshops involving the end-user beneficiaries and partners. In the agricultural sector, I have personally been part of three very big co-creation workshops, where we had around a hundred participants and five to six moderators. We had two to three FPOs working in the same sector. We had 50-plus farmers from different regions coming together and our role becomes that of an effective mediator. A project in India with ANM [auxiliary nurse midwives], that focused on pregnant women and mothers' care is an example where our work was all about uncovering a number of bureaucratic barriers that were not allowing care to get to many of these vulnerable women in rural regions. It's important to remember that a decision maker in these systems might have six or seven layers of hierarchy between them and the end-users as in the example of ANM and pregnant women. Our goal in such projects is to bridge the gap between the decision makers and the end-users. That's how we try to make a contribution and manage, but I would not claim our approach works all the time.

Jesper: I would say we have a third user in the project you mentioned, the citizens of Canada. The dynamics of the different levels of government are pretty complex. We tend to start with changemakers, who are the activists, if you will. We let them be the subject of social learning. We might engage with the executives that give mandates and open the door for them to become active in new ways, or we may facilitate processes for middle management to take real ownership of the projects' needs. This group becomes instrumental in the successful execution of the intervention. Finally, we also engage with other stakeholders outside of government. All of them have a role to play if we want to see relationships shift for the better. Again, there is a lot of social learning in this kind of endeavor.

Another related factor depends on how one defines success criteria and how one decides to focus on some of these relationships or social elements. I believe that aspect of the work has been one of the critical challenges of any effort I've been a part of, because you start learning the need to adapt as these relations play out over time. When it comes to design work, I guess how you involve users and design with users are critical questions to ask oneself at the front end of developing services or systems.

That said, in terms of the actual policies that may ensue from these design interventions—especially if they are focused on systems change rather than small-scale service solutions—the periods to see impact can take years. There's just a long lead-in time. Many of the seeds for change that we planted ten years ago, when I was part of the MindLab team, are only now manifesting in the Danish Government's policies.

Regarding funding, I'd say that the legitimacy perspective matters: what you can take credit for. Accomplishing a cohesive articulation of this remains a considerable challenge. These considerations are at the center of many of our conversations in the design for the public sector arena; some of the folks leading some of the systems work in design and policy happening now are pretty inspiring. Some of the work we've been doing is to begin to define or have a better language for intermediary outcomes in terms of systems change and which stakeholders will see the positive impact. So this might not be an outcome for the citizens yet, but the likelihood of good outcomes in a continuous way for the citizens will increase if X or Y happens over time or we see signs like this and this and this in the way that the organization is operating, and so on.

> **Jennifer:** You all seem to be advocates of long-term partnerships and projects—most of the examples you've given go well beyond one year. How do you all handle partner fatigue for long-term partnerships and projects?

Fumiko: We try to extend our projects across multiple years unless we face an annual budget constraint. As long as there are intentions and interest to collaborate on both ends, we typically sustain our relationship regardless of achieving an initial project's goals. In one example with the Hiroshima Prefecture, we collaborated for five years. Eventually, we had so many different industries we were engaged in within the prefecture that the partnership evolved into a focus on incubation and entrepreneurship. We would finish one phase and then shift into another joint vision. So multiple projects resulted from that initial project, perhaps helping us avoid the fatigue issue. Our partners often say, "Once we can get hold of you, we don't want you guys to go." That said, our ultimate goal is that our partners will eventually manage fine without us.

> **Nandana:** I love this question. I have experienced ecosystem fatigue, which happens if we continuously engage partners without giving

Design for Social Innovation

them anything in return. We expect our partners to provide our innovators access to the ecosystem, to co-create and pilot the project. But, if that doesn't happen, the partnership fails. Partnerships need to be about reciprocal relationships where we simultaneously give and receive.

Then there is the issue of organizational changes, which we touched on earlier. It sets us back every time because we have to start a new relationship. The setbacks are pretty common and problematic with government work. When people at the top change, the overall agenda changes, and we essentially have to start over, which can be counter to our work and quite disruptive. I like to describe effective partnerships in the social sector as a slow-cooking method. People need to realize it takes time to see results. Achieving impact requires frequent and continuous engagement at every level to reach the end-goal together.

Jesper: We try to balance a fringe project or a training activity with a portfolio of projects where we are working strategically to prioritize professional development efforts that are highly complex. As far as the lead-in time, a lot goes into positioning the partnership in the right way. At least, in theory, what we end up working on is just helping people do what they have to do, but more efficiently.

As a field overall that intends to make a positive impact and "does good," we haven't adequately addressed the fallout of partnership fatigue. I also understand why partnership fatigue occurs, given the positioning and delivery of this work to date has not always met its aspirations. In general terms, the point of partnerships is leaning into this notion of sharing risk, sharing what's at stake. There could be other reasons, like bringing in funding from new sources or accessing new points of information or resources. But, for us as designers and design organizations, the motivation has to go beyond "we are going just to come in and help out." There has to be a proper integration of shared values and shared commitment. That integration is vital if we are to seek social impact beyond the confines of a discrete project.

Navigating
Partnerships

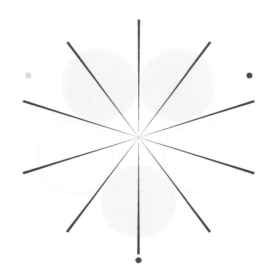

Mapeo Digital

Mapping risks to improving quality of life in Guatemala City

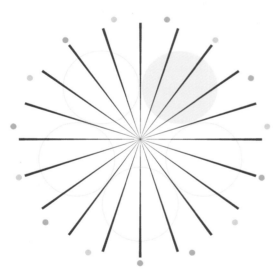

Digital Impact Square

Rooting technical solutions in the context and social needs of India's underserved populations

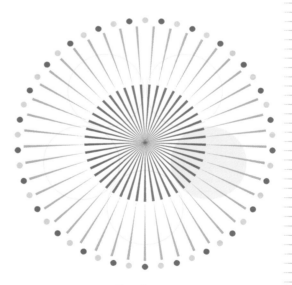

Izmirsea

Reviving residents' connection with the sea

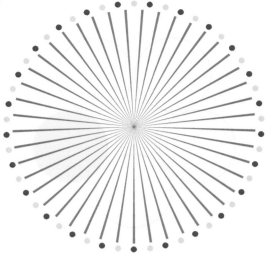

Spiro Wave

Expanding hospitals' capacity to care for patients during the COVID-19 crisis and beyond

XSCHOOL

Enhancing regional resilience by incubating new products, services, and businesses

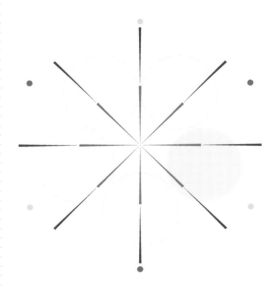

The Nest

Sharing study spaces to improve outcomes for Tel-Aviv-Yafo teens and their families

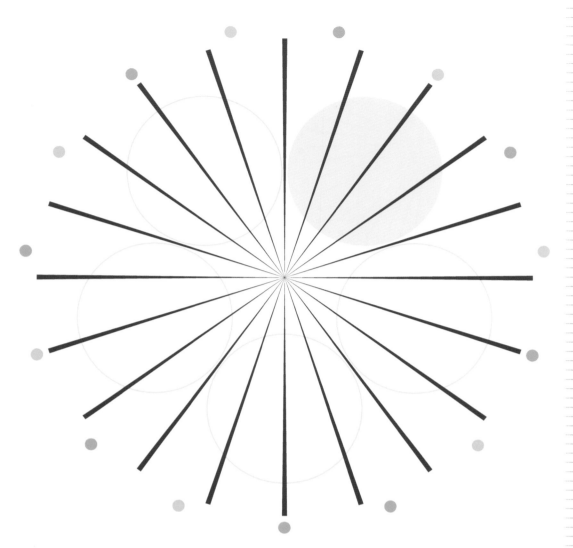

Duration
March 2016–present

Location
Nashik, India

Categories
Health and Wellness
Education
Social Entrepreneurship
Skill Development
Rural Innovation

Designer
Tata Consultancy Services

Partners
Multiple

Designer Organization Type
● Non-Profit

Team Size
● 11–20

Design Quotient
● 21–40%

Project Costs
$100k–$500k

Source of Funding
Foundation/Non-Profit/
Endowment

Funding Mechanisms
Unspecified

Impact Measurement Methods
Quantitative: Growth in Product/
Service Adoption or Usage,
Number of Projects Initiated,
Number of Financially Viable
Projects

Mediums
Organizational: Innovation Lab

Design for Social Innovation

Digital Impact Square

Rooting technical solutions in the context and social needs of India's underserved populations

Over the past two decades, social innovation in India has largely been concerned with the idea of scalability, when the focus is on serving the poorest populations. While that strategy has been successful for businesses, any social endeavor has to contend with a complex heterogeneity of 8 major religions, religious subidentities, 36 regional subcultures, and 23 official languages. Against this backdrop, large-scale, "copy and paste" solutions tend to exclude local communities or have limited impact. Is it possible to combine locally rooted services in India's less developed areas with highly scalable technology?

In an attempt to answer that question, the Tata Consultancy Services (TCS) Foundation created a non-profit initiative called Digital Impact Square (DISQ). It is an open social innovation center and "pre-incubator" whose mission is to support young entrepreneurs while developing a culture of social innovation among local communities. DISQ emerged from a multi-stakeholder collaboration in 2015 when the government of Nashik, a city of 1.5 million people, set out to remodel the experience of the Hindu religious festival of Kumbh, which is one of the largest public gatherings in the world. The festival is attended by 30 million devotees, temporarily multiplying the population of the city by 20 times. A group of social innovators, engineers, civic organizations, and city officials participated in a hackathon to design businesses, apps, and other inventions to aid crowd management, access to transportation, lodging, food, and other amenities that made the Kumbh a planning success. By bringing together a community of makers, academia, local administration, and civic groups, the "Kumbhathon," as it was called, sparked interest in a collaborative hub in Nashik.

DISQ alumni interacting and sharing their experience with a new batch of innovators

TCS Foundation saw an opportunity to build on the momentum of these partnerships and created DISQ. DISQ's living lab in Nashik invites students and youth to work on challenges such as health and hygiene, education and skills, financial and personal security, energy, water, and the environment, food and agriculture, housing and transportation, and citizen empowerment. Responding to the desire for scalability, digital technology is always part of the solution but applied in a way that is sensitive to local context and traditions.

After forming teams of participants, DISQ provides extensive mentoring, access to potential partners, office space, and seed funding. Each startup/prototype takes a bottom-up approach, working closely with the ecosystem to develop low-tech solutions seeking high social outcomes. Three pillars summarize DISQ's philosophy. They look to maximize empathy, possibility, and value. The goal is to achieve sustainable social innovation startups in a time frame of 12 to 18 months, from ideas to investment.

One such project is Maatritva, by a team of DISQ participants who subsequently founded the company Preleaf Technology. According to UNICEF, "the direct causes of maternal deaths are well known and largely preventable and treatable", however, access to prenatal care and specialists in rural India remains a grave concern. Maatritva ("motherhood" in Hindi) is a mobile health platform designed for use by frontline healthcare workers in rural areas. By simplifying data entry and analysis, the app helps nurse-midwives deliver care more efficiently through timely identification, tracking, and referral of high-risk pregnancies.

During the co-creation and participatory design process, the Maatritva team discovered and addressed local constraints like functionality in areas of zero mobile network connectivity and those beyond the reach of public transportation. The digital interface was also designed in regional languages, built around the needs of midwives and medical officers who use it for decision making. As of today, Maatritva has recorded more than 1,400 users and has impacted the lives of close to 60,000 pregnant women.

Since its inception in 2016, DISQ has mentored over 300 young entrepreneurs from 70 cities across India. Collectively this group has launched ten social startups, of which six, including Maatritva, have matured into independent entities as of Summer 2020. In sum, these organizations have aided or been used by some 750,000 people, by DISQ's count. DISQ's lasting impact on society is likely to be through the culture of social innovation it fosters, especially in the cities left behind during India's rapid development in the last decade.

Images: Digital Impact Square

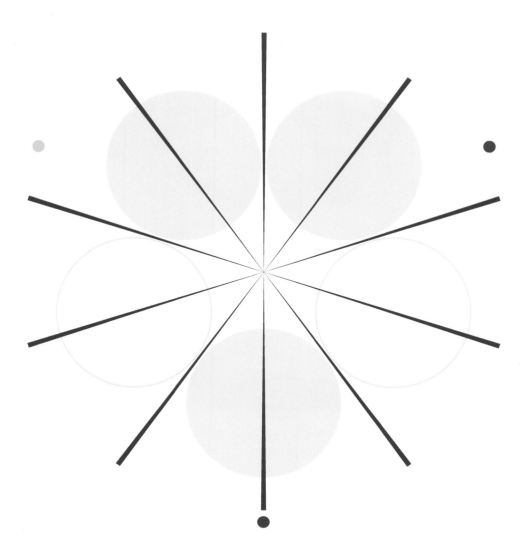

Duration
May 2016–August 2017

Location
Guatemala City, Guatemala

Categories
Social Justice
Policy
Risk Management
Community Engagement
Collaborative Action

Designer
Perpendicular-Social Innovation
Lab

Partners
Observatorio del Derecho a la
Vivienda
Techo Guatemala

Key Contributors
Ónice Arango
Andrea Valladares
Sabrina Vega

Designer Organization Type
• For-Profit

Team Size
• 2–4

Design Quotient
• 81–100%

Project Costs
▭ $25k–$100k

Source of Funding
▬ Foundation/Non-Profit/
Endowment

Funding Mechanisms
Grant

Impact Measurement Methods
Qualitative: Observed
Community Participation

Mediums
Digital: App, Network
Experiential: Workshop
Organizational: Service

Mapeo Digital

Mapping risks to improving quality of life in Guatemala City

For the 1.5 million people living in informal settlements in Guatemala, improvements to housing, infrastructure, and other basic services are critical. The informal nature of these areas makes it difficult for government and NGOs to act, because the baseline data they rely on, such as accurate maps, are often missing and hard to create, which compounds the difficulties that outsiders have understanding the needs and realities of such communities.

Perpendicular, a social innovation and urban research lab in Guatemala City, is working to apply new technologies to these challenges through their Mapeo Digital (digital mapping) project which provides a light-touch way to map both the physical and social geography of settlements. A key aim of the project is to build collective knowledge and capabilities among inhabitants of informal settlements so that they are empowered to advocate for their needs to the formal power structures around them.

In 2016, an informal settlements census was conducted by Techo Guatemala, the local branch of the youth-led Chilean-founded NGO that works together with families living in settlements to overcome poverty and exclusion throughout Latin America. Community data collected through short interviews with leaders allowed them to learn about land tenure, community leadership, security, and economic activities in more than 300 settlements in the Guatemala City metropolitan area. Meanwhile, a like-minded organization in Mexico, Observatorio del Derecho a la Vivienda, was developing technical and methodological methods for using drones to quickly build accurate maps of settlements.

Techo Guatemala, Observatorio del Derecho a la Vivienda, and Perpendicular joined forces to pilot a way to better understand informal communities and the systemic issues that limit their urban integration and development. Mapeo

Aerial view of an informal settlement captured by drone

Digital operated in four communities: Peña de Oro, 5 de Noviembre, Arzú, and El Campanero.

The process can be understood as broadly following three phases. During the first phase, the area is mapped using drones and community members are invited to contribute their knowledge on top of the map. This identifies physical and social threats to the settlement and surfaces existing vulnerabilities, such as sanitation, flooding, social challenges. It's not just challenges that are mapped at this time. Existing positive capabilities such as strong local leaders are also identified. In the second phase, these mappings are analyzed, synthesized, and validated through community workshops. Altogether 217 people participated in Mapeo Digital, which accounts for more than 20% of the residents of all the four communities surveyed. Findings are packaged and shared back to the community, as well as relevant government and NGOs, in the third phase.

Through the team's hybrid methodology combining technology—such as drones and apps, as well as discussions and workshops in the community—the result is shared ownership in a set of clearly presented priorities that blend hard data and local knowledge. Quantitative data including aerial maps and census data that is more accurate than official counts help convey the reality of informal settlements both grounded in the perspective of its inhabitants and in a manner that also "speaks the language" of formal organizations such as government and NGOs. This makes it possible to more quickly identify effective opportunities for collaboration, capacity building and cross-sector investment and escape the cycles

Design for Social Innovation

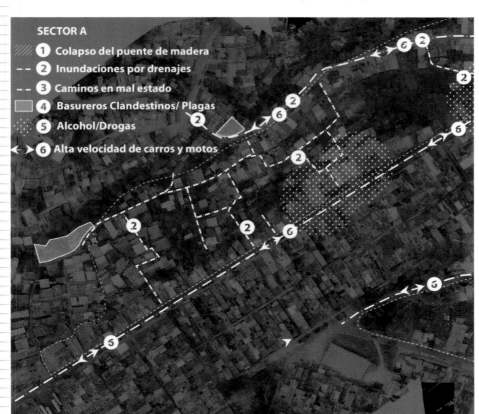

SECTOR A

1. Colapso del puente de madera
2. Inundaciones por drenajes
3. Caminos en mal estado
4. Basureros Clandestinos/ Plagas
5. Alcohol/Drogas
6. Alta velocidad de carros y motos

Annotated map of an informal settlement derived from drone footage

During the first phase of the process, community members annotate a drone map for challenges and opportunities

Images: Perpendicular– Social Innovation and Urban Lab

Volunteers for Techo Guatemala meet with families as they collect more accurate data for the community

of endless diagnosis that can occur when organizations from the formal economy try to make sense of informal settlements.

Perpendicular has validated the efficacy of the method by checking in with the four communities after seven months to identify how families and communities took action. The outcomes include efforts by the relevant municipal governments to install street lights in order to help reduce the risk of violence, as well as (at a community level) the strengthening of the desire among members to work as a collective on issues that influence everyone. Perpendicular and their partners launched Co-Mapp in 2017, which offers a toolkit and app for others to reproduce this process.

Design for Social Innovation

"We can leave a better community for our children, learning about the needs of the community, not focusing only on ours, but [also] those of our neighbors."

Participant, Arzú community

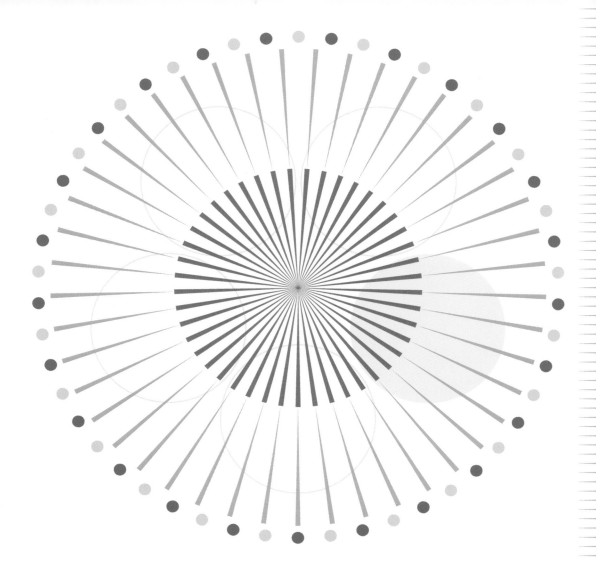

Duration
  2012–present

Location
  Izmir, Turkey

Categories
  Social Justice
  Policy
  Quality of Public Life

Designer
  Izmir Metropolitan Municipality,
  Directorate of Urban Design
  and Aesthetics

Partners
  Multiple architects, city
  planners, landscape
  architects, industrial
  designers, and engineers

Key Contributors
  Hasibe Velibeyoğlu
  İklim Sarı
  Elif Kocabıyık

Designer Organization Type
  ● Government

Team Size
  ● 50+

Design Quotient
  ● 81–100%

Project Costs
  ▷ $1MM+

Source of Funding
  ▬▬ Government
  ▬▬ Self-Funded

Funding Mechanisms
  Self-Funded

Impact Measurement Methods
  Qualitative: Surveys
  Quantitative: Headcount/Time of
    Participation

Mediums
  Spatial: Urban Design

Izmirsea

Reviving residents' connection with the sea

The city of Izmir is located on the Aegean Sea in the westernmost part of the Anatolian Peninsula, where it has witnessed 3,500 years of urban history as one of the oldest port cities of the Mediterranean. The Aegean Sea sits as the calm backdrop of the city's Mediterranean lifestyle and plays an important part of Izmir's culture. However, Izmir's strong connection to the sea has been weakened by rapid urbanization which included the construction of large apartment buildings along the waterfront, blocking visual and physical access, as well as sea breezes.

Izmirsea is a strategic urban design project initiated by the Izmir Metropolitan Municipality that aims to increase the quality of public life by focusing on everyday human experiences and reviving residents' interaction with the sea. As Professor İlhan Tekeli, proponent of the project, describes, "This initiative... looks to set forth a transformation that is egalitarian rather than hierarchical, multi-voiced rather than single, and incorporated in the urbanite's life along with the city rather than in the name of it."

The goals are many: increase residents' connection with the sea; sustain the lifestyle and identity typical to a coastal Mediterranean city; provide "wholeness" to the city; enhance site-specific parks and recreational areas and services; provide common spaces where people from different socioeconomic backgrounds can mix; increase public awareness and appreciation of design; and bring a great number of designers together for collaborative design process.

Izmir's Metropolitan Municipality coordinated a series of well-attended, multi-disciplinary, collaborative workshops and conducted public questionnaires that aimed at creating a design and culture strategy for the city. The Izmirsea project was funded and initiated by the Municipality as one of the outcomes of this effort, which was then pursued within five defined regions along the waterfront. Multidisciplinary design teams for each of these five regions were created

and the teams coordinated while developing their design proposals, to be carried out through consecutive stages of projects big and small.

Following a questionnaire-based survey, design teams learned that the Bayraklı region has low and diverse socioeconomic levels, high levels of migration, and a weak connection between its coastal and residential areas, leading to The 'Bayraklı Waterfront Urban Design Project.' Now complete, the success of the project can be witnessed through the vitality of the public space, including widely used mobile phone charging stations and food kiosks, higher numbers of young people spending time in public, an increase in cyclists, as well as the popularity of picnic areas, playground areas, and public art.

Beyond the quality of the new public spaces, the design approach helps address larger social and environmental challenges. Spaces that are responsive to the needs of residents and local business help to diversify social and cultural activity, and utilizing local materials and industries improves the environmental and economic sustainability of the work.

**Images: Izmir Metropolitan
Municipality, Directorate of
Urban Design and Aesthetics**

Design for Social Innovation

**Renovated
seaside**

Before

After

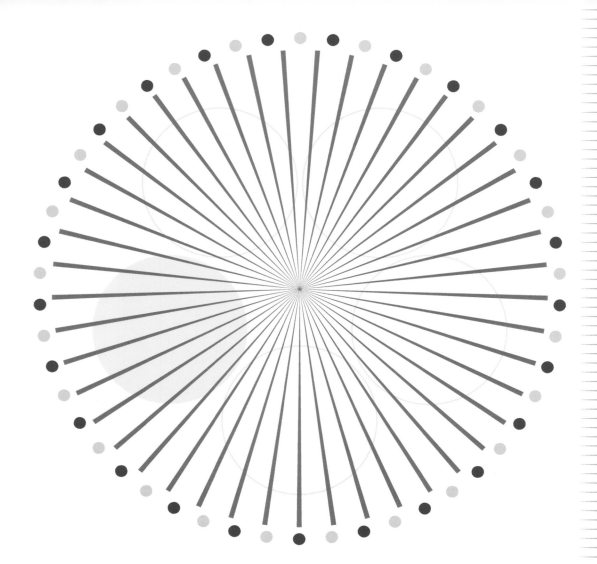

Duration
    March 2020–present

Location
    New York City, USA

Categories
    Health and Wellness
    Humanitarian Affairs

Designer
    Spiro Devices

Partners
    Newlab
    10XBeta
    Boyce Technologies

Key Contributors
    Scott Cohen
    Marcel Botha
    Charles Boyce

Designer Organization Type
    ● For-Profit

Team Size
    ● 50+

Design Quotient
    ● 0–20%

Project Costs
    ▭ $1MM+

Source of Funding
    ▬ Government

Funding Mechanisms
    Fee for Service
    Grant

Impact Measurement Methods
    Quantitative: Cost Savings,
        Growth in Product/Service
        Adoption or Usage

Mediums
    Physical: Medical Device

Spiro Wave

Expanding hospitals' capacity to care for patients during the COVID-19 crisis and beyond

As COVID-19 began to spread rapidly in early 2020, a massive global ventilator shortage was anticipated. Not only were ventilators hard to find, they were also expensive, limiting access for hospitals in rural America and other global contexts that had lesser purchasing power, smaller stockpiles, and limited access to critical equipment in general.

In response, a diverse team from Newlab, a community of experts and innovators applying transformative technology to the things that matter, 10XBeta, a product development firm, and Boyce Technologies, a design-for-manufacturing company, came together to form Spiro Devices. Their goal was to design a new type of emergency ventilation device that could be rapidly produced at scale and would meet the demands of the current crisis.

As Charles Boyce, the founder and CEO of partner Boyce Technologies, stated, "There's a lot you can't see in a model, and if you can't manufacture something at scale, it doesn't matter. It's not going to have an impact." The Spiro Wave device was inspired by the open-source MIT Emergency Ventilator Project that had been developed prior to the COVID-19 crisis, and the Spiro team refined this concept and built on the previous research.

They identified two main barriers to production of typical ventilators that were prohibiting supply from meeting the spike in demand initiated by the crisis: traditional ICU ventilators are expensive (generally upwards of $30,000 per unit), and time-consuming to produce due to the complexity of the design and supply chain. This pointed to the need for a new device with a simplified design that would allow it to be low cost and rapidly manufacturable. From the outset, the team worked directly with clinicians—the ultimate end-users of the devices—

Marcel Botha, chief product officer of Spiro Devices, and clinical advisor Dr Albert Kwon test a device during the R&D process

Image: Elizabeth Hasier Photography

to understand the functional and technical requirements. The device underwent rigorous testing to adhere to medical device protocols as required by the US government's Emergency Use Authorization standards and functioned successfully in early animal trials.

The final result is a low-cost automatic resuscitator that helps hospitals expand their capacity to care for patients with critical ventilation needs. Spiro Wave is considered a "bridge ventilator" that allows hospitals to expand their capacity to care for patients that require invasive mechanical ventilation in emergency situations and reallocate conventional ventilators for patients with more sophisticated needs. The cost of Spiro Wave is under $5,000, approximately one sixth or less than a traditional ventilator.

The design automates the pumping of an existing "bag valve mask manual resuscitator"—a medical accessory ubiquitous in most hospital settings—to provide basic mechanical ventilation and supplemental oxygen to patients with acute respiratory failure. The automation of this process, which would otherwise be done by hand, frees up human resources, expands the functionality, and increases quality control. The device has basic programming and sensing to ensure it is pumping at the appropriate rate for the patient in need, meeting the minimum sufficient clinical functionality to satisfy the essential needs of healthcare providers in emergency situations.

The project started in March 2020, and the device received Emergency Use Authorization through the Food and Drug Administration in April. To date,

Design for Social Innovation

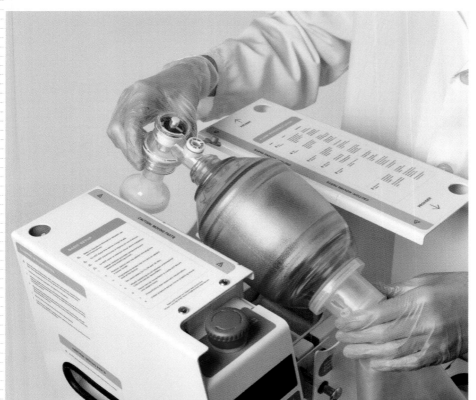

Spiro Devices has produced and distributed 3,000 devices to New York City and its hospitals through a partnership and purchase order with the New York City Economic Development Corporation. They continue to work toward wider national and international distribution in order to expand the impact globally and deliver devices to hospitals that need them most. Though the project started as an effort to create an affordable ventilation device to address the immediate needs of the COVID-19 crisis, it has become clear that the device also has significant utility beyond this crisis as an emergency ventilation device: it can deliver critical respiratory and ventilation functionality in everyday ambulatory and hospital settings, and the team plans to continue development of the design for additional use cases. As New York City Mayor Bill DeBlasio affirmed, "This is New York City ingenuity at its best... These bridge ventilators that have been created are part of what will protect us now and into the future."

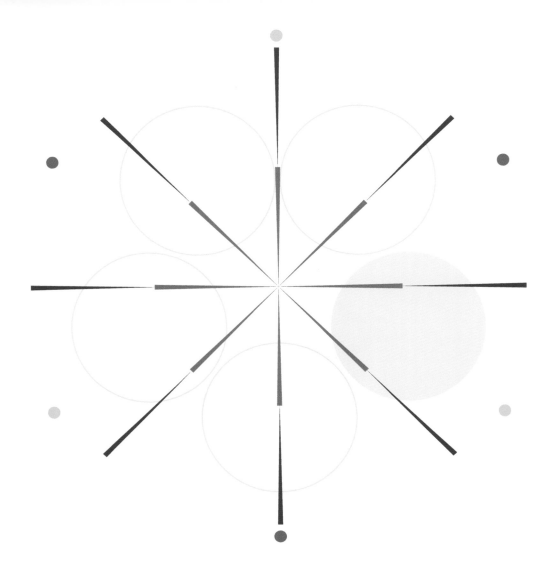

Duration
July 2015–May 2016

Location
Tel-Aviv-Yafo, Israel

Categories
Economic

Designer
Tel-Aviv-Yafo Municipality

Partners
Tel-Aviv-Yafo Education
Administration and
Community Administration
Bloomberg Philanthropies

Designer Organization Type
● Government

Team Size
● 5–7

Design Quotient
● 21–40%

Project Costs
▭▷ $1k–$25k

Source of Funding
▬ Government
▬ Foundation/Non-Profit/
Endowment

Funding Mechanisms
Unspecified

Impact Measurement Methods
Qualitative: Stakeholder
Interviews
Quantitative: Headcount/Time of
Participation, Surveys

Mediums
Spatial: Interior Space

The Nest

Sharing study spaces to improve outcomes for Tel-Aviv-Yafo teens and their families

The high cost of living in Tel-Aviv-Yafo has become a burden for many, and especially young families who are also paying education and childcare costs for their children. For parents of older children, private tutoring to supplement classroom instruction is desirable but costly. After identifying this challenge during research into issues faced by middle and lower-middle-class families in the city, the innovation team ("i-team") within Tel-Aviv-Yafo municipal government sought to prototype The Nest, an idea for new shared study spaces. Tel Aviv was one of 13 cities selected to participate in Bloomberg Philanthropies' innovation teams program in 2015.

The Nest concept emerged from research and co-design activities involving parents, children, school staff, municipality workers, and people from private and third sector organizations. As an alternative to expensive after-school activities The Nest provided a safe and welcoming place for students to study together and relax. The space also made it easier for students to take group (versus individual) tutoring lessons, which reduced the cost to families.

Nests were designed within existing community centers, rather than schools, and were open daily. The space was designed to enable students to sit in groups, alone, on a sofa, or at a bar depending on how they wanted to interact with others and their needs for quieter spaces to focus. It was also hoped that this environment would increase social mixing between students, resulting in them getting help from peers they didn't know beforehand.

Over the course of a one-month evaluation, the team tracked the number of attendees, the duration of their stay, and retention rates to measure success. They also conducted interviews throughout the prototyping phase and gathered feedback through a final survey one week after the prototype concluded.

According to the i-Team, 88% of users stated that the space enabled them to study better because of the learning atmosphere, and the service saved a total of $40,000 that would have otherwise been spent by the families whose children (133 in total) used the space. Students appreciated the space as a "comfortable, quiet place" that's accessible, and one respondent remarked, "It's really amazing that the municipality is doing this for us, and everything for no cost."

Funded by the municipal government, the project was executed as a lightweight prototype with rented equipment, but other factors curtailed the experiment. A more significant challenge proved to be identifying spaces that could be rented for just four to five months a year in a city as densely populated as Tel-Aviv-Yafo. Today, The Nest is a prototype that has come and gone, but findings from the experiment have been repurposed by study spaces in schools and community centers.

Images: I-Team Tel-Aviv-Yafo

Design for Social Innovation

The Nest supportted studying alone or together in small groups

Flexible seating arrangements, were provided to give students choice

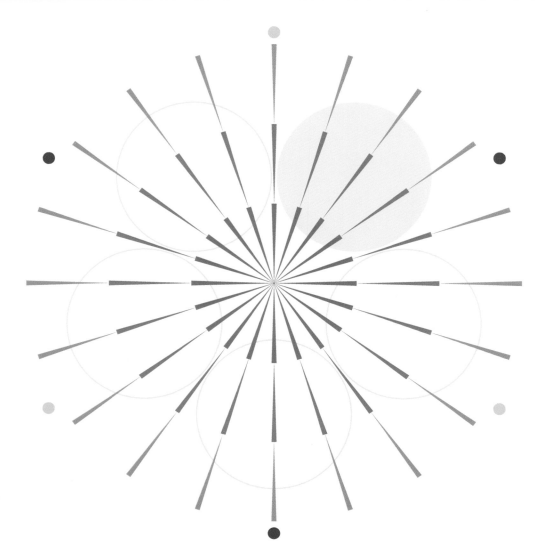

Duration
  Four–month-long program every
    year since 2016

Location
  Fukui, Japan

Categories
  Education
  Identity
  Economic

Designer
  Re:public Inc
  UMA/design farm
  MUSEUM
  Design Studio Binen Inc

Partners
  Fukui City Local Government
  Fukui Newspaper Company

Key Contributors
  Yuki Uchida
  Yuma Harada
  Tomomi Tada
  Morifumi Sakata

Designer Organization Type
  ● For-Profit

Team Size
  ● 5–7

Design Quotient
  ● 61–80%

Project Costs
  ▭▷ $100k–$500k

Source of Funding
  ▬▬ Government
  ▬▬ Private Company
  ▬▬ Crowd Funding

Funding Mechanisms
  Fee for Service
  Crowd Funding

Impact Measurement Methods
  Qualitative: Observed Formation
    of New Social Networks
  Quantitative: Number of
    Projects Initiated, Number of
    Financially Viable Projects

Mediums
  Organizational: Incubator

XSCHOOL

Enhancing regional resilience by incubating new products, services, and businesses

Japan has the world's oldest population and is also one of the most urbanized countries on earth, with centers like Tokyo and Kanagawa growing at the expense of dwindling populations in smaller cities and rural areas. Set against the backdrop of these long-term trends, disasters such as the Great Hanshin-Awaji earthquake in 1995 and the 2011 tsunami and subsequent disaster at Fukushima Daiichi Nuclear Power Plant have catalyzed an interest within Japanese government at the national and local level to support social innovation efforts that provide additional local resilience to supplement government activities in normal times and crisis situations alike.

The government of Fukui, a city of 260,000 people located on the Sea of Japan, asked "think and do tank" Re:public Inc to encourage consumer spending and tourism by publicizing the city's strengths. Many local governments within the country have developed marketing campaigns to address similar concerns, but the XSCHOOL team took a different approach. XSCHOOL sought to create a system that would connect Fukui's industry and its people to other parts of the country. Designers and entrepreneurs were invited to join an incubator program where they would work with local industry in Fukui to co-create new products, services, or businesses. In the process, this system created opportunities for city dwellers to re discover the resources and lifestyles of Fukui and, by extension, other smaller cities. Now in its fifth year, each iteration of XSCHOOL has partnered with different local industries such as ceramics, food production, construction, recycling, chemicals, and textiles.

The structure of XSCHOOL creates three opportunities for positive crossover. First, by purposefully connecting Fukui to other regions around the country, it brings individuals with different perspectives and lifestyles together. Second, It provides a co-creation field across the boundaries between industries and genera-

tions. Young creatives and experienced people in traditional industries meet each other. And, third, participants come from across the country with diverse backgrounds such as architecture, anthropology, finance, childcare, and more. With diverse disciplines, mixed geographies and lifestyles, and many ages involved, the program develops a creative community as a whole to seek new ideas, helping everyone to see Fukui in a new light—no longer just a center of traditional industry and lifestyles.

Through field trips, discussions, lectures, and prototyping, the group seeks to understand the potential of the city. In addition to newcomers discovering Fukui, this process also helps locals rediscover their own resources. For example, in researching the textile industry, they dug into its 1,500 years of history in Fukui, visited and interviewed factories in various stages and scales of production, including fabric, dyeing, and sewing.

Several product and service businesses prototyped during XSCHOOL have been realized subsequently. These include: an activity calendar product designed to keep kids motivated to learn during summer break; and a new way of packaging traditional foods, to be more inviting to tourists who are unfamiliar with them. During the first four years of the program, 20 new projects have been launched, with 40% of them still in operation or for sale.

While the products are important indicators, Re:public's broader goal in the design of XSCHOOL is to enhance the regional resilience of Fukui. The incubator program helps accomplish this by creating cross-sector networks motivated

by the creation of new business opportunities, resulting in stronger and more diverse networks, as well as products that can be developed and generate economic/social activity. Taken as a whole, this represents a "social infrastructure" for creating new value in the region and enhancing regional resilience. With 150 people who have been involved in the incubator program thus far, the network is growing. As one participant described, "Until now, Fukui was completely irrelevant to my life. Now, my body instinctively reacts every time I read or hear the city on the news. I can no longer ignore Fukui's presence."

"I realized newcomers and locals change through challenges with people from diverse backgrounds. If people change, the industry changes. And, if the industry changes, the future of the region also evolves."

CEO of a local company

Navigating Partnerships

**XSCHOOL
included
classroom
sessions and
field research**

**Walking tour
guided by local
historians**

Design for Social Innovation

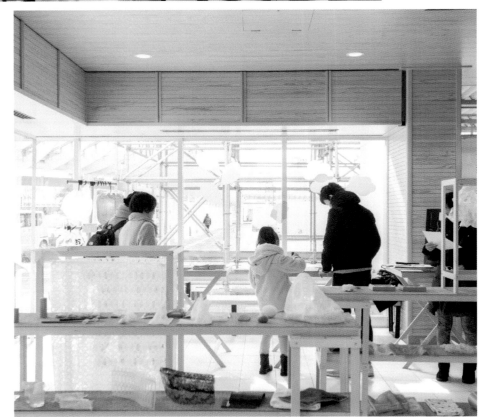

An exhibition created by XSCHOOL participants

Images: Re:public Inc

Mediums of Change

Debbie Aung Din, Jan Chipchase, and Ramia Mazé, with Bryan Boyer

In contrast to traditional areas of design, social innovation is concerned with producing outcomes—health, happiness, equity, and the like. Yet the crafting of objects, media, ephemeral experiences, and organizations is inescapable. In this roundtable, social innovation is catalyzed through books, photographs, moonshine, documents, games, curricula, policy experiments, and breakfast. Throughout the cases in this book an even broader set of mediums are identified. Whether tangible like a book or ephemeral like a workshop, these mediums serve as vessels to contain intentionality. Different outputs and outcomes rarely happen without different inputs, so what are the inputs that make a difference, and how are they communicated?

The word "mediums" as it is used here is purposefully borrowed from artistic practice, where it refers to the specificity of making art with a particular type of media, such as lead pencil, acrylic paint, or cast bronze sculpture. Media have their own tendencies and affordances. If you want to achieve photorealism, paint with oil or use a camera to take a photograph. If you want to depict energy, the grit and imprecision of charcoal encourages the artist to work at speed, literally pouring energy onto the paper through its medium. Artists discuss and debate the limitations and proclivities of various mediums, and the best amongst us artfully overcome or stretch those limits. Design for social innovation has historically had a difficult relationship with tangible things, because the work is not about making artifacts, but about making change. Exquisite graphic design or artfully crafted documents are not the primary focus, and yet they are almost inescapable. Things are nearly inevitable, but what kind of things are appropriate for each project? And how should they be crafted? When working with a government organization, should the expectations of that group be accepted as the norm, or should the limits of their definition of "meeting" or "workshop" be transgressed to make a point? These are some of the questions that Debbie Aung Din, Jan Chipchase, and Ramia Mazé explore in the following discussion.

In design or social innovation, mediums of change act as vessels or vehicles for enabling individuals to see the world differently and ultimately take action in ways that differ from their personal or organizational status quo. "Lots of people acting differently together" is a clumsy way to describe it, but this is one of the ultimate goals of social innovation. The mediums employed by designers in this book help them focus and scale the impact of their work. Occasionally a meaningful conversation is just what's needed to help someone see new possibilities and commit to action. But that almost always needs to happen with many people, in multiple contexts, across various geographies and times. In those situations, the medium of change becomes a critical decision. How do new insights live in the world? How are new possibilities made more durable than the spoken word? Is it possible for our work to outlive the moment of blinding insight, or even the designer's lifetime?

Debbie Aung Din

I am co-founder of Proximity Designs, a social business operating in Myanmar that delivers affordable and innovative products and services for farm families living in poverty. I've also been engaged in design and economic research in Myanmar since 1995. My previous work has been with NGOs, USAID, the UN, and the World Bank.

Jan Chipchase

My name is Jan Chipchase and I am the founder of Studio D, a discrete international consultancy working at the intersection of research, design, strategy, brand, and public policy. Based out of Tokyo, I spend a lot of time on the road.

Ramia Mazé

I'm Ramia Mazé, and I'm joining this conversation from Helsinki, Finland, where I work as a design researcher and educator at Aalto University. Shortly I'll be relocating to University of the Arts London as Professor of Design for Social Innovation and Sustainability.

Bryan: Let's start with the story of Paddy to Plate from Proximity Designs, led by Debbie, and Studio D, led by Jan. What was the project?

Debbie: When we first started in 2004, the Stanford D school was also starting out with its course on designing for extreme affordability. We were basically one of their first partners and we went on to work together for about eight years. At that time we were also very new to design and we didn't have our own team or lab, and so it worked fairly well. We had some existing irrigation pumps that had never been looked at from a user point of view and needed help.

These projects lasted with grad students from January to June, but they would spend only one week during spring break with us and then the rest of the time were remote. After a while we developed our own in-house expertise and we sort of "graduated" from using graduate students, because they were also juggling their own schedules and other commitments. Some projects actually continued after the six months' engagement and we had a few graduate students come for the summer and it worked out really well [to have designers in-house]. They made huge contributions, but we felt like we needed to pivot to something more intensive and that was more full-time.

Jan: You were about 350 people in the company at that time?

Debbie: Yes, [and now] we're about 1,000. We have three businesses and a customer base of about 700,000 farm households across the country, in more than 10,000 villages.

Jan: When we first started working with Proximity, it felt like a small and chaotic organization with a big beating heart and you were working out of that large apartment close to where you are now. It feels like Proximity is on a similar trajectory to kind of classic startups in the sense of growth and reach, and it's just with a different set of metrics, but in terms of headcount it's that kind of speed of growth. And so, Debbie, when you speak of maturity and knowing what you wanted, part of that is the growth of the organization and starting to have organizational functions [inside the company] that are specialized. You were looking for a group that could work alongside you to bring more depth to certain aspects of your work.

Debbie: Mm-hmm.

Bryan: The Paddy to Plate project resulted in a "codex" to the environment that you're working in. It describes the context and the realities of your customers basically, as well as part of the system that they exist within, in terms of pricing dynamics, regulatory dynamics, etc. Can you tell us about why a codex was important to you?

> **Debbie:** Before we got into paddy or rice farmers, we were mostly working with vegetable growers and small-plot irrigation systems. We were thrust into working with rice farmers because we were the largest farm recovery service provider after a huge cyclone ripped through the Irrawaddy Delta, killing 150,000 people in 2008, most of whom were rice farmers. We pivoted to rice farmers and realized that we needed more in-depth knowledge of the rice farming ecosystem before we started designing services for them. For us internally, [the Paddy to Plate project helped us gain] foundational knowledge we needed.
>
> We also felt that in Myanmar there has been very little focus on the farmers themselves [from the Agriculture Ministry and agriculture businesses]. It's all about getting rice production up regardless of what the farmers think or feel, and so the reports are very dry and do not really provide an understanding [of the farmers]. Looking at it from the lens of the farm family is a very novel perspective for the development community and the agriculture business community.

Bryan: Was the choice to make a book part of a conscious influence strategy in that community of decision makers? Were there other components to it?

> **Debbie:** Yes, definitely a conscious strategy. We also did events and invited people in the agriculture business community, the development community, and the government. The event was highly designed so that it wasn't like the usual dry gathering. We really tried to immerse people into the world of paddy growing, so there were a lot of exhibits and interactive stuff going on. It had a party feel to it. We've done four or five events like that in the community, and we've kind of gotten a reputation for that. Everyone wants to come to our book launch or product launch or whatever it is. It's part of our branding, I guess.

Jan: Another thing that we've always done when working together with Proximity is we take a lot of photography. We probably generate somewhere between 8,000 and 18,000 photos in a project and downsize that to about 250–300 photos, where we have the legal and moral right to share.

Each of the projects ends up with a photo archive and they make their way into Proximity digital assets, that get used in various ways on the website through to reporting and, in fact, if you have the opportunity to visit Proximity Designs HQ, some of the photos from Paddy to Plate and other projects are displayed in large format, floor to ceiling. I think that's an example of what you talked about Bryan, building a foundational understanding [of your customers]. Inherent in [the Paddy to Plate book] as an artifact and the photos on their walls is the tonality of the organization and its ethical stance about how it wants to engage the world and be engaged with. Proximity takes a very human-centered approach to encountering its customers that follows the company's ethical standards. For instance, data is collected in a respectful way. We're very, very careful about photos with children. And, if you engage any human in the book, it should be very much as an equal. You're not looking down on them as subjects.

> **Bryan:** I want to go back to something Debbie mentioned. You've chosen to express yourselves very deliberately in the book itself, and the events, and it sounds like in your office, all to show a deeper level of engagement with your customers, the farming community. I want to poke at this a little bit, if you'll allow me I understand the book and events as a way to collect and then communicate this core piece of content that was important for maybe the next phase of the Proximity Designs' work with the right human tone. Why not a film?

Debbie: The process of writing and putting it down on paper was a good discipline for our team to think through everything and really understand the material and all the experience of the research. Having it on film, [the team] would not capture and internalize all of those details that you can in a written document.

> **Jan:** We also have to be comfortable with trading off the quality of the research with the impact of having a camera crew: a boom mic, someone with a camera, the inevitability of retaking a shot, and so on.
>
> Our research is very, very fast-paced. I know there are videographers that can work at a fast pace, but fundamentally they change what the research project is, so we made a conscious decision not to go down that route. It's not always going to be the right answer, but so far it seems to have been the right answer for what we've been doing.
>
> But I do want to mention another aspect of this project. When working with Proximity we have the Studio D team of two to four people and then we have the Proximity team, which is typically three to six people, plus some coming in and out. We like to cleave the core Proximity teammates away from the mothership a little bit, so that they feel like they're part of this new project team. One of the ways that we do that is running little side projects that we keep secret from Proximity.

"Would the World Bank ever make moonshine? No! ... I love finding that kind of edge of things that reflects the DNA and... becomes a touch point to discovering the depth and rigor of the research."

On this one, after we concluded the final presentation, we said that we have a small gift, and presented moonshine that we had produced. We did this for a few reasons. For one it's what farmers do. They make this kind of "gut rot," high alcohol content, "maybe it'll make you blind" moonshine. So we thought: what would it look like if we package that up into something that was equivalent to fine wine? It was an interesting design challenge. The second reason is, it's a great way to have the Studio D team and the Proximity team come together and work on a project that is separate from everything else, but we know it will bring joy later on. We didn't make many bottles of this, but if you go to Proximity's office you will find a bottle in an alcove. I share because this is another example of the love and attention to detail that goes into a project that is not part of any spec at all. It was just, let's do this. A few hundred dollars to get things printed up and designed and commissioned. Would the World Bank ever make moonshine? No! Would Proximity ever make moonshine? Probably, but some of your funders might kind of like look at it and go, "Oh, hold on a second." But can your subcontractor make moonshine and package it up with Proximity? 100%. I love finding that kind of edge of things that reflects the DNA and is definitely not something that you would expect to find within a standard project, but then becomes a touch point to discovering the depth and rigor of the research.

Ramia: The idea of mediums is very interesting. How, where, and why do things travel through mediums? What happens when those things travel from one place to another and are meant to be carried on by others, elsewhere, who did not start or fund or manage the project? I'll give you one example.

DAIM [an acronym for the "Design Anthropological Innovation Model"], a project initiated by Joachim Halse, Eva Brandt, Brendon Clark, and Thomas Binder, then at the Danish Design School, involved several design consultancies, industrial partners, and the Copenhagen regional waste authority. They studied and intervened in a wide range of the different practices involved in waste handling—from "fieldshops" with consumers at the

Design for Social Innovation

local mall, with homeowners, with teens on social housing estates, with garbage handlers at the local dump, and teachers engaging with the waste authority in their curricula. Why, how, and where did recycling happen? What, or who, was seen as the problem? How were different stakeholders treated? They looked from different perspectives, including that of those stakeholders who are too often (and incorrectly) stigmatized as being part of the problem.

The DAIM team documented their interventions through various mediums, such as live blogging in the mall and teens' self-documentation of local garbage practices. Finally, a DAIM "box," which packaged together and contained documentation of the interventions as well as open methods and tools for further inquiry and ideation, was handed over to stakeholders, including the waste authority.

I visited a couple of years after the DAIM project concluded. By then, the municipal waste authority had opened up a kind of "learning lab" inside the incineration plant, where schoolchildren were coming to learn about the waste issues that were inbuilt into their educational curriculum. I met one of the project participants on behalf of the authority, who dusted off the box. While the box wasn't used actively or in the lab, there was a clear learning and continuity in terms of the participatory and game-based methods built into the installations and activities in the lab. He drew a mind-map to narrate a web of impacts and traces of the projects afterwards.

It seems to me a great success that the municipal waste authority had evolved their own mediums, including the lab, the schoolteacher guides, and teaching materials. They had also produced their own set of inquiry and innovation methods, in the form of a kind of small, polished and branded, spiral-bound notebook. We're used to designers making tool kits for clients, but they made their own! For other social innovation initiatives, this is promising and raises new questions. When, where and how does the client take over new knowledge? Which bits from the design process become ingrained and continue? In fact, they had hired two extra people within the municipal waste authority to take on the job. So it was a very interesting example of the transference from a design-led project—from the designers and researchers—to institutionalization of the learnings.

> **Bryan:** Can we pause for a minute and ask Debbie if Proximity would use props, for lack of a better description, in a similar way to bring your findings into meetings with counterparts in government?

"We take our irrigation pump products to meetings. In the early days, the director general of the Ministry of Agriculture said, 'Oh, I want one of these.' And we said, 'Sure, could you buy it and pay for it?'"

Debbie: Definitely. We take our irrigation pump products to meetings. In the early days, the director general of the Ministry of Agriculture said, "Oh, I want one of these." And we said, "Sure, could you buy it and pay for it? It's $20." And most government officials would expect you to give it to them for free, but we said, "No, we're a social enterprise and farmers pay for it. So we want to be able to tell our staff and farmers that you yourself, paid for it, too." The book has also been really great for meetings and giving it to donors as well. One of the main program coordinators [at a funder] calls the book "the Bible" and his copy is just completely dog-eared.

> **Bryan:** These artifacts have a role to play in catalyzing the "transference" that Ramia mentioned. Did the DAIM project consciously start with the box as an artifact and then create larger systemic change? Was it intentional or a lucky coincidence?

Ramia: DAIM was intentional. They were using design methods and design anthropology methods of documentation, observation and amplification of local bottom-up practices to show what was actually happening in Copenhagen at the time. The box was full of documentation but also contained workshop materials such as a scenario-based "design game." The game is a way to structure a workshop in which stakeholders externalize "this is how it is now," propose "this is how it could be," and explore pathways to get there. The DAIM team had quite specific ideas about the craft and the artifacts in the box, such that aesthetics had a purpose in getting the contents to matter. In the end, I think some things transferred. Some of the engagement with inquiry in the field, with diverse participants, with collaboration and learning methods—these transferred.

Since you mentioned the word "film," Bryan, another project that I've studied in South Africa may be useful here. *One Table Two Elephants* is simultaneously an award-winning film and an example of "cinematic ethnography," created by Jacob von Heland and Henrik Ernstson. It is free for use and accompanied by scholarly and teaching materials. As they put it, "the film follows biologists, hip-hoppers and a revivalist urban shaman, to explore how race and nature are intertwined in the postcolony" in

Design for Social Innovation

townships and between them, in the contested open spaces left by barriers that used to separate the racial groups during apartheid.

As cinematic ethnography, the ethnographic part is a lot about listening to the different voices, claims and experiences. And about trying to reveal who's doing what and empowerment. The cinematic part is about intervention—making those invisible and different voices and actions widely visible. This kind of project reveals the politics of the kinds of social innovation project we're talking about, in which going in as a designer, as an educated, foreign and white person, is inescapably problematic. Perhaps this film is an example where the creators took quite a different role, in a way, listening, recording, and spreading, more like the role of researchers.

> **Debbie:** We've found that the listening is very important, and so is being opportunistic. You just hit when it's hot. To give you an example, a few months ago we were asked by the government in Myanmar to teach human-centered design thinking in an hour. Their view was, "OK, you have an hour and it's PowerPoint slides." We thought, "Oh, we don't know how much to push the envelope and change the whole meeting," but we did as best we could and it was so surprising to see buttoned-up government officials really come alive and get into brainstorming, sticky notes, and all this kind of stuff. It was a real surprise to us but they really soaked it up!

Bryan: How do you think about the role of participation? How do you bring stakeholders into the project? What's the balance between wanting to produce something, an experience, an artifact, a publication, versus the desire to have participation and some kind of open-endedness where you're putting people on their toes. How do you balance those?

"There are also problematic uses of the term 'participation,' which actually silence and oppress the ones that are already doing meaningful things but would never use the term to describe their work."

> **Ramia:** I speak from the Nordic countries, where I've working myself with participatory design for many years, but this is a movement enduring and growing since the 1960s. The Scandinavian countries is where participatory design emerged, and now it's spread in various ways and forms, and popularized for political and commercial

rationalities and so on. Municipalities in Finland have been heavily investing in a participatory "design game" called the Participation Game. The City of Helsinki produced the game in collaboration with the design consultancy Hellon, and some of my colleagues at Aalto University.[1] It's a physical board game with structured activities for civil servants to think about and plan for how they could include more participation in policy making initiatives. It has been tested by tens of thousands of civil servants across the country.

Given this rich history and wide adoption of participatory approaches, I'm interested in the nuances, differences, and issues that arise in different practical experiences with participation. What do practitioners mean by "participation," what they do with the information, buy-in, and the web of relations that emerges through participatory processes? These kind of "democratic experiments" are also risky, so practitioners need to think really carefully, rather than cut-and-pasting. This is true everywhere, but perhaps especially in very sensitive contexts like South Africa.

Without sensitivity, participation can be very tokenistic. It can be placatory and look fantastic on the public relations brochures. There are also problematic uses of the term "participation," which actually silence and oppress the ones that are already doing meaningful things but would never use the term to describe their work.

Jan: Maybe I could share a little bit of the tension that we see as a consultancy. Essentially, we are paid to go in and work for a certain amount of time on a project. And there are things in a contract that say you have delivered this or you haven't delivered this, so that you can be judged upon that, paid or not paid, and slapped around if you haven't done what you're supposed to do.

It's important to have [the contract] in place; otherwise, you can't really go anywhere and support people. As a studio, we think a lot about designing the design experience. That starts with the way that we frame our relationships with [our clients and collaborators]. Most clients want to come in the field, we have a role in the Studio, which is "no tourists." Every client that comes into the field with us is put to work. We put this now in contracts, as well.

There's a certain amount of gluing and synergy that needs to happen before the momentum is in place and, if someone comes into the team and they're taking calls and other things, it's sucking the energy out of the team, so the "no tourists" rule has no exceptions. When we design the design experience, we typically rent an apartment or small guest house

Design for Social Innovation

and the team lives together, they cook breakfast together, all of that kind of stuff. This experience is very strong from a trust-building point of view when we're working with clients. I think a lot of consultancies feel a lot of pressure to always be the smartest people in the room, and often that pressure leads to consultants bullshitting their roles. We are hired in and we're paid to do things, but it's a two-way street in terms of knowledge. We are not experts in everything. Our clients are there, too, and they are contributing.

Once you come out of a high-intensity project like this, it shapes the team. It shapes the identity of individual team members and the relationships between people from different cultures. In that sense, the people that come out of the projects are shaped by the work, they're shaped by the ethical stance, and they become cultural "flywheels" for the project themselves. So, when they go back into their organizations, they can articulate the project goals and outcomes extremely well. They articulate it not because they're being paid to articulate it, but because they believe in it. Debbie, what's your take on that? Because you're the partner in many of those. I'm curious, what's your take?

> **Debbie:** From the very beginning we were very intentional about framing our relationship with poor rural families. What is that going to look like? And we knew we wanted to be equals, and so the best way for us to structurally do that was to treat them as customers where they have a say whether the product or service we're providing is valuable to them or not. We get immediate feedback [via the market], so that has been extremely important. Part of our DNA is to treat people as customers. It's built in. They have ownership and buy in from the get-go. When we design products and services for them, we're constantly trying to get their feedback on how to make it better so that they are interested in buying our offerings. This can be quite different from the aid community, where people are not seen as customers, but more as beneficiaries or charity recipients.

Bryan: That makes sense in your context, but when the same "customer-centric" language is used in government it makes my skin crawl. Citizens are not customers! Ramia, does the game have anything that helps a civil servant understand the people that they're serving?

> **Ramia:** The terms "consumer" and "citizen" as interchangeable is very problematic. Citizens should not only or primarily be seen in terms of market consumption. A general intention of the Finnish government and therefore the Participation Game has been to increase the human-centeredness of government, which has been explicit in the national strategy of the Finnish government for many

years. Design is even mentioned in the government's 2016 Strategic Program! In 2015, the think tank Demos Helsinki and my colleagues at Aalto University produced an influential white paper for the Prime Minister's Office, *Design for Government: Human-centric for Governance Through Experiments.*

Between 2015 and 2019, the Prime Minister's Office established a unit, an "experimentation framework" and a funded platform Place to Experiment between 2015 and 20 with this task. There were a couple dozen projects, of which the most publicized was the "basic income experiment." The projects were mainly proposed by individual citizens or civil society groups, and funded as experimental pilots. This is a very interesting example both of governmental as well as citizen-led social innovation. And it can also potentially be understood as design. Place to Experiment is one of the 12 projects featured in the Finnish Pavilion at the XXII Triennale di Milano.

Bryan: This is a good reminder that one of the most important mediums of change is being thoughtful with how you spend your money and where you personally make "investments," even if they're small.

Ramia: Finance is one of the main, traditional instruments of government—that is, taxation or subsidies. But how the government allocates their budget is central to its operations and, obviously, to society. I think the idea of what's been called a "culture of experimental governance" has been a really big shift in how government works. In this case, it's not about the massive roll-out of huge programs implemented by various authorities, but investment in niche and experimental projects from bottom-up and relatively small stakeholders.

Bryan: If we try to connect this point to the experiences at Proximity Designs, how have you managed to inculcate a willingness and ability to be experimental among your team of 1,000 people, Debbie?

Debbie: This continues to be a challenge for us internally, especially in a society like Myanmar, where the educational system just teaches people to do rote thinking and really squashes creativity. The teams that work with Jan have a steep learning curve. It's like boot camp for them, and we see huge jumps in the individuals who embed on Jan's projects, so we choose them carefully when we put together the team. Then, in terms of scaling the rest of the design thinking, we have Proximity school, an in-house initiative that is both online and in person, where all of our staff learn critical thinking, growth

Design for Social Innovation

mindsets, and other things that really lend themselves to creativity and design thinking.

Bryan: What are the open questions we can carry forward?

Debbie: Right now we're immersed in COVID operations. How do you do design when right now we're remote? That will be our challenge, because so much of our name and our operations is very much on the ground and being proximate.

Ramia: The issue of proximity is really pertinent. This issue comes front and center in design for social innovation, because of the long-standing critique of the kind of parachuting and "colonial" resonances of designers and development agencies acting in distant parts of the world. How does it work? What does it mean to design for others faraway? What is the medium through which different things happen at a distance? Who does what? For whom, and for whose benefit? In what place? What are the assumptions, what is owned, what is handed over? What is used (or not) after you're gone? What did they do for themselves, having engaged but long after, as in the DAIM example? Where are resources and decision-making power in the process?

Jan: How do you bring together people that don't necessarily share all the same viewpoints and ethical stance and cultural ones, particularly when you're running international projects? How do you bring teams together in such a way that they'll trust one another enough to have honest conversations, to work through the shit, to get rid of egos, and come out of it stronger so that they can then work together?

1   Since the time of this essay, Mazé has become Professor of Design for Social Innovation and Sustainability at London College of Communications, University of the Arts London.

Mediums
of Change

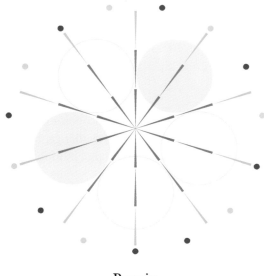

Beegin

*Fabricating more accessible beekeeping
systems for farmers, beekeepers,
and bees*

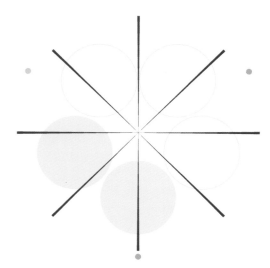

Game-Based Menstrual Hygiene
Education

*Destigmatizing menstrual health with
inclusive and interactive approaches*

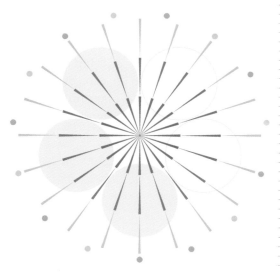

MAFA

*Reconceptualizing preschool
classrooms as open-ended
learning spaces*

Design for Social Innovation

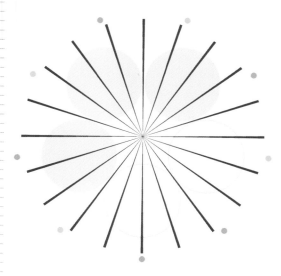

Paddy to Plate

Understanding the needs and context of entrepreneurial paddy farmers in Myanmar

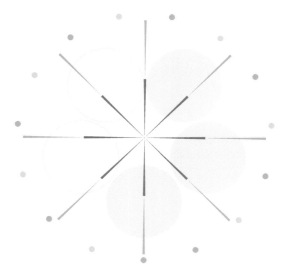

Right2City4All

Inviting youth to help design safer public spaces in Kosovo

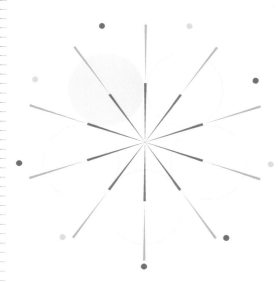

Brazilian Government Supplier Registration System

Procuring government services without wasting anyone's time

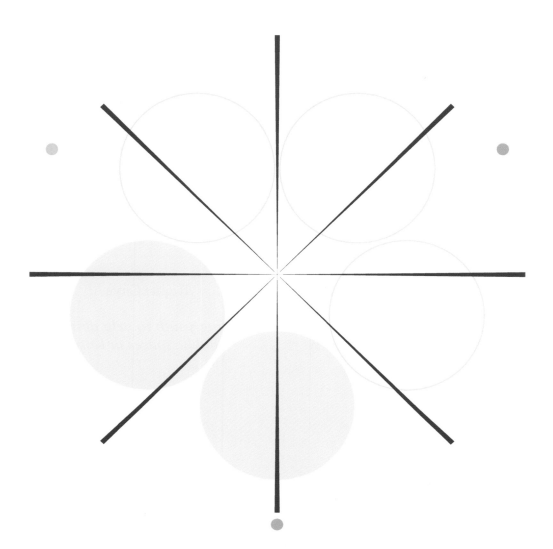

Duration
November 2016–March 2017

Location
Nairobi, Kenya

Categories
Identity

Designer
Nairobi Design Institute

Partners
WASH United

Key Contributors
Pauline Kanana
James Maina
Agnes Ogallo

Designer Organization Type
● Academia

Team Size
● 2–4

Design Quotient
● 81–100%

Project Costs
▷ $1k–$25k

Source of Funding
▬ Foundation/Non-Profit/
Endowment

Funding Mechanisms
Fee for Service

Impact Measurement Methods
Qualitative: Stakeholder
Interviews

Mediums
Experiential: Training
Physical: Game, Teaching Aids

Design for Social Innovation

Game-Based Menstrual Hygiene Education

Destigmatizing menstrual health with inclusive and interactive approaches

High-quality menstrual hygiene education remains a challenge in Kenya, particularly for low-income women and girls. Access to sanitary products is also limited for a majority of the girls and women living in low-income areas. For example, approximately 65%[1] of women and girls in Kenya are unable to afford buying sanitary products. Consequently, many young girls often experience a great deal of stigmatization coming from family members, fellow classmates, teachers. Adults who disseminate menstrual hygiene management education have an important role to play in changing the norms to be supportive, but this role is often overlooked.

WASH United, a not-for-profit organization that works to end the sanitation and hygiene crisis in Sub-Saharan Africa and South Asia, created a Menstruation Hygiene Management (MHM) curriculum that addresses proper hygiene and good practices during menstruation. In 2016, they brought in Nairobi Design Institute (NDI) to identify ways to improve their current approach, including the methodology and structure of running MHM training sessions. NDI works to foster a new generation of innovators through an immersive human-centered design innovation program that teaches African youth how to best apply design-led innovation within their communities.

NDI started by getting to know WASH United's primary end-user: young girls 9 to 13 years old who live in low-income areas with limited access to information. The team invited other stakeholders such as the MHM facilitators (adults who teach the youth) from community-based partner organizations and clients, to collaborate throughout the design process. During this research the team identified that some of the challenges with existing MHM curriculum stem

from difficulties experienced by the facilitators. Traditional classroom setups contributed to a loss of concentration or a fear, on behalf of the youth, of asking questions because of the group setting. Exclusion of boys from the sessions exacerbated this by limiting their understanding of MHM topics and creating stigma towards girls. New teaching and learning approaches were needed.

The research allowed NDI to reframe the goal of the project to focus on the need to improve the overall MHM training experience for all parties involved by suitably equipping facilitators with the right tools that encourage participation from both girls and boys. This would be accomplished by designing an experience that would normalize the conversation around MHM and other topics related to puberty. Through workshops with WASH United and their implementing partners, NDI led the co-creation of low-fidelity games related to different MHM topics. A subsequent usability workshop allowed for testing with end-users to inform high-fidelity prototypes and the final design.

The final output was a visually appealing game designed with familiar tropes of board games such as dice and a game board. Playing the game with an adult facilitator creates easier openings for the participating children to learn without personal embarrassment or stigma. The game creates opportunities for them to ask questions and learn. Additional materials are provided for facilitators so that they can calibrate their teaching to the needs of the students.

Three months after implementation, Nairobi Design Institute measured the impact of the game by conducting contextual and group interviews with facilita-

Design for Social Innovation

tors and participants. They discovered that facilitators found the new curriculum simpler and more efficient to use. Youth participants also enjoyed the game as a way to learn about their bodies. The team also observed a shift in perceptions, from youth treating menstruation as a secret to openly talking about it with peers and elders.

> *"I used to hear that menstruation causes bad odor. I now know that it is normal and caused by poor hygiene, so I'm no longer worried because I know how to better take care of myself. I will share this knowledge with my sister when she starts menstruating."*
>
> Rose, 16 years old

Participatory design session with facilitators

Images: Nairobi Design Institute

Design for Social Innovation

**Testing
low-fidelity
prototypes with
participants**

**Testing
high-fidelity
prototypes
of the MHM
roundabout
chart with
participants**

Mediums of Change

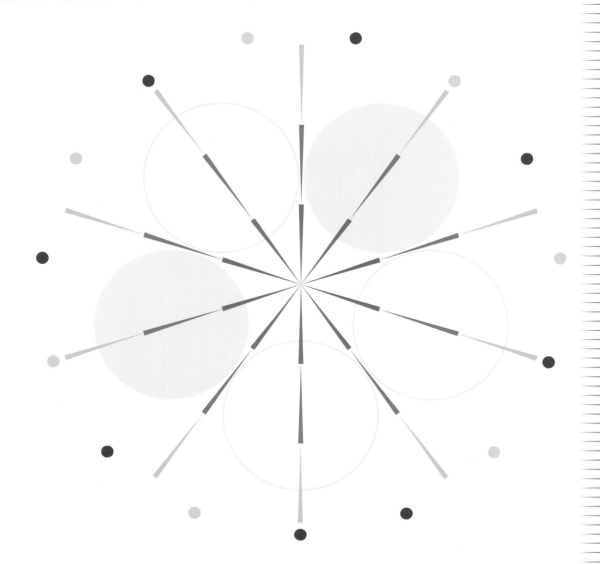

Duration
 June 2015–ongoing

Location
 Johannesburg, South Africa

Categories
 Economic

Designer
 Ivan Leroy Brown & Angus
  Donald Campbell

Partners
 Small-scale farmers
 Expert beekeepers
 University of Johannesburg,
  South Africa's Design Society
  Development DESIS Lab and
  the Department of Industrial
  Design

Designer Organization Type
 • For-Profit

Team Size
 • 11–20

Design Quotient
 • 0–20%

Project Costs
 ▷ $25k–$100k

Source of Funding
 ▬ Government
 ▬ Private Company
 ▬ University

Funding Mechanisms
 Unspecified

Impact Measurement Methods
 Qualitative: Evaluative Case
  Study
 Quantitative: Key Environmental
  Indicators, Growth in Product/
  Service Adoption or Usage

Mediums
 Physical: Beehive
 Organizational: Business

Beegin

Fabricating more accessible beekeeping systems for farmers, beekeepers, and bees

In 2019, the World Bank declared South Africa the most economically unequal society in the world.[1] Within this context, Beegin is designed to provide a tool for financial empowerment, essential for undoing existing racial inequities, while simultaneously nurturing a healthy local ecology. It supports emerging and expert beekeepers, as well as bees themselves.

While a student at the University of Johannesburg, Ivan Brown, under the supervision of Angus Donald Campbell, head of the Department of Industrial Design, wanted to promote more sustainable beekeeping and identified opportunities to improve the livelihoods of marginalised small-scale farmers. The individuals he identified wanted to keep bees, but lacked the skills and equipment to do so. Brown made this the focus for the final project in his Bachelor of Industrial Design studies, continued to develop it during his Master's studies, and, finally, into a commercial enterprise.

Beegin's design research methodologies were borrowed from Timothy Prestero's design for outcomes,[2] which is a participatory methodology that focuses on manufacturability, distribution, and actual use to help to ensure a product's delivery and uptake. Brown paired this with the concepts of Appropriate Technology[3] and the Capabilities Approach[4] to further embed the design outcomes in the South African context. He partnered with a group of six expert- and five emerging beekeepers to identify key issues, which included: theft and vandalism, lack of finance, diseases and pests, limited land and space, and lack of knowledge.[5]

A key finding that emerged was the way that ineffective hives limited the potential of individual beekeepers. A series of beehive prototypes, each going through multiple iterations, refined the design for lightweight concrete hives. These were distributed to all 11 beekeeping partners for field-testing over one honey-production season, which generated further insights for the refine-

ment of the prototypes. The final design considered the beehives as part of a socio-technical-ecological system, including the bees, the tools, and materials for the making of the hives and their potential for business creation. It was optimized for protection, adjustability, ease of inspection, site, harvesting, manufacture, thermoregulation, and material properties.

A key innovation in the final Beegin hive was its material, which is a light-weight concrete composite. The thickness and the use of lightweight fillers resulted in the beehives having much better insulating properties than traditional wooden hives. On testing, it was found that bees in the insulated Beegin hives needed to expend less energy on heating and cooling, which enabled them to put their energy into honey production, yielding an increase of up to 40%. The Beegin hive can be locked to reduce theft and, in the event of disease, they can be non-destructively burned to remove pathogens and mites. These qualities give the Beegin hive better longevity than wooden alternatives and therefore reduce cost of lifetime ownership.

Beegin hives can be manufactured without in-depth technical training thanks to proprietary vacuum-formed molds and simple instruction manuals. Beegin does not sell the hives directly but sells molds and instructions that can be followed by local entrepreneurs, thereby reducing the embodied energy of the supply chain needed to deliver hives to remote areas. Beegin provides a better hive for bees, which in turn aids the farmers, who rely on their pollination activities, and introduces new economic opportunities for the entrepreneurs who manufacture and sell their own Beegin hives.

Design for Social Innovation

1   "Poverty & Equity Data Portal," accessed April 4, 2021, https://pover-
       tydata.worldbank.org/poverty/country/ZAF.

2   Timothy Prestero, "Design for People, Not Awards," June 2012,
       www.ted.com/talks/timothy_prestero_design_for_people_not_awards.

3   Barrett Hazeltine and Christopher Bull, *Field Guide to Appropriate
       Technology* (Amsterdam; Boston, Mass.: Academic, 2003).

4   Martha C. Nussbaum, *Creating Capabilities: The Human Development
       Approach* (Cambridge, Mass.: Harvard University Press, 2011).

5   "Situation Analysis of Beekeeping Industry," accessed April 4, 2021,
       www.apiservices.biz/documents/articles-en/beekeeping_regional_situa-
       tional-analysis.pdf.

Images: Ivan Brown

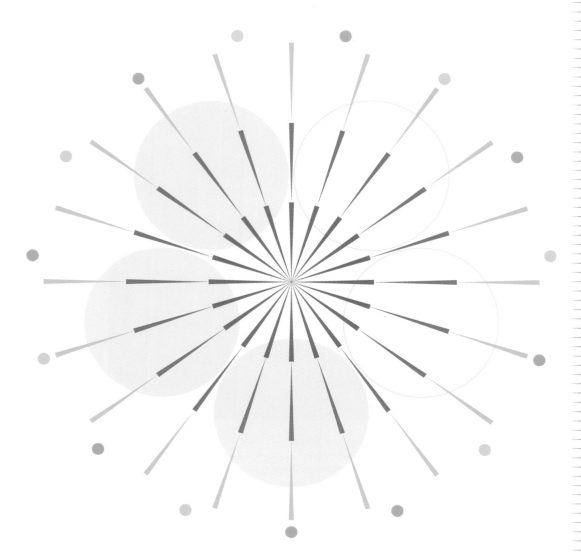

Duration
  2012–2017

Location
  Chile

Categories
  Education

Designer
  Pontificia Universidad Católica
  de Chile

Partners
  Junta Nacional de Jardines
  infantiles de Chile (JUNJI)

Key Contributors
  Patricia Manns
  Alberto González
  Cynthia Adlerstein
  Edgardo Moraga

Designer Organization Type
  • Academic

Team Size
  • 11–20

Design Quotient
  • 21–40%

Project Costs
  ▷ $100k–$500k

Source of Funding
  ▬ Government
  ▬ Private Company
  ▬ University

Funding Mechanisms
  Unspecified

Impact Measurement Methods
  Quantitative: Evaluative
  Assessment

Mediums
  Digital: App
  Experiential: Education
  Physical: Furniture

MAFA

Reconceptualizing preschool classrooms as open-ended learning spaces

More than 200,000 children aged 2 to 4 years attend preschool in Chile, according to data from 2018, and, while these early years are known to be important, the current environments available to them are designed according to an outdated model which does not take into account contemporary knowledge about how kids learn. To improve Chilean public preschool education, the Modelamiento del Ambiente Físico de Aprendizaje initiative ("Physical Learning Environment Modeling System" in English, and referred to here by the acronym "MAFA") was created by Pontificia Universidad Católica de Chile with the goal of developing modernized learning environments. As an interdisciplinary research team including the design school and education faculty, MAFA's goal was to design a system of physical learning environments for preschoolers that is flexible for teachers and students. These spaces emphasize teamwork, identity, coexistence, empowerment, and negotiation as part of the learning experience.

MAFA's research established two main hypotheses. First, because contemporary preschool pedagogies embrace loosely structured experiences, traditional ideas of "furniture" and how a "classroom" should look were inappropriate to the task. Therefore, an interdisciplinary team that could rethink these spaces from scratch was necessary. Second, preschool classrooms cannot be designed for rote educational experiences more common in older classrooms, such as kids sitting neatly in chairs quietly listening to a teacher. Rather, these educational spaces should be designed as places for "living and learning," according to organizer Patricia Manns, which means they must be flexible and open-ended.

MAFA's response to these dual hypotheses was to rethink the furniture of the classroom as a set of modular "practice supports." The term purposefully rejects traditional interpretations such as "chair" or "table" and instead pushes children and adults alike to engage in a process of creativity and discovery to

Each child finds their place to socialize, read, play, or eat breakfast in the MAFA classroom

make use of the supports during various learning activities. As one early childhood educator who was involved with the project put it, "The Tables are armchairs, they are desks, they are beds, they are tables, and a host of [other] things."

The process of making sense of how to use the furniture becomes part of the educational experience. Each classroom has a 3-D-printed scale model of itself that encourages children and educators to negotiate how they will transform their own physical environment as they move from one learning experience to the next. Educators are invited to use MAFA App, a mobile app that allows them to share teaching and learning experiences as the physical environment changes within their own classroom. This helps teachers learn from each other and collectively make the most of the learning environments.

The MAFA system was implemented in 25 experimental classrooms of socially disadvantaged and highly vulnerable communities. These MAFA classrooms were compared to a control group using an evaluative model developed by the MAFA team as well as the widely used Early Childhood Environment Rating Scale coming from the US. Both rating scales showed statistically significant improvements in the MAFA classrooms. Further validation came from the pedagogical communities such as preschool teachers, education technicians, administrators, and international experts who specialize in education and design. This feedback allowed the team to demonstrate a substantial increase in the quality of children's learning environments, while also using the feedback to refine the system.

Design for Social Innovation

Today, the MAFA system has been implemented in 30 preschools, where more than 1,500 children have been educated in their learning environments. The team plans to apply a similar approach to kindergarten, first grade, and second grade classrooms.

> *"[Catholic University and Center UC] have been pioneers in research and, above all, in systematizing advances in initial education through this perspective, which allows us to visualize the need to reflect on learning environments."*

Fabiola Mánquez, director of the Education Quality Department at JUNJI

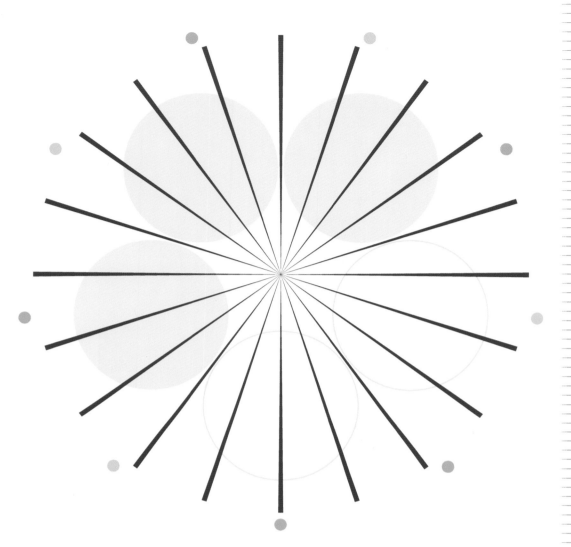

Duration
  February–September 2015

Location
  Myanmar (Shwebo, Pyay,
  Danubyu, and Nyaungshwe)

Categories
  Economic
  Agriculture

Designer
  Proximity Designs and Studio D
  Radiodurans

Key Contributors
  Jan Chipchase
  Phyu Hninn Nyein
  Lauren Serota
  Su Mon
  Nge Oo Mon

Designer Organization Type
  ● Non-Profit

Team Size
  ● 8–10

Design Quotient
  ● 61–80%

Project Costs
  ▷ $100k–$500k

Source of Funding
  ▬ Foundation/Non-Profit/
  Endowment

Funding Mechanisms
  Grant

Impact Measurement Methods
  Quantitative: Surveys, External
  Impact Evaluator

Mediums
  Digital: SMS
  Organizational: Service
  Physical: Book

Paddy to Plate

Understanding the needs and context of entrepreneurial paddy farmers in Myanmar

In a country such as Myanmar, where 70% of the population depends on agriculture, access to advances in farming technology and techniques is vital to improving living conditions. The team at Proximity Designs knows this reality from a close vantage point, as a local social enterprise that designs and delivers affordable, income-boosting products that are informed by the insights and aspirations as well as the entrepreneurial capacity of rural families.

The difference between being local and truly understanding the context and needs of the users of your products can be a wide gulf. Though Proximity already had significant expertise and experience in this area, they chose to invest in anticipation of future products and services by partnering with consulting research, design, and strategy firm Studio D Radiodurans to develop in-depth ethnographic research. The two teams had already worked together for a number of years, building up trust in each other's capabilities. It was from this base of mutual respect that they took on their largest collaboration, Paddy to Plate, with the goal of identifying ways that Proximity Designs and its partners could provide meaningful products and services for smallholder rice farmers in the future. The result was an in-depth "almanac" that explains the needs, aspirations, and context of smallholder rice paddy farmers in Myanmar.

Paddy to Plate began with research into the challenges of smallholder paddy farming practices in Myanmar during each stage of production. The team sought to learn how farmers decide to invest and manage risk, in addition to the practical challenges of running a working farm. Beyond individual considerations, they also took into account the backdrop of tensions and opportunities at a national level in a country experiencing rapid economic change.

The study generated 1,839 observations and insights (and 19,227 photos) aimed at helping the team identify opportunities to support farmers and those in

the farming ecosystem. On-the-ground interviews, data collection, and synthesis involved 12 people working over six weeks. The team used qualitative and empathic research techniques including in-depth contextual, ad hoc, group and subject matter expert interviews. The team leveraged Proximity Designs' extensive field presence to immerse themselves in existing products and services. This approach supported a stronger empathic understanding of paddy farmers. In-field synthesis took place in three ways: informal debriefings after each research session; daily full-team debriefings to discuss key findings, possible process improvements, and goals for the following day; and on-site meetings to create a high-level, synthesized summary of findings for the location. All of this was boiled down to 22 opportunity areas.

Based on the findings from Paddy to Plate, Proximity Designs took the lead in developing concepts, and designing services that cover almost all of the opportunity areas. Potential projects were piloted. To date, four mature services have grown out of the insights from Paddy to Plate: soil testing and treatment, digital agronomy advice, nutrient management, and crop protection.

The Soil Health Diagnostic Service gives farmers affordable, accurate recommendations on the correct amounts of fertilizer to apply. This reduces unnecessary input costs, increases farm productivity, and restores the health of their soil. Another example is Shwe Phyo ("Golden Sprout") that is a digital service that uses text messaging to share vital information, such as fertilizer scheduling and quick response for pest and disease problems.

Proximity Designs regularly conducts rigorous impact assessments. Their in-house social impact team operates as a quasi-independent unit to assess the impact of all products and services and draws customer insights. They quantify customer satisfaction, assess changes in household incomes, and recommend opportunities for improvements. In June 2019, Proximity contracted an independent external evaluation. The study confirmed the findings of their team: a farming household can increase its net income by an average of US$335 a year, after receiving Proximity's farm advisory services. Since 2015, more than 166,000 paddy farmers have adopted their agronomy practices, generating a total of over US$55 million in additional farm incomes.

In addition to these direct and measurable outcomes, Paddy to Plate also provided less tangible contributions that help Proximity Designs build and maintain a deeper connection to their work and the people who the social enterprise serves. This can be seen in Proximity's external connections, such as using the Paddy to Plate research to expand their advisory team from two townships to 30 across the country. The research also helped internally, by creating more meaningful connections between members of the Proximity Designs team. Though not a planned outcome of the project, the publication that resulted from Paddy to Plate is now used to rapidly on-board new team members as Proximity grows. Assets from the research have also been utilized in unexpected ways at the company headquarters, from floor-to-ceiling photographs, to a bottle of "moonshine" made during an exploratory phase of the project.

Mediums of Change

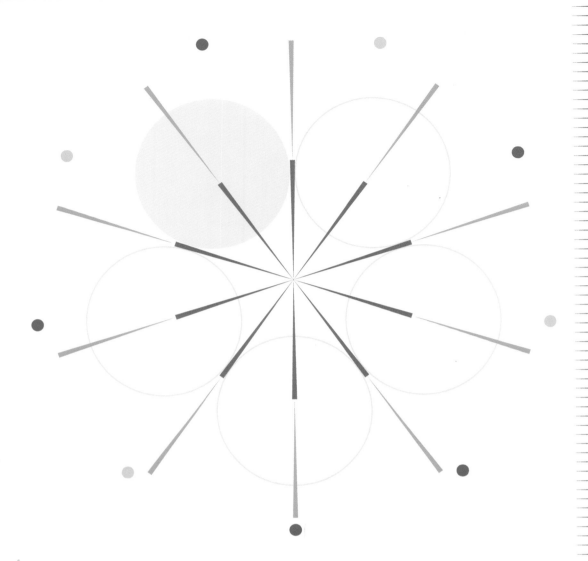

Duration
   May–July 2017

Location
   Brasília, Brazil

Categories
   Economic

Designer
   GNova (Government Innovation
      Lab of the Brazilian Federal
      Government)

Partners
   Ministry of Planning (currently
      Ministry of Economy)

Key Contributors
   Joselene Lemos
   Wesley Rodrigo Lira
   Daniel Rogério
   Iara Endo
   Manoela Hartz

Designer Organization Type
   ● Government

Team Size
   ● 8–10

Design Quotient
   ● 0–20%

Project Costs
   ⊳ $25k–$100k

Source of Funding
   ▬ Government
   ▬ Self-Funded

Funding Mechanisms
   Self-Funded

Impact Measurement Methods
   Qualitative: Stakeholder
      Interviews
   Quantitative: Cost Savings

Mediums
   Digital: Website

Brazilian Government Supplier Registration System

Procuring government services without wasting anyone's time

Like many countries, Brazil has a standardized system through which companies bid on and contract for work with the Federal Government. In 2016, the Federal Audit Office (CGU) highlighted criticisms of the system as requiring a complex registration process with many documents inputted from users. If all this effort delivered better results, it may be worth it, but instead CGU found that this increased costs for suppliers as well as being costly for the government to maintain. Unreliable information stemming from manual data entry and the system's idiosyncratic registration system, which involved a combination of online and offline activities, were some of the biggest complaints. Users saw the registration system as plagued by red tape, according to a "public services census."

As a laboratory for government innovation focused on developing creative solutions for public problems, GNova was asked to help. The team collected information about users' experience through in-depth interviews and observational research. Four types of users were interviewed: suppliers, registration units, purchasing and bidding units, and partner institutions. In total, approximately 30 people from 25 institutions were part of this process.

While GNova initially hypothesized that the problems were technological, their interviews helped them to identify problems that were not obvious to managers and that may not have surfaced otherwise. For instance, it was impossible to cancel a user's registration. Recovery of lost login and password details was also plagued by difficulty.

When GNova delivered their research to the government in a clearly mapped and visually engaging document,[1] the Ministry of Planning, who "owns" the Unified Supplier System, undertook a redesign of the registration process with

The tedious registration process before the redesign required a significant amount of paperwork

the goal of improving the user experience and making the complete process available online. Suppliers no longer needed to deliver physical documents in person, the 1,855 brick and mortar registration locations ceased to exist, and some 4,000 public servants who worked in these units were reassigned to other activities. Deactivating these units alone would generate savings of $R65 million in the first year of operation of the system, according to the Ministry's estimates.

Efficiency gains within the government were paired with benefits to the individual businesses and business operators. The indirect costs on behalf of registering companies who are recording and maintaining their information in the system decreased to a quarter of their initial levels, as stated by the Inter-American Development Bank.

GNova's post-project evaluation identified benefits that are harder to quantify. As one partner described, "without the field research with GNova, we would have had another result, another product... making very little progress in transforming the service compared to what it was before. [Gaining] user insight [helped us] try to go further, looking for the best without being limited to what was possible in terms of time and resources." The project was recognized by Brazil's Innovation in Public Service Award as one of five winners out of 70.

1   GNova, "Projeto SICAF: Mapa de Insights," n.d., https://repositorio.enap.gov.br/bit-stream/1/3404/1/SICAF_Mapa%20de%20Insights.pdf.

GNova team seen while developing their online system

The team produced a map of insights that includes recommendation for management, communication, and registration systems

Images: GNova

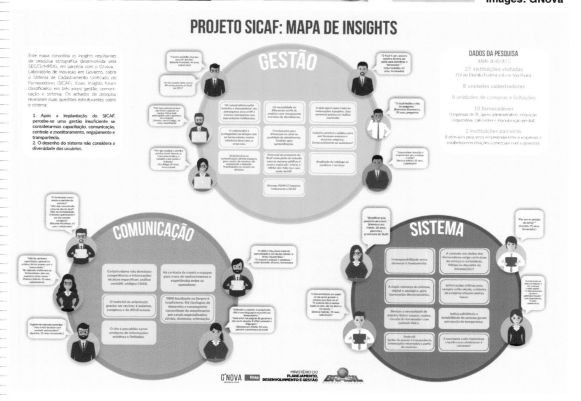

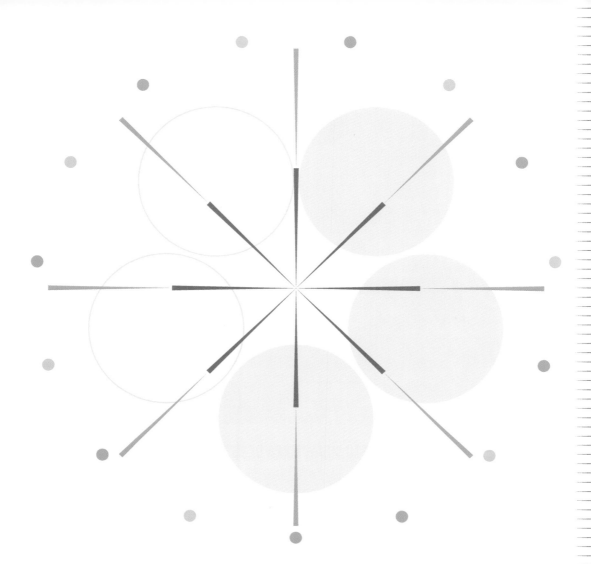

Duration
   July 2017–June 2018

Location
   Pristina, Kosovo

Categories
   Social Justice
   Policy
   Public Safety

Designer
   UN Women Kosovo Office and UN-
   Habitat

Partners
   Municipality of Pristina (Department
      of Strategic Planning and
      Sustainable Development;
      Department of Public Services,
      Protection and Rescue)
   Kosovo Police
   Regional Emergency Operations
      Center

Ministry of Internal Affairs
University of Pristina, Faculty of Civil
   Engineering and Architecture
Kosovo Women Network
Open Data Kosovo
Girls Coding Kosova
UN-Habitat
Block by Block Foundation

Key Contributors
   Vlora Nushi
   Armenda Filipaj
   Simona Shwitter
   Anisa Bina
   Rozafa Kelmendi

Designer Organization Type
   ● Non-Profit

Team Size
   ● 11–20

Design Quotient
   ● 21–40%

Project Costs
   ▭▷ $1k–$25k

Source of Funding
   ▬▶ Government
   ▬▶ Self-Funded

Funding Mechanisms
   Self-Funded

Impact Measurement Methods
   Qualitative: Participant/Client/User
      Feedback

Mediums
   Experiential: Training
   Organizational: Service
   Spatial: Urban Design

Right2City4All

Inviting youth to help design safer public spaces in Kosovo

Kosovo is one of the poorest areas of Europe, with a long history of conflict between its Albanian and Serbian populations. Kosovo's cities have experienced rapid growth in recent years, and there is a growing need for well-designed public spaces that can be enjoyed by everyone. Opportunities for residents, including women and children, to cast their voice in how these public projects are developed, however, often remain limited.

The UN Women Kosovo Office works on gender inequality issues and for this project cooperated with UN-Habitat, whose Block by Block initiative provided a promising starting point. Block by Block uses the Minecraft video game as a tool to engage youth to imagine futures for their communities. It gives neighborhood residents the training and platform to participate and contribute their ideas through a collaborative process. To date, it has been used in more than 37 countries.

Working in partnership with the Municipality of Pristina, the country's largest city, Right2City4All was developed as a collaboration with local institutions and universities, including the national government, local police, and leading women's groups.

The collaborative project team, led by UN Women Kosovo in collaboration with UN-Habitat, started with an audit to understand how different population groups understood the role of urban design in their everyday safety in the city. Troubling factors were identified, such as insufficient lightning, poor sightlines, unused spaces, lack of walking paths, poor infrastructure, and maintenance.

Fifty-eight young people used the Minecraft video game to propose ways to make Pristina's City Park safer. Klodeta Krasniqi, a program officer with UN-Habitat, observed, "using this tool really empowers youth in the process. The youngsters take leadership because they know the game and it brings them

Views of the recreated Pristina City Park in the Minecraft video game

very close to reality." This was the first time such an approach was used in Kosovo. Proposals included repurposing abandoned houses for youth and cultural centers, adding walking and jogging trails in the park, improving public lighting, developing urban art, and expanding the focus from the park alone to include the park and nearby streets.

The result was a more comprehensive perspective on Pristina's public spaces, by combining observations of how spaces are used today with proposals for how they may be reimagined in the future. Assessments of perceived safety in public spaces led to concrete design possibilities for improving safety and accessibility in selected public spaces. New ideas for reporting and responding to physical and sexual harassment in public space were also put forward.

Beyond developing a shared understanding of the precarious reality of Pristina's public spaces, UN Women Kosovo worked with institutional partners at the systems level to support their transformation toward greater action on public safety and inclusion. This included activities such as sensitization training for municipal officials, police officers, and civil society organizations to understand the realities of harassment in public spaces and mainstream gender as an important consideration for urban policies. Right2City4All also established a partnership between the police and Open Data Kosovo and Girls Coding Kosova to use the "WalkFreely" online platform[1] as an official reporting mechanism for sexual harassment and violence.

According to Vlora Nushi, the officer in charge at UN Women in Kosovo, "This project was the first concrete step towards creating safe, inclusive, and accessible public spaces in Kosovo in line with the Sustainable Development Goals and with a specific focus on gender-sensitive urban planning."

During a Minecraft charrette, observations and insights from safety audits are shared with the group

"*For me, the most amazing part was to see how well they understood and conceptualized the recommendations from the safety audit. Everyone included different urban solutions to improve safety and perception of safety.*"

Klodeta Krasniqi, program officer with UN-Habitat

1   http://iwalkfreely.com/.

Youth use the accessible medium of Minecraft to create their own solutions to the concerns identified in Pristina City Park

Local police participate in the efforts to address issues of public safety in Pristina

Images: UN-Habitat

Measuring Impact

Stuart Candy, Chris Larkin, and Joyce Yee, with Mariana Amatullo

How is society's capacity to innovate furthered by design? This substantive question is at the core of this roundtable discussion and, in many ways, underpins one of the chief motivations for this publication. Measuring the impact of design in driving social innovation forward is an endeavor that remains fraught with difficulty. We can point to a number of reasons that account for the elusive nature of the task.

First of all, the social innovation field is more complex than traditional industrial and technological innovation, partly because it happens at the crossroads of multiple sectors and disciplinary boundaries. The necessity for collaboration across a coalition of funders and stakeholders is part and parcel of addressing interrelated social challenges successfully, whether in financial literacy, the well-being of refugees, or the redesign of public services, all exemplified in the cases we profile in this section. As Chris Larkin from IDEO.org points out, the collective nature of this work can make it difficult to establish theory of change models and account for their impact. Furthermore, a significant portion of knowledge flows from practitioners working in contexts of high complexity and often doing so frugally with scant resources. Given that many of them are "laying a path down while walking it," it can be challenging to codify common patterns of success or failure. Besides, the context of where social innovations are being implemented is, by definition, diverse, and as a result, understanding parameters of success can vary depending on the stakeholders engaged.

Second, while there is a growing body of research in design for social innovation, we still suffer from a lack of cumulative learning. We seem to relish celebrating pilots and novel projects without necessarily always taking a systematic view to capture replicable insights and the many nuanced considerations that characterize this work. In this sense, as Joyce Yee offers in light of her ongoing work with the DESIAP network and her research with the Young Foundation, embedding a learning-centered evaluative practice and a trust-based approach to working with communities might represent effective ways forward. In addition, the temporality dimension that underpins social innovation work contributes to the difficulty related to evaluation. From his vantage point as a futurist, Stuart Candy highlights this challenge of zeroing in on what is "knowable" and subject to assessment and measurement. In this regard, because the issues that social innovation tackles do not have finite starting and ending points, the processes of uncovering culturally appropriate opportunities and finding solutions do not always square with the bounded timelines of a design consulting engagement. We know that the implementation phase of social innovation initiatives represents a critical juncture to account for impact and iterate on processes that drive long-term adoption in a given community.

What complicates matters further is that this is also the phase where design's presence is typically at a deficit. Social change takes time and leaves behind transformed social relationships that are hard to quantify. Design project commissions are rarely funded to enable designers to bear witness to these phenomena. Once a project's deliverables have been completed, design teams typically hand off the project to partners; the funding is seldom there for them to revisit outcomes downstream. This constitutes a double loss: with designers out of the equation, they lose the opportunity to learn from and iterate on the inevitable complications that arise in this phase, and they seldom have access to spot insights that might inform new protocols for assessing impact. Fortunately, and as we can surmise from the discussion, we are starting to see an increased recognition by funders that optimization of social outcomes often does require a critical and ongoing design presence, especially in system and organizational change initiatives.

Third, and lastly, evaluation methods for these design practices are in their infancy. As a consequence, the philanthropy and social sectors that fund and commission this work turn to measurement frameworks that do not always align with "designerly approaches of knowing." As all three roundtable discussants highlight, this makes for evaluation results that can exacerbate power asymmetries between Global North and Global South considerations and miss the relational dimension of the design contributions that emerge. Ultimately, they may fail to translate the value of the design methodologies, techniques, and problem-solving approaches in play. In this regard, it is not entirely surprising that new approaches to social challenges might require that we pay attention to new metrics and re-imagined indicators. Only then will we be in a position to answer with creative confidence this question: what does success look like?

This roundtable discussion took place in July 2020 and was condensed and edited for clarity

Joyce Yee

I am a professor of Design and Social Innovation in the School of Design at Northumbria University. We're based in Newcastle upon Tyne, up in the northeast of England, and my research looks at the role of design in supporting organizations and communities to be more creative and innovative. Part of that work is around the use of design in social innovation practices, particularly in an Asia Pacific context. Along with a colleague at RMIT, Yoko Akama, I co-founded a network called Designing Social Innovation in Asia-Pacific (DESIAP). It is a virtual learning platform, bringing together researchers and practitioners who are using design to support social innovation.

Stuart Candy

I am an associate professor in the School of Design at Carnegie Mellon University (CMU) in Pittsburgh, Pennsylvania. I'm a professional futurist, and I help many types of organizations think and feel their way through events that haven't happened yet, in order to try and make wiser decisions. On the curricular side, part of what I do at CMU is weave foresight through the Design curriculum so that it can become a normal part of what designers do; to think about design decisions they're making in the present in the light of alternative possible future states. On the practice front, I was initially drawn to working in a design context while a grad student in the futures program at the University of Hawai'i at Manoa. Although the field had been around for decades, my colleagues and I were always explaining to people what it was, which suggested that maybe it wasn't quite living up to its potential. And so, both in an effort to make what we do more clearly understood to the public, and to help make an alternative futures orientation more legible and influential as organizational practice, we started designing and staging experiences intended to feel like they were actually happening within various alternative futures, as opposed to having people merely read written accounts of what those worlds might look like. That turned out to work extremely well for galvanizing conversation in a different and deeper way. It led to what we came to call Experiential Futures, a transdisciplinary and transmedia canvas for manifesting ideas about possible futures using all sorts of media and environments—a video, a set of postcards, an immersion, a game; whatever fits the challenge at hand. And that's the angle from which I'm approaching the question of social impact in design.

Chris Larkin

I am the Senior Director of Impact at IDEO.org. My role is to support our three studios—in Nairobi, New York, and San Francisco—with Impact theory, thinking, and measurement, and how to bring that meaningfully into the design process, as well as trying to establish evidence around the value of design to make a case for what it is that design can do in the social sector and international development space. My background is in social and organizational psychology. I worked in social and behavior change research and programming for many years before joining IDEO.org—which is actually the first place that I'd really worked with design in an intentional way. Before that, I was working more in the media and communications space, and applying that type of creative practice to challenges of social and behavior change.

> **Mariana:** Welcome to you all. It's fair to say that this field of design for social innovation, design for social change, design for social impact—the nomenclature can vary—has been evolving and maturing in the last decade. And the issue of quantifying impact and value is a key question that we are always wrestling with. I would like to start the conversation by asking you each to reflect on how you're approaching this big question of value and measurement? How does it manifest for your research and your teaching, for your practice?

Joyce: As a designer, proving the value of design is a constant pursuit: you present your portfolio and say, "Look at my previous work, how it brought value to these organizations." Yet it's often really hard to quantify. My sense is that hasn't changed, to a certain extent. My first engagement with trying to assess the value of design came when I was working on a service design project about ten years ago. We attempted to use social return on investment (SROI) to evaluate the outcomes of a new, digitally mediated training service introduced to support the existing on-site training offered by the company. SROI is basically an accounting version of ROI, but is aimed at quantifying a social and environmental value by placing financial proxy values on impacts identified by stakeholders. In principle, it sounded perfect, enabling us to capture impact recognized by stakeholders to be important, in an accounting model that businesses understand. In reality, it was far more challenging than we thought. Apart from being very time-consuming and requiring quite in-depth knowledge of the approach, it was extremely challenging trying to assign financial proxies to social impact. For example, we found an improved sense of well-being and motivation in staff but these outcomes proved difficult to assign a convincing financial measure. So my first experience of using a cost-benefit model to evaluate the impact of design signposted many of the future challenges that I would encounter ahead.

Within the social innovation space, evaluating impact has been a continuing topic of concern. Discussions with practitioners through the DESIAP network often highlight the incongruities in applying a Global North model to different cultural contexts in Asia-Pacific. We encounter the same narrative when discussing the challenges of impact evaluation, where the issue of power asymmetries of aid means that evaluation is often top-down and

Design for Social Innovation

driven by the funder's agenda. This leads to a gap between how outcomes are reported against predefined criteria versus the impact that practitioners are seeing on the ground.

The emergent nature of social innovation means that the primary purpose of conducting evaluation is to understand what has been done, what has been achieved to date, and how best to progress the work. What we realized is that our practitioners are already embedding evaluative practices in their approach to design, through multiple iterations and prototyping. As a consequence, what we found helpful was to develop a propositional framework to represent the range of evaluative practices already being practiced. The framework, which we call Designing Social Innovation Evaluation, reinforces the core principles of building trust, participatory collaboration, and being grounded in place, culture, and locality. I'm currently working with the Communities Driving Change team at the Young Foundation in the UK to embed a learning-centered evaluative practice. Our aim is to encourage the use of evaluative practices as a way to iteratively learn and improve project outcomes.

Encouragingly, we are starting to see funders responding to this need. There is an increasing move towards a more trust-based approach, where outcomes and impact are co-created. It is built on a trusting relationship with the fundee, which then manifests in multi-year non-restricted funding with streamlined paperwork and reporting, enabling agility, and quicker response to changing context. So there is a definite perspective shift in how impact and value are being considered in social innovation.

> **Mariana:** That's a great issue to think about, the relationship and the institutional models of funders, and how that impacts practice and evaluation. Chris, what's your experience and perspective on this question?

Chris: The international development sector and social sector are, as Joyce said, extremely evidence-driven and there's pressure for data and evidence for what design is doing—the value of it. A lot of that is driven by the need for cost-effectiveness in terms of where the investment goes. But there's also increasing buzz around different innovation approaches. So, there's a dual evidence burden that I've been trying to work on with IDEO.org, and it's one that separates the design process from solution effectiveness. I've found it necessary for our organization to try and push for that clarity and separation and not see design as an intervention but rather as a methodology. And, actually, I've pushed back against the ways in which evaluative approaches have been applied, because design never takes any one shape or form. From one project to the next, it looks different every time. Yes, there's a set of design thinking processes and certain practices we will always do around insights or synthesis processes, and, obviously, the craft side of design. But I would argue that the investment in different stages, and the processes that we pull from, always looks different. So that's been one kind of framework. In terms of what we've been doing, the most activity around measurement has definitely been in the adolescent reproductive health space, which is part of a larger portfolio in the global health sector, and where there is strong interest for a data, and evidence-driven based approach.

It's an interesting position to be in as a design firm because we don't implement the solutions that we help to design. We tend to hand things off, and we'll come back in maybe to help optimize or do light stewardship supporting a client partner that we've worked with. But, essentially, the measurement sits with that partner. But we have been working with teams to make sure that any solutions we design are measurable, taking more accountability for that and making sure that we're developing theories of change and logic models that describe a change pathway, trying to guide the metrics and methods that our partners can use to track progress, and handing that off with anything that we do. And then we also liaise with independent evaluators that are increasingly working in this space.

I do a lot of work to help translate for independent evaluators, who are trying to look at design and what value it has brought or how it has played out in an organization, around what the design intent was or how designers may have talked about what they were doing. It's about navigating those perspectives, and I guess one of the pieces of work that I'm doing now is to try and dive more deeply into the design process and the experience of design at an organizational level. The challenge is to look beyond the solution itself that we've been brought in to work on and to see what else has an organization gained. How have their ways of working changed? How have they started to look at problems differently as a result? And that's where the difficulty lies in the evaluation space where those frameworks don't really exist yet. As an evaluator, there are very few clear frameworks to say, "These are the things you should be seeing if this has been done well." So that's something that I'm trying to pivot to a little bit more now in my work. What can we contribute to this space as a design firm with a responsibility to actually create that learning, offer some of those frameworks for others to use?

> **Mariana:** Stuart, you're coming in with a very different trajectory and position and in a field where you're also engaging with a lot of design artifacts, design research processes, and working also at an organizational level where people come to you, navigating uncertainty. Can you talk a little bit about how this question of measurement is entering into our field and reflect on the perspectives we've

Design for Social Innovation

heard so far? I'm hearing questions of translation and gaps in both of these first very rich statements.

"Assessing or evaluating or gauging impact can take many different forms, and measurement is just one kind of approach, which carries with it a particular set of assumptions about how to try to know what change has occurred, and even what is knowable."

Stuart: A key question that comes up for me is this: when is it appropriate to measure, as opposed to engaging in some other kind of evaluation? This reflects Chris's point about design being methodology rather than intervention. That resonates for me partly because the essential thrust of futures work—as a perspective, as a mindset, as an array of conceptual resources—has to do with how people approach time, which is not necessarily an easy thing to measure. It's also a kind of perspectival or cultural shift that might unfold over a much longer period than individual projects or interventions typically do.

So I want to tease apart the question of measurement versus assessment. I don't see those as interchangeable terms. Assessing or evaluating or gauging impact can take many different forms, and measurement is just one kind of approach, which carries with it a particular set of assumptions about how to try to know what change has occurred, and even what is knowable.

The question of impact became a focus for me in a previous life working full-time as a consulting futurist, part of an in-house foresight and innovation team within a global design and engineering firm, Arup. Our role faced in two directions at once. Part of it was externally oriented; proposing and delivering work to external partner organizations. And it was also partly internally oriented; encouraging and enabling our colleagues to think longer-term about the kinds of projects we were doing. What might be the future needs for a cultural institution like an opera house, or a hospital, or a university campus—all of these categories of buildings and infrastructure that the company was involved in bringing to life—a decade or a generation from now? In both of those modes, internally and externally facing, the center of the work had to do with relationships. What's the quality of the relationship between yourself and your team, and the people you're serving and traveling alongside? This is something you have to think about a lot, but that is not necessarily easy to measure. In futures work, the quality of the relationship is particularly important because it's a situation where you can lead a horse to water, but you can't make it drink. You can't force people to think long term. All you can do is try to create conditions that engender a different perspective. This means it's not just relational practice, it's also invitational. Evaluating how you're doing requires attending to the quality of the relationships that you're having, whether you get invited back after a first engagement. It's one of the most important questions for a consultant who makes their living by helping people, and I guess I say this because I want to make space in our conversation for the question of how we can evaluate, gauge impact, and arrive at judgments about the quality of things we do, without assuming that that necessarily means putting a ruler next to them.

> **Mariana:** And you're touching on this question of time and temporality that is core to your field. Joyce, how does the factor of time play out when it comes to social innovation and design and working with communities and trying to demonstrate value? What are some of the opportunities and barriers there?

"Impact will also occur beyond the program duration. I'm personally interested in the transformative nature of these initiatives and how social innovators are fundamentally changed because of their involvement in the program."

Joyce: Stuart has brought up a really important point. Temporality is a key aspect of designing that we don't often acknowledge as problematic. Typically, a design project has a start and an end point. However, we found that this consultancy model doesn't really work in a social innovation context. Problems encountered by the community persist prior to and extend beyond the project duration. When you leave or when you extract yourself many of the issues will still remain. It then becomes really important to consider how your interventions play out over a period of time beyond your contribution. Additionally, when you are working with a community, you're continually having to build new relationships and maintain existing ones. Relationships don't end just because the project has ended. We often hear of practitioners still keeping in touch with the community long after the project has been completed.

Within the issue of evaluation, that's even more problematic. A lot can happen over the course of a program which may be years long, so the initial criteria of measurement may no longer make sense. Impact will also occur beyond the program duration. I'm personally interested in the transformative nature of these initiatives and how social innovators are fundamentally changed because of their involvement in the program. However, it is hard to know when this kind of transformation will occur; often it emerges after the program ends. So, in relation to impact measurement, that's a real challenge to capture impact beyond the program duration.

> **Mariana:** Chris, would you build on that, from the perspective of IDEO.org and the work you're doing?

Chris: The concepts of "relationship" and "invitation" are important elements. We've found that some of the most effective work and solutions come from design engagements where we've gone back time and time again over a period of one to three years to help a partner optimize, to re-examine what we've done with them, and determine if, maybe, a service or a product innovation has become redundant, or to ask what we might have missed, or what the new present or future requires. I don't believe you can do that—a six-month design engagement and handoff—unless you have embedded some design skills or capacities within an organization. It's really hard to step away. There's something valuable in being able to come back. It takes a while to learn about the solutions that are going out into the community.

For example, we've had some partners on health projects where, in the immediate term, the solutions were more expensive to implement up front, but over time these costs came down. So that point of asking, "Where do you optimize? Where do you come back in?" and allowing space for that innovation to find its feet, is important. But, in terms of designers being at the table to help that process, that's based so much on the relationships and on having been able to quickly show value and be there with a partner to understand where is it that we can come back in and help and that they're able to identify where they do and don't need us back in. There's a timing piece around relationship and implementation, but also to what Joyce was saying about the change in outcomes over time. Increasingly, when we work on bigger social change challenges or look ahead to applying design to more systems change, that change doesn't happen quickly. We're designing solutions to shift things like social norms, which we know could take ten years or generations to really change. We're often designing something that just can't be measured in a three-year grant cycle. The question is how to preempt that limitation, and come to the table and ask, "What's the way around this, and how do we maintain a commitment to something that could be really effective?"

Stuart: To Chris's excellent point about the really big changes being slow to happen, it's important to add that they don't move at an even pace either. It's very often a nonlinear process. They don't happen steadily such that this increment of effort corresponds neatly to that increment of observable change.

This reminds me of a wonderful recent article by Rebecca Solnit about the racial justice uprisings happening across the United States and around the world, called "The Slow Road to Sudden Change." She says: "You can think of it as a bonfire. Or a waterfall. The metaphor of the river of time is often used to suggest that history flows at a steady pace, but real rivers have rapids and shallows, eddies, and droughts. They freeze over and get dammed and their water gets diverted, and sometimes the river comes to the precipice and we're all in the waterfall. Time accelerates, things change faster than anyone expected. Water clear as glass becomes churning whitewater. What was thought to be impossible or the work of years is accomplished in a flash." Not only is that a beautiful expression of the concept, but it's also incredibly important for the conversation we're having. If we're interested in trying to evaluate the impact our efforts are making, we need to realize that, in many cases, for the things that matter most, it's going to take an enormous amount of really slow, long, patient effort in order to create the conditions for a "sudden change."

And I realize that this is kind of what has happened with the recognition of futures or foresight as a field, as well. You've probably all heard about it quite a bit in the last five years. It wasn't on many people's radars a decade ago, although it dates back to the 1960s at least. Likewise, the slow, patient work of civil rights activists and the Black Lives Matter movement, over years and years, laid the groundwork for this change in social attitudes that pollsters are saying represents one of the fastest shifts in values ever seen in the American population. Similarly, with other things we care about and want to change. There are slow periods where the effort put in doesn't necessarily produce an observable corresponding outcome that, say, funders might be eager to hear about. As my former Arup colleague, Dan Hill, said about the strategic design work that he, Bryan Boyer, and others did at the Helsinki Design Lab at Sitra, it's more of a squiggly line than a straight line between intervention and outcomes.

Design for Social Innovation

Mariana: Connected to this question of temporality and change, there is also the question of scale. We've talked about the resource constraints and the institutional logics that many of these funders and partners are following in terms of accountability. If we propose a design process or project that fails, depending on the sector we're in, that could cost lives. How are you each seeing the pressures around questions of scale in your work, and how does that connect to this question of expectations around evaluation, of what success looks like? I wonder, Joyce, if you can start reflecting on that through the work of the network and your research?

> **Joyce:** We tend not to focus on scale because we just don't believe it's always beneficial. Many of the practitioners that we speak to focus less on scale, and instead on sustainability, on how the impact can be sustained. Initiatives are mainly community-led and community-centered, and you often can't scale the idea; what worked for one community doesn't necessarily work for another. For them it's much more about how to make it locally specific, adapting what they have learned into a different context.

Chris: We see a lot of similarities with what Joyce is saying. We practice human-centered design, and there's an inherent tension between human-centered design and scale. Because when you're digging deep to look at a group or a segment and design bespoke ways of connecting, and designing something that fits with their desires, is that the right entry point for someone to try and scale that? If it's urban women that you've designed for in a context, to try and scale that to a rural context is likely not going to work. There's an immediate problem with scale within that. Generally, where we've seen solutions successfully scale, it's really more about adaptation; it's never replication. It's always about redesigning—sometimes it is about redesigning for that end-user, but often it's about redesigning for a new implementer. When there's pressure from the outset for scale, or there is a need and a desire for it, I think that has to be recognized right at the beginning. Unfortunately, very often, the space given for research or understanding the context that we're designing for isn't big enough to do that kind of learning, to process across all the potential different contexts from the beginning.

This speaks to the need of working out further how these programs are structured and come together. I do see some positive signals. Like some of the programs that we've worked with—A360, for example, is a program dealing with adolescent and reproductive health run by PSI—and they have focused a program on young, married, rural girls, a very specific population. As they look to try and scale this across Ethiopia, they're adapting that model as they go, but still for that population, rooted in the needs of that group. My perspective is that there's something quite Western in the idea of scale: the concept that you can just take a project, roll it out, and, if it's successful, replicate it.

> **Mariana:** Earlier, Joyce touched on the influence and impact of a Global North, or Western perspective that so often dominates the conversation around so many of these issues. Both in the team we've assembled here and the case studies we're examining, we're attempting to take a deliberately pluralistic approach to this discussion. Recognizing the tension that this dominant perspective often creates, I wonder what ideas or insights you have about what might move the needle in terms of shifting this Global North-Global South dichotomy? Stuart, from some of the work you're doing with large organizations such as the United Nations, how aware are they about those tensions when they bring you in?

Stuart: This actually ties to what I was just thinking about scale because to me scale can't be divorced from the ethical orientation and commitments of the organization that you're working with. As a practitioner, this is a question I'm very interested in. What are, to use Donella Meadows' language, the places to intervene in the system that stand a chance of having a bigger or more meaningful impact? These are not necessarily just the largest partner organizations. One has to make a judgment about how much good they're going to be able to do in partnership. The kinds of organizations we've preferred to partner with over the last few years include, as you say, the United Nations Educational, Scientific, and Cultural Organization (UNESCO), the United States Conference of Mayors, which comprises mayors from all over the country, or the International Federation of Red Cross and Red Crescent Societies (IFRC; that's the experiential futures case study that we contributed to this book). We need to ask: how do these organizations think about and support their highly diverse constituencies?

To me, the core premise of futures practice, in the tradition I'm operating out of, is to serve as a container for pluralism. It's futures with an "s" for good reason: both that the future hasn't happened yet, so it could be many different things, and that the space of alternative futures is itself a commons that belongs to literally everyone. It should be cultivated to make space for everyone, speak to everyone, and recognize that the future is co-created by us all. In the case of the IFRC, which has national societies in basically every country on the planet, this ultimately means having to address the futures of humanitarian aid through the lens of every geography and society. It's radically plural in its very composition, and that requires a commensurate pluralism of perspectives in the processes that are used to arrive at decisions, I think that's part of why our efforts to introduce foresight there were able to move so far as such high speed.

Design for Social Innovation

Mariana: Joyce, do you want to bring your lens into this? You've already touched upon it a little bit.

Joyce: I always see myself first and foremost as a designer. On one hand, I am interested, motivated, and completely obsessed with design, because I believe it has tremendous power to do good. But at the same time, as a researcher, I'm also very critical of the way in which design is used. That criticality is important because I see my role as surfacing and challenging a number of assumptions: how design is used, how we learn about design, how we teach, how we apply it. And that's particularly important in a non-European context. Because, certainly in Southeast Asia, there's a widespread, implicit assumption that "The West is the best"; that anything that comes from the West is good, better in terms of quality and substance than something that might arise or be created locally. And that applies to how design models and "design thinking" and design processes have been adopted. It's very much, "Let's just use this model." Of course, there's some local adaptation, but some of the adaptations are quite superficial. What we're trying to do in our work is to recognize culturally specific practices, indigenous ways of knowing and values, and seeing how that transpires to what we can recognize as designing. We don't immediately label what we see as designing but instead take out time to understand how their practices manifest. Although some elements are quite similar to what we feel designing is, we are always looking out for the cultural nuances in how it is being used and applied. Similarly, we bring that criticality to our criticism of current evaluation methods, because it has all these implicit assumptions tied up with it.

We touched on this earlier—the idea that, if we can measure things, they become knowable. But this assumes that there is only one way of knowing. It's important to acknowledge there are other ways of knowing and being. I'm Malaysian, but I have now spent more of my life in the UK than in my place of birth. I'm trained in the Western design tradition, so I'm susceptible to describing and defining design in its most dominant industrialized model. This is why I'm trying to step back and be much more critical in my conceptions of design. As an educator and a researcher, my role is trying to ask different questions that concern other world views and offer frameworks that help us embrace difference and accommodate heterogeneity as its central condition.

Mariana: And for you, Chris, you have been investing in this question a lot in terms of taking a reflexive approach. How are you addressing these tensions and how is it changing with a studio in Nairobi, for example?

Chris: One of the biggest shifts in how we're thinking about our work is around this idea of moving from empathy to actual lived experience, and to making the design lead someone who's much more closely embedded in the context, or at least the region within which we're designing. Building up the Nairobi studio has been an effort to have an East Africa hub within which we can bring in design talent, from Kenya and then other countries within that region, to do the work. At the same time, sometimes people conflate human-centered design with participatory design, and I don't think IDEO.org's approach has ever been a community design or participatory design model. But we are definitely looking much more toward seeing what a really meaningful co-design model looks like with people in their communities.

That's been true even in the work we're doing in the US, recognizing that the designers working on challenges of poverty and inequity here often do not have the educational or class backgrounds, or experiences, of those things. We've pushed to actually bring people who are affected by these issues into the process. Also, on this topic, is a recognition of the need for more discipline integration, the need for a plurality of perspectives. That's less of a Global North, Global South question, but related in that it addresses design being open to other areas of expertise and being able to break established patterns and allow other voices to be heard. There's an appetite for capacity to be built off the back of a design engagement so that, when the design team moves away, there is a team that's able to continue the design work and actually adapt some foundations that we've put in place for the solution and take it forward. The challenge there is finding the right way to build that capacity. What can you do in tandem with a design engagement versus intentional capacity building? That's just one of the tensions that we play with right now, and look out to where's the right place to try and invest and support and grow to make that a reality.

> **Mariana:** Turning back to the question of measuring impact, we talked about frameworks, but what do you see that excites you in terms of possible indicators that might make the field in this area stronger? What are the steps you're taking in your own practices, in your research, or changes that you're observing that you have hope for that will help move that needle?

Chris: One of the steps that I am taking internally is to push us to be much clearer around the way design has been leveraged, and be really clear that one design project is not the same as the other. You can't bundle them all together and then ask, "What is the value of design?" I see the external evaluators who are doing that work are becoming much more versed in design. The same sets of people and consulting evaluation firms are doing repeat projects, measuring and evaluating design within unique contexts, and that massively increases the frameworks that they've got. We have projects where we're still working on very incremental innovation—where we are working to improve, say, user experience or how to increase the reach or engagement with something—and others where we're coming in to actually find new ways, new framings or tackle behavior change that's really deeply rooted in social norms or other kinds of structural inequities. Being clearer about how to separate those two distinct modes, and look at them as different types of design projects, a different set of cases is crucial. My hope is that we can start to perceptively separate that work and look at these as different ways of applying design. If we can see them through that lens, I think we can extract greater insights about when design has value and how.

> **Joyce:** What gives us hope is that there is a subset of organizations and communities of practice that are open to change. Our framework aligns well with funders looking to be more community-driven and responsive to change. The work that we're doing with organizations like the Young Foundation—indicates to me that there is an appetite and that organizations are open to finding different ways to better understand the impact of their work. Our next step is to advocate its use alongside a pre-existing program of evaluation that has to happen to fulfill other institutional requirements. While the advocacy aspect is still challenging, my sense is that you can only do it by showing examples. It's an aspect that we are working on going forward.

Mariana: This question of "demonstration" is coming up a lot. Stuart, what do you see that gives you hope?

> **Stuart:** Well, let me give a broader answer, because what's interesting about design is that it is such a broad umbrella for many different kinds of activities. Without reducing it to a binary, I see a tension or a spectrum of activities that offer cause for both hope and alarm depending on how those tensions are managed.
>
> The spectrum includes very empiricist engineering subcultures, like human-computer interaction, and A/B testing, and this very numbers-driven "show me the data" discourse. At the other end, we might say there's more arts- and discursive-driven work, perhaps seen most prominently in what we come across in speculative and discursive design; designers giving themselves permission to speak about the world, not just to solve problems that their companies or clients present. And those different activities are grounded in different epistemologies—to echo what Joyce was saying—different types

of knowledge, different assumptions about what is knowable, what's valid or important, what's solid enough to base decisions on.

Design's umbrella has expanded in recent years, with more and more people identifying what they do as design, spanning that whole spectrum. There are decisions to be made about how we position the work that we're doing at any given time, and therefore what the appropriate measures of impact and kinds of conversation to have about that work are. A couple of years ago I had a terrific conversation with Jeff Bardzell, now at Penn State University, where we were talking about this tension in relation to the human-computer interaction cluster on the one hand, and the speculative design cluster on the other. And he said something that stayed with me, that there's a temptation in the latter context to apply justifying or grounding strategies that are actually appropriate to software, but not appropriate to try to change how a community sees itself.

We need to make decisions, not just on the basis of what is pragmatic or expedient from a credibility standpoint because it's clear that the data-driven paradigm currently has more prestige in academic culture, but rather on the basis of what is "epistemically appropriate," as he put it. And so, to answer the question of where I see hope, it's in that very awareness seeping into the design conversation. Maybe we are learning to differentiate between cases where trying to establish something empirically is appropriate, versus cases where it's more appropriate to engage in what our design futures colleague Anab Jain calls "slow critical activism"; that kind of Solnit mentality of the slow road to sudden change. You can't expect ambitious change efforts to yield results that you can measure overnight, or even at the end of a two- or three-year-long project. You're planting seeds that take longer than that to grow. But I see hope in the increasing literacy of, and self-examination of, design as a field.

"We have an even bigger challenge coming that touches on systems change and how we apply design within that larger complexity. The more that design starts to integrate other disciplines really intensively, the shape of it changes. This is quite promising."

Design for Social Innovation

Mariana: Thank you. I think this has been an insightful conversation, and I just wanted to offer you each a round of final reflection. Any parting words?

Chris: In response to the question about what's coming next for our field, I feel we're seeing progress in how we measure design as we're practicing it right now. It's true that design is expanding, that the system is changing as we're in it. We have an even bigger challenge coming that touches on systems change and how we apply design within that larger complexity. The more that design starts to integrate other disciplines really intensively, the shape of it changes. This is quite promising. But the two, the shape of design and the kind of outcomes that we're trying to look at, are shifting.

Joyce: I think it's a question of confidence. We have done enough to show that design is worth using. We believe in our process, which often entails many rounds of iterations, prototyping, and learning. Of course, we need to stay grounded and humble, but should be more confident in advocating that a design approach is inherently evaluative.

Stuart: Although I've voiced some concern here about defaulting to scientific or social-science-envy-driven forms of design evaluation, it's really a matter of deciding what's appropriate for the case in question. I'm very excited about a project I've been working on around bringing possible climate-disrupted futures to life immersively, using extended reality (AR and VR), with a colleague who's an ethicist and another who's a behavioral scientist. The project entails not just creating those experiences, but also figuring out what difference they make to the people who have them. This is where a behavioral scientist's mode of evaluation comes in. I'm excited because we very rarely get to do that in experiential futures work; it's more often a matter of planting seeds and hoping some of them grow.

But, in our urgency to legitimize ourselves, we should be careful not to lose sight of the truth of our experience. For example, when people ask me, "How do you know that an experiential scenario is any good?" I would ask them if they've ever been to a party, and they say yes, and then I ask them if it was a good party. And they can tell you if it was or wasn't. I mean, we have experiences, and we can usually evaluate them without the benefit of an exit survey. This might be a very mundane example, but a party is a gathering of people held to accomplish something in terms of relationship and community, and we tend to know when it's working or not. So there is space here for different degrees of formality and procedure in how we evaluate what we're doing, and they shouldn't all default to the most rigid or buttoned-up end of the spectrum. There needs to be pluralism in our strategies for reflecting on and evaluating what we're doing.

Mariana: Well, thank you all for sharing your perspectives here today. And I enjoyed that party metaphor because I think, in this age of COVID-19 and quarantines, we probably have all missed the positive impacts of that kind of experience!

Measuring
Impact

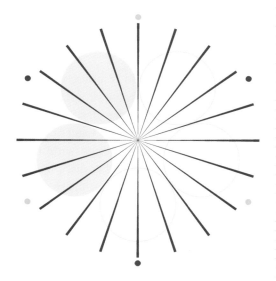

Hospitable Hospice

*Envisioning a new model of
end-of-life care*

City of Rain

*Constructing a more sustainable water
paradigm for Mexico with rainwater
harvesting*

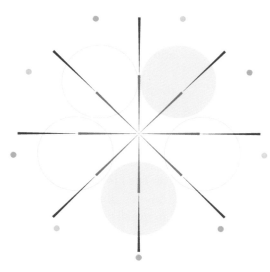

La Transfo

*Creating public innovation labs within
French city governments to improve
public services*

Design for Social Innovation

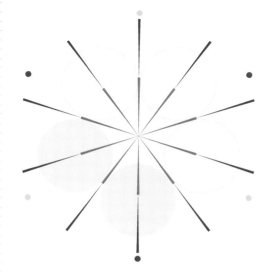

Acciones de Paz

Forging new bonds through the co-creation of open-source furnishings in abandoned public spaces

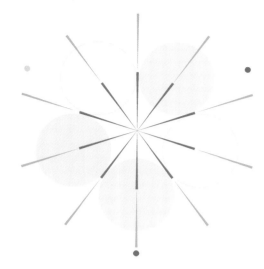

Throwing Car Culture Under the Bus

Inspiring and empowering youth to choose public transit

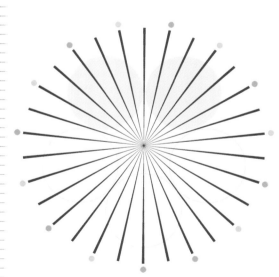

Kuja Kuja

Establishing better feedback loops between refugees and humanitarian organizations

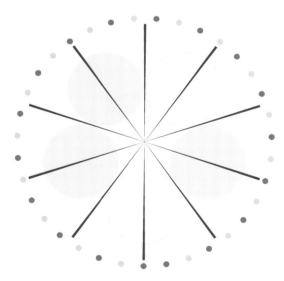

The Future is Now

Futuring to transform the world's largest humanitarian network

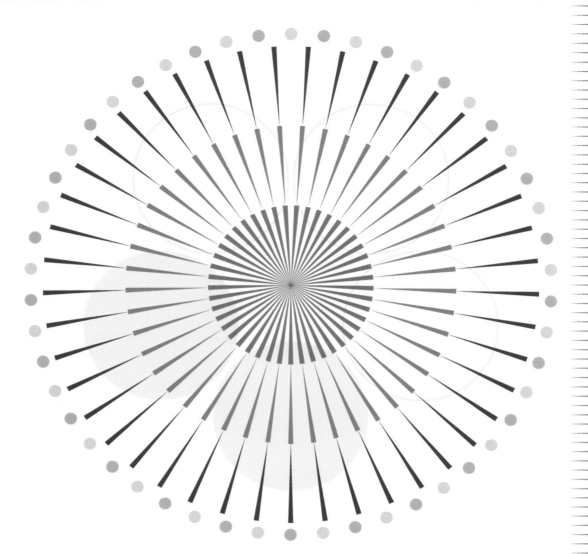

Duration
2006–present

Location
  Mexico City and
    other Mexican states

Categories
  Social Justice
  Environment
  Education
  Policy
  Resilience

Designer
  Isla Urbana

Partners
  Users
  Material providers
  Fabricators
  Rainwater specialists
  Mexico City's Ministry of the
    Environment

Designer Organization Type
  ● Non-Profit

Team Size
  ● 50+

Design Quotient
  ● 61–80%

Project Costs
  ▷ $1MM+

Source of Funding
  ▬ Government
  ▬ Private Company
  ▬ Foundation/Non-Profit /
    Endowment

Funding Mechanisms
  Fee for Service
  Grant

Impact Measurement Methods
  Qualitative: Surveys
  Quantitative: Key Environmental
    Indicators, Surveys

Mediums
  Experiential: Training
  Physical: Rainwater Harvesting
    System, Training Manuals

City of Rain

Constructing a more sustainable water paradigm for Mexico with rainwater harvesting

According to The Nature Conservancy, Mexico City is the third most water-stressed city in the world. Of the 2.6 million homes in the capital, 36% endure water shortages on a regular basis and a growing number of homes are subject to water supply cuts.

Isla Urbana's goal is to develop rainwater harvesting technology for residents of Mexico City that will allow urban dwellers to capture rainwater on their roofs, clean it, and store it—thus increasing their water provision and resilience to frequent water cuts. Rather than providing a product, Isla Urbana works toward their mission by offering a rainwater harvesting system which complements hardware with education and community partnerships. Their rainwater harvesting systems continue to evolve, based on conversations with the communities that use them in both urban and rural contexts.

Being low cost, durable, locally manufactured, easy-to-use, and capturing quality water are central to the product's development. Equally important is the project's roll-out; Isla Urbana initially focused its efforts on low-income, water-scarce areas of the city and built its rainwater harvesting systems there. Today, Isla Urbana's rainwater technologies and implementation methodologies can also serve multiple sectors of society, helping individuals understand natural water cycles more deeply.

The team's qualitative research revealed that many people living in the low-income southern periphery of the city were suffering from chronic water shortages, yet were experiencing flooding during the rainy season. That same year, Isla Urbana piloted their harvesting system in the home of one of the families who had participated in the original research. Rain was harvested from a

70 square-meter section of roof and passed the water through a simple treatment system into a cistern. The results surpassed expectations by supplying approximately 70,000 liters of water, enough for a family of seven to live entirely from rainwater for eight months. Isla Urbana's harvesting now reliably provides five to eight months of a family's water in urban contexts, and a full 12 months in rural communities.

The organization continues to grow its program by creating strategies that target the best potential users for large-scale government-funded projects and locating high-need areas with adequate rainfall to be captured. The approach includes providing training tools and manuals needed to maintain their systems, growing adoption of the system through informal talks and house visits, and follow-up evaluations that test water levels and quality. Alongside residential-scale installation and training, a "Rain School" program fundraises and installs system and educational programs for public schools throughout the country, leading a group of primary students to celebrate with a cheer: "From north to south, from east to west, we will take care of our water whatever the cost."

Isla Urbana has grown over the past ten years by working with a broad range of partners, including private sector, government, and community stakeholders. To date, they have installed over 20,000 systems, directly benefiting 120,000 people and harvesting more than 900 million liters of rain every year for human consumption. The same quantity of water poured into 500-milliliter bottles and laid end-to-end would circle the earth nearly nine times.

Design for Social Innovation

In 2019, in partnership with Mexico's Ministry of the Environment, Isla Urbana installed 10,000 systems in the Iztapalapa and Xochimilco areas of Mexico City, both with serious water problems. Mexico City's Rainwater Harvesting Program, designed and launched by Isla Urbana and the Ministry of the Environment, is projected to install over 100,000 rainwater systems in the next few years, and Isla Urbana continues to promote and support the expansion of rainwater harvesting throughout Mexico.

> *"My concept of a beautiful day has changed: beautiful days are cloudy days because it means it is going to rain."*

Rafael Parrao, Iztapalapa, Mexico City

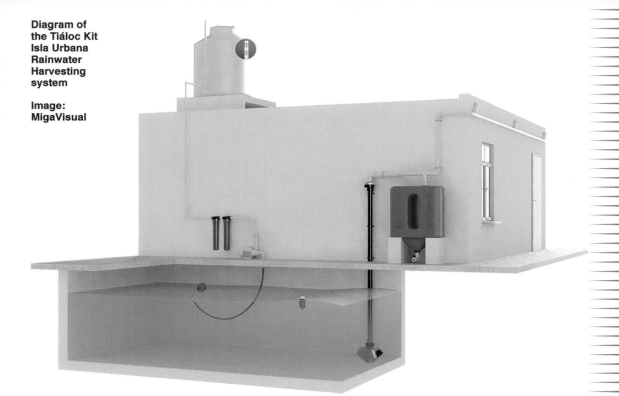

Diagram of the Tiáloc Kit Isla Urbana Rainwater Harvesting system

Image: MigaVisual

Family members pose for a photo with their their newly installed rainwater capture system

Image: Pilar Campos

Design for Social Innovation

Neighbor seen with blue Isla Urbana system in the background

Isla Urbana has also installed their systems in rural areas

Images: Isla Urbana

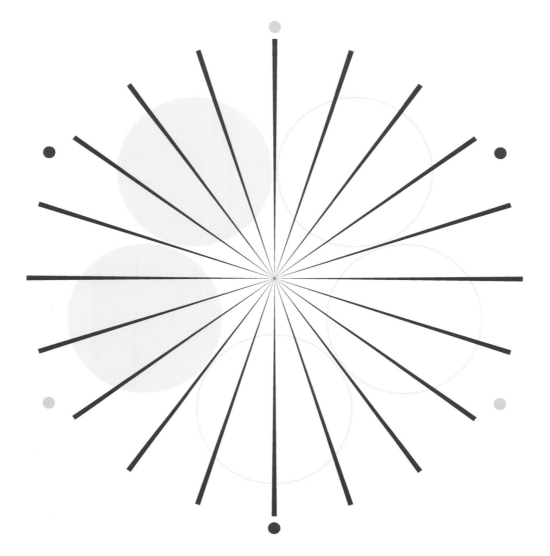

Duration
2013 (nine months)

Location
Singapore

Categories
Health and Wellness

Designer
The Care Lab

Partners
The Lien Foundation
The Ang Chin Moh Foundation
St. Joseph's Home
Assisi Hospice
Dover Park Hospice

Designer Organization Type
● For-Profit

Team Size
● 5–7

Design Quotient
● 81–100%

Project Costs
▭ $100k–$500k

Source of Funding
▬ Foundation/Non-Profit/
Endowment

Funding Mechanisms
Grant

Impact Measurement Methods
Qualitative: Awards Received,
Adoption by the Organization
and/or Other Organizations
Quantitative: Volume of Media
Coverage

Mediums
Digital: E-Book
Physical: Book

Hospitable Hospice

Envisioning a new model of end-of-life care

Reaching the end of life can be challenging in countless ways and includes many decisions and difficult conversations. Hospices provide essential care and comfort for people who are in the process of dying, yet they often have a negative image in society. Patients and families typically undergo sudden transitions between hospital, hospice, and funeral service providers, an experience that can be bureaucratic and isolating.

In 2013, the Singapore government was increasing the capacity of eldercare facilities to meet the needs of an ageing population. The Lien Foundation saw an opportune moment to rethink the experience of end-of-life care, such that new insights and ideas might also inform this national push to boost residential care facilities. They proposed a design-driven approach to creating a future vision for inpatient hospice building and service standards in Singapore. The project built on their commitment to invest in innovative solutions and to convene strategic partnerships that address social and environmental challenges. Along with their partner, the Ang Chin Moh Foundation—a non-profit organization that works to enhance the perception of death and bereavement, they asked The Care Lab—an international network of designers-turned-activists who work to transform the world of care—to work on this project. Together, they aimed to integrate new products, services, spaces, and communication strategies into a new model of hospice care while demonstrating the value of design in a sector that is not accustomed to such innovation approaches. As Mr. Ang Ziqian, the founder of the Ang Chin Moh Foundation, stated: "This is the first time a project like this is taking place in Singapore and in the world. It examines end-of-life care in totality—from the start of getting hospice care, to coping with dying, and to what happens after death. It is important to extend the continuum of care beyond death and to support families in their transition when death arrives."

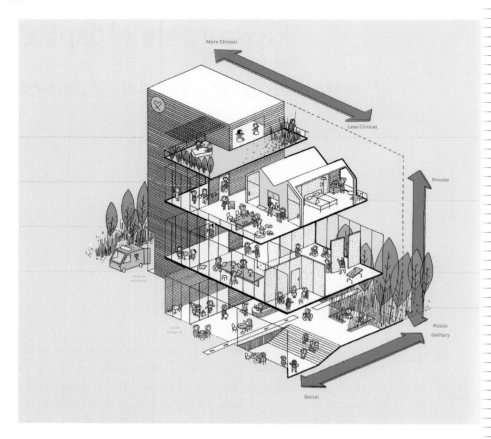

The Care Lab's design approach is empathic and multifaceted, which enabled them to unpack complexity and break the silence around this taboo subject in Singapore, where hospices are still seen as "Death Houses." Their sequence of research activities provided them with an in-depth understanding of end-of-life care: secondary desk research, expert interviews, and on-site ethnographic fieldwork with patients, families, and care teams from three hospices and one funeral service provider. The focus was on the patient journey from the point of referral and entry into an inpatient hospice, including the moment of death and through the family's bereavement process.

A major research constraint was the need to recruit patients and families in a sensitive and timely way, working through trusted relationships that existed with hospice staff, and recruiting patients just prior to fieldwork. They designed research methods to safeguard the privacy, safety and comfort of patients and their loved ones at all times, and had to be flexible enough to work around the unpredictable workflows of staff in hospices where situations can change in an instant. The team had to be intellectually and emotionally prepared for the site visits, in addition to feeling safe, supported, informed and equipped throughout the research process.

The collaboration resulted in Hospitable Hospice, a first-of-its-kind look to redesigning the experience of death and dying. It comprises seven core concepts that are presented in the project e-book and that can be downloaded from The Care Lab website, including: Care Central, a new type of care setting that

brings together palliative care for a community, coordinating hospice home care, day care, ambulatory and in-patient care; Open Hospice, a service platform that ensures Care Central is integrated into the community via a range of outreach services and programs; and Giving Patients a Voice, an idea that is central to the hospice experience, is the uniqueness of each patient's story, situation, and personal choices. Twenty-four Universal Experience Design Principles underpin these ideas and are being used as building blocks to create new end-of-life and long-term care experiences in Singapore, Spain, and beyond.

This new model of hospice care that has since been implemented in two locations, at Assisi Hospice and St. Joseph's Home in Singapore, has inspired eldercare services worldwide. Hospitable Hospice is located within the community rather than the outskirts of the city and has a stronger presence in the community through events, volunteer opportunities, and online interactions. It provides personalized care for patients, and it helps people navigate the end-of-life journey. In Spain, this work has inspired a network of private nursing homes to introduce new protocols and practices and training into its services. An additional eldercare hospital is being built, with its service and space design plans being inspired by the work, and it has informed a local city council in its aging strategy and planning. By co-designing with patients, families, care teams, and experts, they showed that design can be a powerful advocacy tool for social change.

The results of this project continue to challenge conventional thinking on what is possible, feasible, and desirable in today's hospice care landscape.

Due to the difficult nature of the conversations, the team developed ways to coax people into discussion

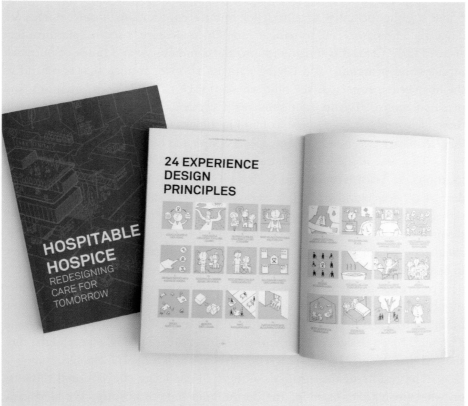

The final report captures 24 design principles to guide the creation of future hospice and care environments

Design for Social Innovation

In Singapore, it was warmly received by leaders in the long-term care sector, where the key insights and concepts of the publication also apply. Each of the three participating hospices involved went on to use the research and design recommendations to inform the design and development of their new facilities and services. While visiting Singapore in 2018, The Care Lab observed that these hospice care teams and the communities they serve continue to benefit from the project: open, innovative, and caring work cultures and practices flourish, while terminally ill patients and their families experience services that are personalized to their needs and provide compassionate care throughout the end-of-life journey.

Beyond Singapore, the project was well received at the Asia-Pacific Hospice Conference. Hospice UK ordered 250 copies of the design handbook to distribute to all hospices in the country, and their CEO, David Praill, considered the book to be "essential reading material for anyone leading a hospice into the future."

"Today's hospices were built for yesterday. Hospices suffer a poor image and are misunderstood. They deserve better understanding from society and fresh insights to meet rising care expectations. The findings not only apply to hospices, they are equally relevant to institutions providing eldercare, like nursing homes. We hope this study will raise aspirations for eldercare facilities and services to be more caring, dignifying and uplifting."

Mr Lee Poh Wah, CEO of the Lien Foundation

Images: The Care Lab

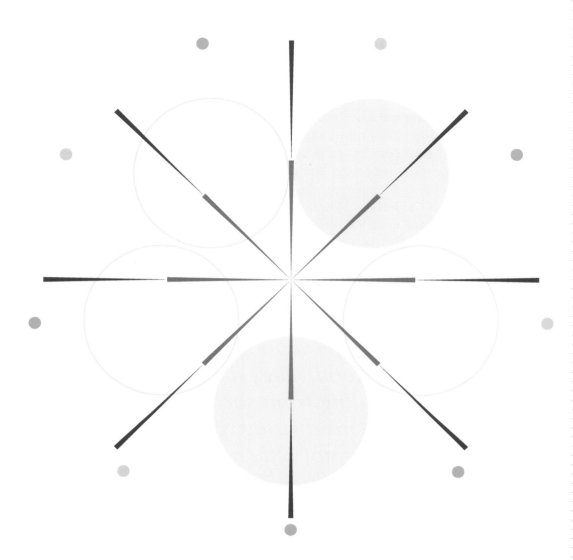

Duration
June 2016–October 2020

Location
France—Paris, Mulhouse,
Dunkerque, Lille, Strasbourg,
Metz, Nantes, Grenoble, and
Rennes, as well as the region
of Occitanie

Categories
Policy

Designer
La 27e Région

Partners
Governments of each city
involved
Bloomberg Philanthropies
I-teams program

Key Contributors
Stéphane Vincent
Nadège Guiraud
Julien Defait
Louise Guillot
Sylvine Bois-Choussy

Designer Organization Type
● Non-Profit

Team Size
● 8–10

Design Quotient
● 0–20%

Project Costs
▷ $1k–$25k

Source of Funding
▬ Government
▬ Foundation/Non-Profit/
Endowment

Funding Mechanisms
Unspecified

Impact Measurement Methods
Qualitative: Stakeholder
Interviews, Assessment
of Change to Internal
Organizational Practices,
Observational Research
Quantitative: Growth in
Products/Service Adoption
or Usage, Participants/
Stakeholders Trained

Mediums
Experiential: Training
Organizational: Innovation Lab

Design for Social Innovation

La Transfo

Creating public innovation labs within French city governments to improve public services

Innovation labs are becoming popular within local governments, but they sometimes struggle to have enough impact on the administration to create lasting change. La Transfo, an experimental program led by La 27e Région ("The 27th Region"), aims to show a more durable model that is grown from within public administrations rather than creating a new team or department. This hypothesis is the basis for the team's work with eight to ten local governments in France who have created or are in the process of creating their own public innovation labs.

La Transfo's goals are threefold. First, for the public sector participants of the program, it provides training where they can learn about and experiment with new innovation skills. Second, for the "hosting" local governments, it's a way to work on real policy challenges by creating proof of concept initiatives. These are doubly useful, because they also create an opportunity for individuals in the training program to gain real-world experience with innovation skills. Third, it's an opportunity for La 27e Région to prototype and test the idea of an innovation lab being driven by existing civil servants—who bring their own contexts, organizations, and challenges.

For each pilot city, La 27e Région recruited a cross-disciplinary team of three professionals (designers, social scientists, cityplanners, etc.) who would spend about two to three days per month for an 18-month stretch. The core works with a group of 20 civil servant "ambassadors" from various departments and fields. Collectively, this forms an ecosystem of collaborators and supports who work together while taking part in practical, hands-on sessions based on real challenges presented by the city.

Réflexe Énergie: tackling energy precariousness in Dunkirk

To date, seven public innovation labs have launched after official approval. Most of the participating local governments have created new innovation positions and are working with public agents who continue to raise awareness and training. Across the seven Transfos, a total of 159 public agents have been actively involved in the program, 1,445 have been engaged with practical cases, and 26 administrative departments have adopted innovation methods that they were exposed to during La Transfo. Across a variety of topics including energy efficiency and temporary urbanism, 29 challenges have been addressed through proof of concept initiatives, resulting in 194 "solutions" (proposals) being developed and 62 that progressed to testing and/or implementation.

When asked about the benefits of La Transfo, a public agent in Dunkirk replied, "At the individual level I gained self-confidence. The collective approach allowed me to value my own skills. With my colleagues, I gained the ability to listen more effectively. With my hierarchy, I learned to ask more critical questions to improve the organization… I believe more than ever in public action!"

The variety of perspectives in this feedback from one individual underscores that there is no "one lab fits all." Through their experience with La Transfo project, La 27e Région believes that, in order for a public innovation lab to really take root within a local government, it needs to rely on available internal resources such as existing staff, stakeholders, elected representatives; that it should be developed iteratively through co-creation; and that training efforts directed toward skill-building and culture change must be customized to the specific context.

> *"La Transfo will help our administration translate our ambition for the metropolitain project into concrete actions."*

Elected representative in Metz

Images: La 27e Région

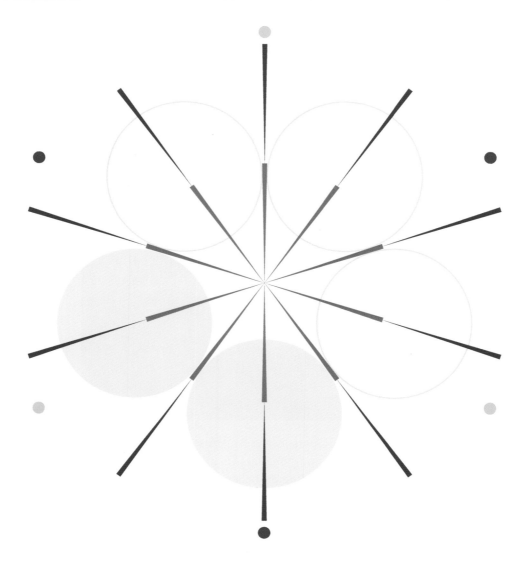

Duration
Two years (year unspecified)

Location
Tumaco, Ipiales, and Madrigal,
Colombia

Categories
Environment
Social Justice
Identity
Policy

Designer
Feeling

Partners
Gobernación de Nariño
Fundación Avina

Designer Organization Type
● For-Profit

Team Size
● 5–7

Design Quotient
● 81–100%

Project Costs
▭ $25k–$100k

Source of Funding
▬ Government
▬ Foundation/Non-Profit/
Endowment

Funding Mechanisms
Unspecified

Impact Measurement Methods
Quantitative: Surveys, Growth
in Product/Service Adoption
or Usage

Mediums
Experiential: Workshop, Event
Physical: Furniture

Design for Social Innovation

Acciones de Paz

Forging *new bonds through the co-creation of open-source furnishings in abandoned public spaces*

Acciones de Paz ("Peace Actions" in English) is a project that sought to revitalize abandoned and underutilized public spaces in Nariño province, Colombia, that suffered armed violence during Colombia's civil conflict. Inspired by the El Campo de Cebada bottom-up commons in Madrid, Spain, Acciones de Paz employed a participatory process to revitalize abandoned public spaces. This included the collective imagining of how public spaces could be used, the design and creation of new outdoor furniture, and inviting citizens to decide the programming and use of those public spaces. While the physical interventions and events are the most visible outcome of this process, the motivation was to promote peace-building through engagement and participation.

Through participatory design, mapping, and other discovery methods, a diverse group of participating individuals including community members, businesspeople, and those from local organizations identified underutilized public spaces and co-created criteria for interventions. Once a public space was selected, new furnishings were developed through opensource collaborations. Designs were considered for their ability to promote peace-building along five key dimensions: political, social, cultural, environmental, and spontaneous playfulness. Spaces were then brought to life through crowdsourced events such as arts and crafts, cinema nights, workshops to generate ideas to improve the city, and so forth.

The team at Feeling, a local design and innovation studio, began by identifying key local stakeholders and establishing a network for the project, and on-site research helped them understand the context and dynamics of abandoned public spaces. From then onwards, Feeling acted as support for a community-led process to air the aspirations and needs of the community itself, for the

community itself. Later in the process, once furniture was designed, it was published in an open-source manual made available on the website of the provincial government. This made it easier for the project to be adapted situationally, as it was implemented in different regions including in the Colombian Pacific coast, near Colombia's border with Ecuador, and in the Cordillera region.

In their final phase of work, the team spent three months measuring impact. The number of visitors to the revitalized parks increased by a minimum of three times their levels. In one case, the new park saw almost nine times as many visitors as before. When asking local women to describe their perceptions of safety in the revitalized park, between 70% and 90% described them as safe, compared to 10% to 30% before.

As explained by a resident of Comunidad Tumaco, where one of the parks is located, the physical interventions ultimately take a backseat to the healing interactions they catalyze. "We never imagined that we would end up sitting with a shared goal here together in this park which had been abandoned. Especially since beforehand we openly were in conflict with one another [laughter]. After we started working together, we realized that we were more similar than different, that we liked the same things, there had just been nothing here before to unify us. Now the park has done that, it has opened the door for us to work together as one family."

"We never imagined that we would end up sitting with a shared goal here together in this park which had been abandoned. Especially since beforehand we openly were in conflict with one another... After we started working together, we realized that we were more similar than different, that we liked the same things, there had just been nothing here before to unify us. Now the park has done that, it has opened the door for us to work together as one family."

Tumaco community member

School children learn about the furniture project

Constructing the agora

Images: Sofia Cabrera

Design for Social Innovation

Aerial view of the installation

Image: Rodolfo Ordoñez

Group prototyping session

Image: Sofia Cabrera

Measuring Impact

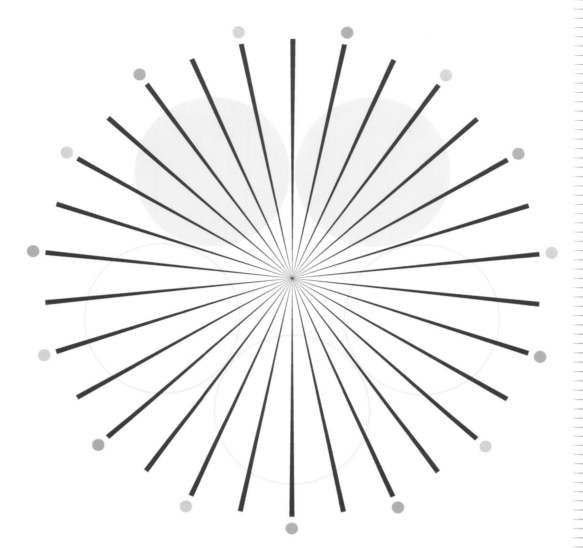

Duration
2016–2017 (initial design work),
2017–present (optimization
and scale are ongoing)

Location
Uganda, Rwanda, Somalia,
Sudan, Columbia, Ecuador,
Kenya, South Africa, USA

Categories
Humanitarian Affairs

Designer
IDEO.org

Partners
Alight (formerly American
Refugee Committee)

Key Contributors
John Collery
Barry Lachapelle
Jennifer Rose
Daniel Feldman
Nathalie Collins

Designer Organization Type
● Non‑Profit

Team Size
● 11–20

Design Quotient
● 41–60%

Project Costs
▷— $500k–$1MM+

Source of Funding
▬— Foundation/Non-Profit/
Endowment

Funding Mechanisms
Fee for Service

Impact Measurement Methods
Quantitative: Response Rate,
Surveys

Mediums
Digital: App, Website
Organizational: Service

Kuja Kuja

Establishing better feedback loops between refugees and humanitarian organizations

There are more than 65 million refugees and displaced people around the world today. Ensuring they get the services they need involves management by international organizations, governments, and communities. Alight (formerly American Refugee Committee), an international non-profit that provides resources and economic opportunities to refugees and internally displaced persons around the world, discovered that humanitarian organizations like their own had stopped thinking of refugees as their primary "customer" and instead became focused on large funders. IDEO.org partnered with Alight to imagine a future where refugees can have a voice in shaping the services provided to them and hold humanitarian organizations accountable.

Kuja Kuja, the output of this partnership, is a public feedback platform that tracks and aggregates "customer satisfaction" responses among refugees in real time. The goal of this service is to create tighter, faster feedback loops between refugees and the organizations that serve them.

The team's goal was to build a foundation of honesty and mutual accountability between Kuja Kuja staff and refugees in Nakivale, a refugee settlement located in the Isingiro District of southwest Uganda. They wanted to create a scalable platform that would surface customer sentiment in meaningful ways, and a customer service model with a set of values and rituals that the Kuja Kuja team could embrace and implement to a high standard. It began with binary data: were the refugees satisfied or unsatisfied?

The IDEO.org design team, made up of three people, worked closely with the Kuja Kuja team in Nakivale and Alight's leadership team in Minneapolis, Minnesota, USA, on all stages of design research, prototyping, optimization and piloting. The team prototyped a number of different services and solution com-

ponents on the journey to designing the platform and branded customer service model.

They initially experimented with an interactive voice response system, mobile text, and even an open mailbox so people could write feedback letters. Through these prototypes the team learned that refugees they were designing for preferred in-person interactions. When the IDEO.org team prototyped mobile texting, they learned that it was not common for people to text, due to costs. Setting up a toll-free number was also cost-prohibitive in Uganda, so the team turned toward a digital platform instead. Beyond questions of access, the team ultimately found that trust was a critical barrier to overcome.

Before demanding information from the refugees, Kuja Kuja needed to help refugees build trust in the system and a familiarity with technology that would inevitably seem foreign. This led the Kuja Kuja team to create a friendly brand that laid a foundation of mutual accountability between Kuja Kuja teams and local residents. Everything—from the name (*Kuja Kuja* means "come, come" in Swahili) to the on-ground-teams (who live in the settlements) to the digital experience—is designed to be as welcoming as possible.

Kuja Kuja staff travel around the refugee settlement with tablets, collecting satisfaction data on an app and suggestions for how to improve service. They aggregate those suggestions into a dashboard that shows aggregate perspectives in real time. The category of water, for example, includes a list of all responses

Design for Social Innovation

Images: Kuja Kuja

collected on that topic. Alight staff—both locally and at the global headquarters in Minneapolis—can keep track of issues and prioritize action.

Since it launched, the Kuja Kuja customer service team has sought feedback from more than 1 million people residing in camps. As Alight describes the objective and ultimate impact of this platform, "Understanding our customer more deeply will allow us to increase the value and impact that its services currently deliver and to make better decisions about new services to design."

Kuja Kuja's platform is entirely public, allowing anyone to see that, for instance, the Kiziba Camp in western Rwanda is reporting an 80% satisfaction rating, up a little from prior weeks, and that water is a persistent theme from week to week. By making this data public, the team intends to enable refugees to hold humanitarian organizations accountable for the quality of the services they provide.

> *"What we discovered was that we can typically get a 20% improvement in customer satisfaction over a three-month period with no additional budget and no additional training."*
>
> Daniel Wordsworth, CEO of Alight

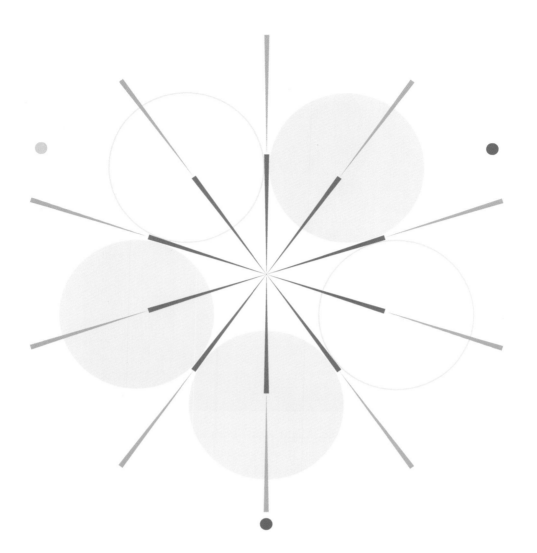

Duration
2012–present

Location
Kingston, Ontario, Canada

Categories
Education

Designer
Limestone District School Board

Partners
City of Kingston

Designer Organization Type
● Government

Team Size
● 2–4

Design Quotient
● 81–100%

Project Costs
▷ $25k–$100k

Source of Funding
━ Government
━ Self-Funded

Funding Mechanisms
Self-Funded

Impact Measurement Methods
Quantitative: Growth in Product/
Service Adoption or Usage

Mediums
Experiential: Training
Physical: Book
Organizational: Service

Throwing Car Culture
Under the Bus

Inspiring and empowering youth to choose public transit

Kingston, Ontario, is a low-density city of 136,000 people located where the St. Lawrence River meets the Great Lakes. One-third (33%) of greenhouse gas emissions in Kingston come from transportation despite a well-functioning transit system. While other efforts have focused on reducing the number of working adults who drive to and from work, Dan Hendry, employee of the local school board and self-educated designer, realized that high school students were not taking advantage of the free city bus passes to which they are entitled.

The idea was good in principle, but Hendry noticed that in practice there were some important barriers. Many students lacked knowledge about the transit system, were unsure where or how to pick up the free passes, or simply did not have enough experience with transit to understand and value it as a source of mobility freedom. As a result, Hendry identified that students were over-reliant on passenger vehicles, leading to a larger carbon footprint for the city.

On their own, bus passes could increase access to transit, but more ingrained social challenges prevented students from taking advantage of that access. Through interviews with principals, teachers, and students, in addition to bus usage data, insights about how to best reach the students began to emerge. Many teachers and parents did not use the bus themselves, so they were not in a great position to be role models for students. Instead, the school board and local transit authority teamed up to create an "orientation program" for ninth graders that focused on encouraging students to master the skills of transit with real-life experiences (and their free bus pass), which, in turn, helps students gain independence and confidence. The insights that led to this program, and the development of the program itself, are the result of the team's participatory, design-led process.

Session leaders personalize transit ridership by sharing examples from their own lives when they have been nervous or embarrassed about lack of knowledge, which in turn creates a space of open discussion for students who want to learn more about the ins and outs of bus ridership. Through this and other discussions, the intent of the sessions is to destigmatize transit as well as to create an opportunity to communicate the many benefits of bus riding across social, economic, health, and environmental dimensions.

In 2012, ninth graders were taking about 34,738 rides on public transit annually; since 2016, yearly rides on public transit by nine to twelfth graders in Kingston has risen to between 500,000 and 600,000. A student from the University of Waterloo, Veronica Sullivan, studied the program for her master's thesis and found that twelfth-grade students, on average, use the transit pass three times more frequently than ninth-grade students, indicating that, as students become older and gain more experience with transit, they become more frequent transit users. In feedback to Hendry and the project team, students report increased confidence in taking independent trips to and from work, volunteering positions, extracurricular opportunities, as well as sports and recreation programs. Direct student feedback provides insights into how the orientation sessions can be made more effective, as well as giving the project team a way to confirm that the qualitative outcomes, such as increased confidence about using transit, are as intended.

The program has since expanded to include a Teacher Field Trip Pass that enables teachers to take their K–12 students to libraries, parks, museums, and

WELCOME STUDENTS!

more. Additionally, over 40 communities across Canada have expressed interest in replicating this program, which led Hendry and his team to create a guidebook for the Federation of Canadian Municipalities to distribute in English and French.

Hendry suggests that "this replicable service provides a meaningful alternative mode of transportation for youth, and can be applied to other mid-sized North American municipalities in the future. They don't require more money or technology. Instead, they require strong partnership with school boards and students."

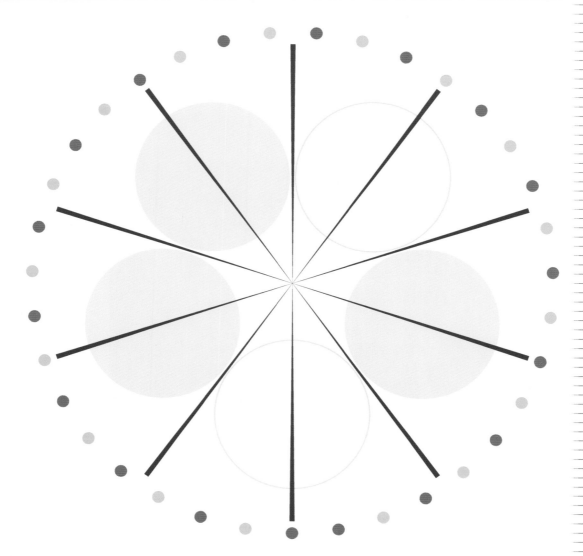

Duration
2017–2019

Location
Global

Categories
Humanitarian Affairs

Designer
International Federation of Red
Cross and Red Crescent
Societies

Partners
Carnegie Mellon University
Situation Lab
Changeist
Edge DNA
Newcastle University Open Lab
Red Cross Climate Centre
Superflux

Key Contributors
Shaun Hazeldine
Aarathi Krishnan
Carlos Alvarez de la Vega
John Sweeney
Stuart Candy (advisor)
Sohail Inayatullah (advisor)
Claudia Juech (advisor)

Designer Organization Type
● Civil Society

Team Size
● 21–49

Design Quotient
● Unspecified

Project Costs
▷ $25k–$100k

Source of Funding
▬ Foundation/Non-Profit/
Endowment

Funding Mechanisms
Grant

Impact Measurement Methods
Qualitative: Adoption by the
Organization and/or Other
Organizations

Mediums
Digital: Website, Social Media
Communications, App
Physical: Game
Spatial: Exhibition

Design for Social Innovation

The Future is Now

Futuring to transform the world's largest humanitarian network

Founded in 1919, the International Federation of Red Cross and Red Crescent Societies ("IFRC" or "the Federation") is the world's largest humanitarian network, with some 12 million volunteers, 450,000 staff, and 160,000 branches across 191 countries. It works to meet the needs and improve the lives of vulnerable people before, during, and after disasters, health emergencies, and other crises.

Recognizing the fast-changing context of humanitarian aid, in 2016 the Federation began exploring the possibility of integrating a formal institutional foresight capacity, to think broadly about how the organization may need to change in order to continue fulfilling its mission in the coming decade. A global Foresight Advisory Board was convened, and an in-house Foresight and Futures team formed.

With partners both internal and external, the team staged an exhibition called "The Future Is Now" at the IFRC General Assembly, held in late 2017 in Antalya, Turkey, and attended by 1,000 senior leaders from around the world. Delegates at these biennial strategic gatherings typically receive thousands of pages of documents to read in advance. In an effort to move beyond traditional written analysis and statistics, "The Future Is Now" revolved around "experiential futures," which is a term used to describe the design and deployment of media, artifacts, and encounters that bring possible futures to life in the present.

Examples from the exhibition included an interactive installation on air pollution, simulating a scenario for Mumbai's air quality in 2030; a special IFRC edition of "The Thing from the Future," an imagination game played in the corridors of the event to prompt exploration of various alternative futures for humanitarian aid; a design fiction hypothesizing the use of artificial intelligence to predict disasters and deploy automatic responses; and a range of "guerrilla" artifacts left

in meeting spaces for attendees to discover, such as business cards for future jobs that might someday exist within the organization itself.

This range of experiential scenarios, grounded in key trends and emerging issues identified during prior research, extended opportunities for strategic conversation to a highly diverse, global cohort of leaders and decision makers. The intention was to help anticipate potential challenges, provoke new ideas, and create a long-term progressive agenda that could lead to system-wide innovation throughout the network.

Following this initiative, the General Assembly, the highest decision-making body of the Federation, commissioned a strategy that for the first time ever would utilize a foresight process, and the Secretary General tasked the Foresight and Futures team with leading global consultation and designing the strategy. A large-scale horizon scanning effort ensued, involving leaders, staff, and volunteers worldwide, through workshops, interviews, and other participation mechanisms. Novel approaches to engagement included a digital game called "WhatFutures," hosted entirely on WhatsApp, and played by more than 4,000 people from 80 countries.

This work gradually yielded a systematic assessment of the possibilities that stakeholders were excited or concerned about, how humanitarian vulnerabilities could look in the coming decade, and what kind of organization would be best poised to navigate them. Over 10,000 people participated in the futures

consultations, and more than 120,000 visited the "Future Red Cross Red Crescent" online platform.

At the next General Assembly in 2019, as the Federation celebrated its centenary, a foresight-informed global strategy was unanimously adopted. The internal team has since expanded, and IFRC formed the Solferino Academy to help disseminate and integrate futures and foresight methods across the world. Numerous national societies have now begun using them in their own strategies and work. In the words of the IFRC's Strategy 2030, "We recognize that new approaches are needed to drive global change. We have a responsibility to use our reach and our resources effectively. To do this we must listen, think and act differently, and be open to learning and adapting along the way."[1]

1   International Federation of Red Cross and Red Crescent Societies, "Strategy 2030: A Platform for Change Global Reach, Local Action," 2018, https://future-rcrc.com/wp-content/uploads/2020/01/S2030-EN.pdf.

Positioning for Growth

Gabriella Gómez-Mont, Indy Johar, and Panthea Lee, with Andrew Shea

If you live in the Japanese city of Ise, you might take part in the ritual to rebuild the Ise Grand Shrine every 20 years. These sacred Shinto wood structures are taken apart and reconstructed in the style common for traditional grain warehouses to preserve Japan's oldest architectural custom. The ritual symbolizes death and renewal and invites community members to participate in ceremonies that strengthen their connection to the shrine. It also provides an opportunity to consider how the world has changed since the tradition started 1,300 years ago. In the shifting field of design for social innovation, how can this example motivate us to re-examine the mechanics of how we work? We have no way to disassemble and rebuild an area of design that has many ways of being practiced, but this roundtable serves as an opportunity to reflect on some of the field's general trajectories and consider how to position it for growth.

The increasing number of new publications, studios, and projects that identify with design for social innovation shows that it has grown significantly in the past 20 years. Recognizable design outputs extend beyond objects, textiles, visuals, and shelters to regularly include invisible services and strategies, among others. This shows the scale that many designers are now working on, and the shift from being service providers to facilitating and making decisions at high levels. But what has driven these changes? If design has evolved in response to the needs of humanity, can it help to steer its development?

In this roundtable, three leading practitioners take stock of the building blocks of design for social innovation: the themes that designers focus on, the actors and collaborations that make it tick, the scales being worked at, and structural elements to support it. Panthea Lee, Gabriella Gómez-Mont, and Indy Johar draw on their wealth of experiences and their knowledge of projects like those in this book—projects that involve navigating complexities by designing responsive processes, those that operate at grassroots levels in addition to organizational and governmental scales, projects that require multi-stakeholder engagement and others that a single designer initiated, those that have predictable bottlenecks and others that move at breakneck speeds to meet urgent needs.

Their insights expose some of the stresses on the field and the need to repair sagging beams, a leaky roof, and holes in the foundation. Do growing pains in the field show that it has been defined too narrowly? Designers are now coming to terms with the colonial legacies of the design practice itself, and are working to see the expertise that sits within local communities. How can we elevate voices that have been marginalized and equitably collaborate with local partners and people? As design diffuses and becomes a core capability for more collaborators, what role will designers play on those teams? How can designers become agile and responsive to the politics and power dynamics embedded in their projects? How do we position our practice towards creating new institutions, platforms, and systems that make the world we want to see? This conversation helps cast our sights towards opportunities that pave pathways for the field to grow over the next 20 years and beyond.

Panthea Lee

I'm the co-founder and executive director of Reboot. My work is usually at the intersection of social justice and participatory democracy, and I often have the honour of covening and supporting diverse, unlikely coalitions of actors—including activists, artists, policy makers, researchers—to center community voices in policy debates and other efforts to reimagine our world. We are a global team, with offices in the US and Nigeria, working in about 30 countries around the world.

Gabriella Gómez-Mont

I'm in the process of launching Experimentalista, a studio specializing in cities, public imagination and system change. We shape-shift to accommodate high-level, transdisciplinary collaborations across the world. Formerly, I was chief creative officer for Mexico City and founder of Laboratorio para la Ciudad, the experimental arm and creative think tank of the Mexico City government that reported to the mayor.

Indy Johar

I am a co-founder of Project 00 and Dark Matter Labs and a senior innovation associate at the Young Foundation. I'm interested in redesigning the bureaucratic and institutional infrastructure of our cities, regions, and towns, to be more democratic and allow for distributed governance.

Design for Social Innovation

This roundtable discussion took place in May 2020 and was edited for clarity and length

Andrew: What do you think about the scale that designers are currently working and where you think they should be focusing their efforts? Can you start us off, Panthea, since you had a case study in the book?

Panthea: From what I've seen, designers working in the social design field, broadly defined, tend to work on individual products, services, and social enterprises that often seem like they are trying to work outside of big institutions and outside of government. They are trying to find creative ways around the system, so to speak.

I suspect this is a result of being disillusioned with the government. People have been long told that government is something they can't possibly understand, policy making is too complicated, and governance is really difficult. As a result, many choose to disengage from established systems and work outside it. This means, however, that the scale tends to be much smaller. But this is often brushed aside, because there is an echo chamber effect which celebrates solutions that operate outside public or institutional infrastructure. Only later in the process, when questions of impact arise, do many designers then think about how to institutionalize and scale the work.

There's a lot of good work to be done with big institutions from the beginning, whether it is on individual initiatives, or programs, or in other ways. If big institutions are not working for us, how do we change that? And how do we take our tools, our knowledge, our understanding of systems and break them apart, to identify the specific problems or leverage points? Then, how do we actually design, co-create, and build the sort of institutions and systems that we want, that then can be the platforms and vehicles for the worlds we want to create?

Gabriella: I'm starting a new organization and exploring these questions all over again, since now I am working internationally. Until a year ago, I was heading Laboratorio para la Ciudad, which was the experimental arm and creative think tank for the Mexico City government. Working in the context of a megalopolis requires a continuous conversation around scale. How to travel the scales of a city was always a part of our existential crisis, if you will, because Mexico City is a 21-million-people metropolitan area, 9.5 million in the city proper. Besides being a gargantuan city, one of the biggest in the world, it's also a city made up of many cities: head three subway stops down from anywhere and you can arrive in a different world. I strongly believe diversity is one of the biggest assets of our delirious city— so much becomes possible in the combination and recombination of all resources and elements. But diversity can easily become divisive, especially in societies with great social inequalities. This is one of the big hurdles in terms of trying to design at scale, at the scale of a megalopolis. Many times the way we think of scale—and how we seek to implement it, scalability—is tied to processes of efficiency and productivity more akin to industrial capitalism than to urban practices and social processes. So the way that we were able to enter questions about scale and scaling had to be multifold. Notions of spatial justice, for example, became core in shaping our work and also our recommendations to other areas of government.

At times we would create experimental prototypes and projects to inspire the administration, like-minded people, or even other cities. And that was our scale. A specific and punctual project in a specific location that could help people experience the city in other ways, and hence create the momentum that is needed to take an idea forward—acupunctural interventions or a provocation of sorts to upend our notion of what we think possible and what is not, to reconfigure public imagination. Other times, we actually needed to work with a city as a whole, like when we crowdsourced the Mexico City Constitution. The Constitution should address all of us, but how to actually add multiple voices and perspectives without an overly cacophonic effect? How to create nuanced participatory scaffolding that takes into account the diversity of the society, the wide range of interests, expertise, and experiences, the natural tensions of a democracy? And how, as the Zapatistas would say, to design a world in which many worlds can coexist?

"We need to move into dynamic and creative governance. People not only electing their representatives, not only deliberating and deciding together, but at times even having an active hand in literally helping recreate the city around them."

We also take for granted that everybody wants to participate in the same way. But that's not always true. Some people want to meet for long meetings over months—like the passionate bike and pedestrian activists that we worked with over many years. Others are happy to give you 15 minutes but not more. Some people complain that there are not more ways to join forces for a common cause. Others talk of civic fatigue. I'm interested in the question of how to give a voice and space for multiple types of participations, to rethink the social-structuring of democratic practices, the civic infrastructure that is needed, not only in terms of a specific scale but also

Design for Social Innovation

to address the shifting relationships between several scales. So I think that we need to start moving beyond limited forms of representational democracy, towards deliberate democracy and then past it, too: we need to move into dynamic and creative governance. People not only electing their representatives, not only deliberating and deciding together, but at times even having an active hand in literally helping recreate the city around them. The scale that is the sum of all of us, in all our diversity.

So we need to stop thinking of participation as a simple single thing, but rather create nuanced and multi-level participatory scaffolding that takes into account very different intensities of participation, very different societies, very different access... because sometimes you can go digital, yes, for example, but what happens in a place like Mexico City where you have a digital divide?

I don't think there is a single solution, but the question of scale always needs to be present in whatever we're thinking about that has any type of social component. We should not be afraid of advancing into complexity, as Panthea was saying. Complexity has to be addressed with participatory initiatives or a response that is adequate for dealing with that complexity, instead of watering it all down and becoming simplistic or linear, as in "the five steps of design thinking to solve anything": from a faucet to a city. This approach makes me suspect.

And that might actually be an important caveat for this conversation. The Lab never thought of itself as a design-fronted lab. We were transdisciplinary in nature. There were a couple of designers on the team, but they were outnumbered by a variety of other people—half my team came from urban and political sciences, the other half came from the humanities; urban geographers working with philosophers, artists with lawyers, for example. So we never really thought of the Lab as a design space per se but rather a transdisciplinary space that looked for urban and social transformation, that gathered diverse communities around common questions, where design was just one of our tools.

> **Indy:** I'd like to start by highlighting the COVID-19 situation so we can point out the underlying weaknesses in the system that it surfaces. About 40 million people have been made unemployed in the United States. In 11% of households, both partners are out of work. We're going to see one of the largest global depressions that we've ever seen, both economically and socially. For example, domestic violence and suicide rates are rising. So I would say that the field of design is evolving because of the nature and speed of changes taking place in the world.

Look at the scale of what's been done globally by governments. Spain is trying to create universal income. You're seeing Bangladesh give about 40% of their people a stipend or basic wage using digital wallets, which were set up in under a week. Togo issued 4 million digital wallets and got money out to citizens in under a week. We've seen extraordinary innovation around the world at a social and economic scale. For all the experiments and small-scale innovations we're involved in, governments have done [a lot] in under two weeks. And one of the things it started to show me is that we're fighting at the wrong scale and the wrong point in the system. The underlying issues weren't necessarily the services, or the products, or the social goods. They were much more structural issues at play. So the kind of hypothesis I want to offer is that what we see happening in our increasingly fragile and vulnerable world is a function of four deep structural issues: our relationship with nature, which is fundamentally that of enslavement; our relationship with each other, which is also a thesis of control; our [abusive] relationship with things, which is a thesis of ownership and not stewardship; and our relationship with the future. I would argue the role of the field is about redefining those relationships and building a movement to redefine those relationships. Some of those things are going to span the everyday cultural experience and some of those are going to span the future of public budgeting. So, from my perspective, the issue is not the scale, but it's actually understanding the kind of transition points in the system and being able to organize the politics of change or design the politics of change to manifest.

Gabriella: I completely agree with Indy. Bringing the political dimension into the discussion is incredibly important. Politics as a return to first principles: how do we want to live together, keep healthy together, play together? And so on. It's tempting to avoid these conversations because they're messy and full of tensions: we're not necessarily in full agreement of what those futures could actually entail. It feels easier to create an app or make a specific service more efficient. But the real questions must go beyond any specific service or technology or innovation. Only when we have first waded through the messiness of the human heart and both the possibilities and perils of coexistence can we then go on to create hybrid and dynamic governance models that intertwine with each other, exponentially, that in turn form other assemblages. Only with a common vision and a lens of equity and justice can we truly unleash the creative and collective capacities of a society, with very different intervention points at different scales, at different speeds, and with the right collaborators.

And, because it's an incredibly dynamic space, I also think that there are new governance structures that need to be created to help orchestrate

Design for Social Innovation

many people coming into and out of this overarching conversation. To Indy's point about COVID-19, yes, we're seeing governments moving at incredible speeds. So acting quickly is part of the equation. I think that everyone who professes the importance of experimentation and of agile processes in government are, on one hand, thrilled with these very quick changes. At the same time, they are warranted worries about this same velocity: because we're also going to become path-dependent for many years to come, in terms of the things that we're putting into place right now, the precedents we are creating. How will we do COVID tracking and navigate the tension between privacy and health concerns? How will we realign global chain supplies? What economic incentives will be given, for what, and to who? How will different political systems the world over accelerate or hinder social justice and environmental issues face-to-face with this global (and legal) grand state of exception?

We do have an opportunity to rearticulate many of the foundations and underlying infrastructures, but I also believe that if we are to travel swiftly in the right direction we cannot skip the political question: who do we want to be, together? That big, messy, question of "us" is the elephant in the room.

> **Panthea:** I appreciate Indy and Gabriella's comments and agree that we need to work on overlapping structural inequities and with Indy's assessment of the four relationships that we need to re-examine. I've been looking for those political and social windows of opportunity to tangibly make that happen. How do we cultivate the ability to identify these political windows, because they can be fleeting and are usually not obvious to the design and innovation crowd, and then mobilize around them?
>
> We work a lot in spaces of contested politics, where exploring tensions around our deepest values, getting into serious debates, and finding common ground is incredibly important. I see now in various spaces I work in that people are quick to embrace co-creation or co-design, but these terms are often misunderstood as throwing a bunch of people into a room and hoping for magic, which doesn't just happen naturally. We need to sequence political debates and structure collaborations very carefully if we want to make something real and lasting. We need to identify the different actors that should be part of that process and know what questions to ask, who to ask, and at which points to ask. To your point, Gabriella, solutions are not going to come from any one sector, organization, discipline, or culture.

So how do we empower artists and activists to challenge structural injustices and to articulate a vision for our future, rather than just protesting on the fringes? After articulating a vision of a radically different future, how do we bring in civic organizations, think tanks, researchers to help us understand and navigate the paths to getting there—using methods that corporate lobbyists might? Because the lobbyists understand the legislative and fiscal mechanisms, the bureaucratic and boring details, the administrative procurement and HR mechanisms to actually make solutions real. We do a great job of talking about what needs to change, but a poor job of articulating how we get our designs, our ideas, our initiatives adopted by institutions with power and resources.

Andrew: What kind of capacities do you think designers will need as they contribute to the growth in this field? Does this require a different kind of designer or a different kind of collaboration?

> **Gabriella:** Like Panthea, I also become uneasy by anchoring what we do within a specific discipline because, as they say, when you're a hammer, everything looks like a nail.
>
> First, my intuition is that we cannot anchor these types of practices to a specific field. That's why I'm quite intrigued in a transdisciplinary practice that facilitates collaboration between many spaces and fields, all while creating its own in-between territory—as opposed to a multidisciplinary practice, where each field works within its own language and with its own tools. I think this is important because I believe that the world needs what I've been calling emerging knowledge structures—beyond existing knowledge—when dealing with new scenarios that entail hyper-dynamic realities. In the example of crowdsourcing the Mexico City Constitution, who's the expert that you call in to actually help solve that? Is it a designer? Is it an anthropologist? A lawyer?
>
> Who do you get around the table when there's no specific expert necessarily, but rather one needs to figure out a way forward by working amongst the gaps between several disciplines, individuals, organizations. Structuring teams around this should be as dynamic as the realities that they're trying to understand. And, as Panthea said, sometimes different people come in and out at different times. How do you gather communities around questions, but also how do you then go forward and make reality malleable? Those two caveats have been very important in the way that we try to structure our own work. Sometimes when we were using notions of spatial justice to think about the urban commons, you need somebody that knows

Design for Social Innovation

GIS. Can a designer be helpful? Yes. But many times it depends on the individual skills. There are as many types of designers as there are brains. Design is a discipline that has tried to bring in a crazy amount of incredibly different profiles.

The second assumption, and perhaps provocation, about new skill sets focuses on the complexity, intersectionality, and the interdependence of so many of these questions that we're trying to address. You need people that not only know how to work in transdisciplinary teams, but who can wear different hats and actually swerve from thinking like a designer to thinking like an anthropologist, for example. Because we need to tailor-make solutions to what we're trying to solve instead of thinking that there's a five-step design process or formula that we can throw anything into. Those skill sets include the ability to create frameworks for those specific realities. We should start thinking more about the knowledge that emerges between individuals and disciplines and not necessarily from a single discipline and its constructs.

Andrew: Indy, you work in a number of different kinds of collaborations and entities. How do you build teams and what kind of capacities do you think will be needed as this field grows?

Indy: I wholeheartedly agree with Gabriella. I am nervous of the label of "designer," which tends to create a boundary. I think of design as a foundational capability rather than a specialization. Some of the best entrepreneurs are designers who create space across multiple intersections. It's their ability to connect these different sorts of flows and to arrange them in particular forms that creates value. These activities are not restricted to an architect, a designer, or the field of design.

There's a fantastically smart community of people who explore how the future can be made rather than just the field. Maybe we should be talking about a mission community—a community with a public mission—rather than a community defined by practice. And, rather than defining ourselves through what I would call practice models, maybe we should try to define ourselves more functionally through our missions. We would have deeper conversations as a result.

I'd also like to go back to where the opportunities are, since we're finding that there are certain conversations that have never been possible before. Like the re-examination of property rights. We're working with indigenous communities in Canada right now to re-imagine the relationship to the land and treaties of land. Whether this is going to be a big enough movement that leads to structural change is a different question but, from where I'm sitting, those sort of conversations are happening right at the top and there's a greater appetite for those structural questions than there's ever been.

Panthea: Gabriella's point about designers being as dynamic and tailor-made as the realities that we're in and designing for is such an elegant summation of what we should be looking for.

When assembling a team for any undertaking, ask yourself: do you have curious people, who draw from different disciplines, who are humble enough to know what they don't know, who are collaborative, and who can weave together different approaches and communities? It's important for anyone working on social transformation to be awake to the world, to understand their position within it, and to be deeply attuned to the politics of any situation that they are brought into.

Ask yourself: who's commissioning you? It's always important to know why any actor is asking for what they want and who gets to benefit from the result—and who could suffer. I think most designers need to have a more considered point of view on what work they will undertake, what they won't, and why.

"[Facilitation] doesn't have to be neutral. Being neutral leads to the lowest common denominator outcome that has a little bit of what everyone wants."

My own work has shifted away from being the designer and towards being more of a facilitator who brings different folks together and guides them as they design, debate, and have difficult conversations. I despised the "designer as hero" narrative that early design media seemed to promote, but I also resisted the label of facilitator for a long time because the ask always seemed to be, "Oh, we need a neutral facilitator." How can we bring in a neutral facilitator? Facilitation isn't neutral! Done well, it's about building connections, holding ground, and driving debates that are values-driven but not biased, since the outcomes need to be respected and seen as fair by diverse stakeholders that might include activists, governments, communities, business groups. But it doesn't have to be neutral. Being neutral leads to the lowest common denominator outcome that has a little bit of what everyone wants. It's a negotiated, compromised consensus view, and those

Design for Social Innovation

are never inspiring nor transformative. Designers know the adage "When you design for everyone, you design for no one" and facilitation work could definitely use more of that perspective.

In terms of a skill set, being able to enable, support, facilitate, and get out of the way, which requires being aware of your own position and privilege, and knowing how to adjust to different actors. It requires knowing how to remain humble and flexible while pushing forward with the intention. And how to see everyone's needs, and priorities, and who they are and hold space for that throughout a process.

> **Andrew:** One focal point of our discussion around the growth of this field has to do with sustaining and growing the work financially. We're interested in learning about models you think can help designers continue working on projects like those we associate with design for social innovation, in addition to future areas of the discipline that might emerge.

Panthea: I'm conflicted about this. We have a couple different models to support the way we work currently. The most prominent in our organization is fee for service, but we also have our own programming that is often funded through private foundations. Then we do pro bono work that we fund ourselves.

We do a fair amount of work with international agencies, governments, and other big institutions. We often see ourselves [working] with institutions that may be more conservative on their social or political positions, but that give us the mandate, the resources, the opportunity to create and scale the change that we seek.

From an impact perspective, it's a mix. Sometimes, this work is less satisfying, because the type of change that we want to see is generally more radical and more structural than institutions are willing to go. We always champion bringing in the voices of civil society and of historically oppressed communities. This is not always a popular view with big institutions, and the processes and solutions they are willing to pay for tend to be more incremental, marginal, narrow, and slow. These are limitations to project-based funding through big institutions or governments who define the scope of imagination. They define the agenda and what the solutions can be, which sometimes forces us to draw a line.

Some of our more experimental work has been funded through private foundations that are active in civic innovation and deliberative democracy. Those give us freedom to experiment. The criticisms of private philanthropy are well known and I have a fair bit of angst as I try to reckon with the hypocrisy: that my work around participatory democracy is funded by those that have accumulated wealth at great societal cost, or that circumvent putting their fair share of money into the pot that we all use to fund public and civic infrastructure. Citizen participation is a big part of what we do, which is often funded by foundations who champion the benefits of people engaging in their democracy to, for example, determine how public funds should be allocated via participatory budgeting efforts. But also, maybe people just want more money in the public coffers so we can pay for good health care and good schools, and so citizens don't have to spend their nights and weekends participating in countless civic efforts for our basic demands to be met.

> **Gabriella:** Funding sources have not budged all that much. Foundations, governments, private companies, private philanthropy, but there is not much else, which I guess is problematic. Crowdsourcing would definitely be one of those switches over the last ten years, especially when it's cause-driven or project-driven. A group of artists recently raised 6 million pesos, which is quite a large amount, for a hospital that did not have proper equipment for COVID.

> This topic is one of the growing pains of the design field. It seems that design is in crisis mode of having defined itself in a constrained way. How do you expand the public's understanding of these new forms of design, beyond graphic design and industrial design, for example. We still need to work with clients to help them understand what newer forms of design mean, like transition design or even service design. It may not be clear to the public what these designers do.

> The Lab offered up a quirky space for these kinds of collaborations. When the Lab folded, some members went directly into the government, some of them started new organizations, and many also went back into academia.

> So perhaps one of the questions, if not an answer or a solution to what was posed, is how do we start thinking about funds for social R&D? And obviously this includes design. But how do the more experimental practices get funded? And who are the organizations that require less strings attached for these projects, or prioritize key performance indicators (KPIs), for example, that many times can be useful, but could cause people and organizations to do things exactly as everything else has been done and doesn't leave space for exploration?

Andrew: How familiar are funders with newer areas of design?

Gabriella: Not at all in Mexico, because they haven't even been incorporated into academia or universities. I know quite a few universities in the US and in Europe already have masters, and Ph.D.s, that look at designs in very different angles. But we haven't even gotten to that space in Mexico yet. So we're still very much in that other more traditional way of thinking about the design field. So that makes it harder to actually create a deeper pedagogy both within the practitioners as well as with the organizations that they could be working with now.

Panthea: I agree. A lot of folks are trained the way that they're trained and then they just get into that pattern of seeing the world. The folks that designers are pitching to need that process translated into a recognizable language, whether it's grounded in design or, ideally, within a broader framework.

And, to Gabriella's point around pots of money for social R&D, I'd be curious to explore that question. Given COVID, there has been some more conversation about this recently in the international development space. Because there's two dominant types of foreign aid, broadly speaking: one allocated for global public goods, like vaccines, and assets outcomes that all of us can benefit from; or bilateral aid, which is country-to-country. While there are studies that show throwing money into a big pot for global public goods is a net positive for all, the countries who might consider putting money into the pot may believe they'd see greater immediate return from investing in bilateral aid instead—for example, the aid can be tied to requests around trade policies, migration policies, or any number of issues that have short-term political consequences.

But there is a huge imbalance between what countries get out of extractive or otherwise damaging bilateral relationships, and what they invest in global public goods. Many Western countries routinely support dictators around the world, and their economies benefit from autocrats that repress democracy. Then they will also spend a fraction of that money to support civil society fighting the closing of civic space that these countries have contributed to. They could just not sell weapons to the dictators that are suppressing human rights defenders around the world.

So I guess what I'm trying to say is: we live in a broken, hyper-capitalist society and almost all money is kind of dirty somehow. So the question is how to both understand the inherent challenges and contradictions of where most funding comes from, and how that can feed into the hypocrisies of the systems you work within as you do the work?

Andrew: Indy, how do you look to support the work you do and how would you respond to this question?

Indy: We don't operate in consultancy relationships with clients. What we try to do is to make mission relationships. So the relationship is to the mission, and people bring different resources to the table in order to make that mission manifest.

This means that the business model of design is less and less priced on the client/agency sort of relationship model, but on a kind of thesis of what is public good and your ability to orchestrate and bring together the agents of different resources that are required to work on it. Mission contracting is increasing in the way we do work, it also stops the designer from becoming passively subservient to the capital owner, and it creates a different model of alignment and accountability, which I think is critical. So the issue is not just business models; it's actually as much about the relationship structures and redefining power structures. That's thesis one.

Thesis two is that it's critical for these missions to have different models of financing. We set up institutions so the design of what we're building itself can have an exploratory business model. We do a lot of work around the business model or the value model of civic goods.

We create new value models that recognize how civic goods create huge amounts of spillover effects. A community garden generates massive amounts of positive social value, reduces liabilities for states or hospitals and other risk-holders, it produces huge amounts of cultural benefits, and it can have resilience benefits. These benefits sit on the balance sheet for people and organizations, and a beautiful park will put significant money on the houses that surround that park. We did some work around the Highline, in New York City, which was looking at how the elevated park generated huge amounts of private land value. In about ten months, the land value increase would've enabled you to pay for the entire Highline.

The problem has been that the value generated by the tangible assets as well as the intangible civic assets is never looked at. For example, how much is the health or the mishealth of a nation worth? The US economy is about to demonstrate this during the pandemic, because the insufficient investment in public health is going to be worth trillions long-term, or even short-term. The values of these public and civic goods need to be re-articulated at a deep societal level. A tree, for example, is currently and historically a liability on the balance sheet of local authorities, yet we know that it generates huge amounts of environmental value and services, human social services, heat island effects, and massive amounts of other benefits.

These civic values have largely been discounted or ignored in preference for private value. In order to create new civic futures, we have to do the deep, boring work of redefining our mechanisms of budgeting and accounting of civic and public goods, in order to actually recast an economy of civic value, which I think is really critical to the field that many of us intersect with.

> **Andrew:** As we think about the future, what remains to be done to help the field of DSI continue to grow?

Gabriella: In terms of the design field, the incorporation of new typologies and new territories for design has been interesting. There seem to be studios and organizations that work in unique ways, such as Reboot, Dark Matter Labs, and Experimentalista, that were more of a rarity ten years ago. I still think they're quite rare and that we need more of them.

I also think that there is more angst than there used to be in the field of design because of the burden to solve all world problems—but not necessarily having the tools to do so, because that's not usually what you get taught in school. A fresh-out-of-university graphic designer might be expected to know how to facilitate a workshop or rethink a supply chain or a street, though they didn't learn those skills in university.

We're in this transition mode of realizing that, to get into especially complex issues, more people need to be around the table. And, as I mentioned before, it's not only the field of design that has to be part of that conversation, but rather a gathering of people from different fields and truly thinking about things from a transdisciplinary perspective. We should rescale the expectations we have for individual designers, and think about what design affords to collaborations with anthropologists and political scientists, for example. And, rather than only moving designers into those other fields, we need to also introduce people from other fields into the space of design, its means, its methods, its madness.

> **Panthea:** I agree with everything Gabriella said. How do designers take their skill sets and be able to play more facilitative roles? How do you get comfortable wrestling with the complexity? They need to learn to bring different actors and different disciplines together, but then not think it is their job to have the answer. Instead, their job will be to create the space and to do the finagling behind the scenes to elevate people and voices that don't usually get a seat at the table.
>
> In the ten years that we've been running Reboot, we've thought about when we want to work with and within institutions of power, and when we want to work outside of them, usually with and between amorphous social movements and grassroots groups that

may or may not have formal structures. Right now, my energy goes towards thinking about how we create new structures and new spaces to reimagine how we understand, connect, and build with one another, whether it's the social R&D that Gabriella was talking about or more radical community-driven development models. I've been looking for political windows of opportunity and negotiating at higher levels of government, and we need those conversations and allies if we're going to try and change systems. But I'm also looking to create new spaces.

We're often trying to persuade the right policy maker, or hope for the brief, or wait for the permission. And I'm tired, of it because there's never going to be the right brief to upend grossly unjust structures. Power likes to hold onto power, and so there is only so far institutional mandates will go in overturning massive inequities. So how can we find like-minded allies, people that share the same vision?

"The construction of complex civic relationships has been a bureaucratic nightmare. We are starting to see what I call the boring revolution, a kind of re-imagination of contracting, that is opening up a field of civic value."

Gabriella: Perhaps, towards the future, an interesting design challenge might focus on how to better design those transition spaces where disciplines bleed into each other. While I say that I don't think that these conversations should be anchored in the field of design, I also don't think that they should be anchored in any other specific field. Do we actually come out as an anthropologist, as a political scientist, as a designer, or as a literature major? Do we come out with the skill set of being able to navigate these territories where disciplines intermingle, where perspectives switch from one to another, and where we can actually create a language that fills in the gaps between those disciplines? I don't necessarily think so. I don't even think that it's a specific problem to design, but rather a specific problem of how we have been siloing disciplines. Of course you do need the depth of knowledge, and not only the generalists and the people that can link the information, but also many times, expertise is required. So that might be a good design question towards the future.

Design for Social Innovation

Indy: I'll address this question by talking about the importance of creating civic value. The role of converting civic assets and civic goods into civic value as a whole is a burgeoning future. The reason why we focused on private wealth and private economies as a function of bureaucracy is because it's easier to construct bilateral relationships of our current legal systems than it is to construct civic relationships, which are always multilateral. The construction of complex civic relationships has been a bureaucratic nightmare.

We are starting to see what I call the boring revolution, a kind of re-imagination of contracting, that is opening up a field of civic value that historically hasn't existed. I believe there is going to be a massive space opening up in these areas. The reinvention of our civic economy is going to be significant and it will probably be the great trajectory of our economy, unleashed by the fact that many-to-many contracting, which is fundamentally a civic value, will become more viable. It is civic value as opposed to private value that will continue to be constructs of society.

One challenge I see is the need to be more critical. We've hit a sub-optimal stable point where everyone starts to co-design with sticky notes and sort of goes, "Right, this is it." But it's not. It's just the beginning of a conversation. We have to reimagine the nature and the function of these civic assets and the operational realities of the assets into the 21st century. Venture capitalists understand the idea of intangible value much better than anyone that operates in the domain of civic value creation. They understand discounted cash flows, a mechanism to look at future value in terms of how intangible values, in combination, create a huge amount of possibility. So I think one of the big questions that we have to ask is: how do we finance civic goods and how do we finance value creation?

Designers spend a huge amount of their time constructing intangible assets. We need to be as eloquent, constructed, and structured as venture capitalists are in their thesis of value formation. We should understand, for example, that the kind of technology behind Uber isn't so miraculous. In fact, what is more miraculous is actually their organization and buying of global markets. Buying markets is what they spent their billions of dollars on, because they knew the kind of intangible value of buying and organizing that market is the real asset. While the future has great potential, it requires us to move significantly outside our comfort zones into forms of civic infrastructure.

Positioning for Growth

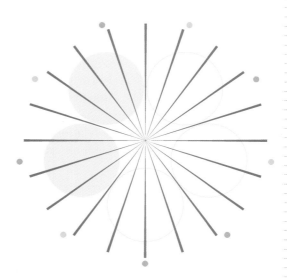

Solo Kota Kita

*Strengthening the participatory
budgeting process by expanding access
to hyper-local data*

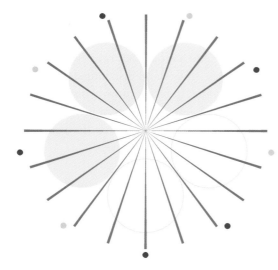

Australia Post Neighbourhood
Welcome Program

*Connecting newcomers to
their community and combating
social exclusion*

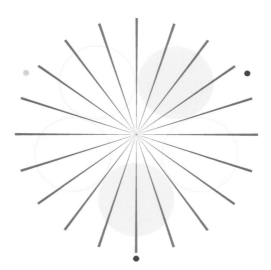

Civil Society
Innovation Hubs

*Countering threats to civil society
through a network of regional "hubs"*

Design for Social Innovation

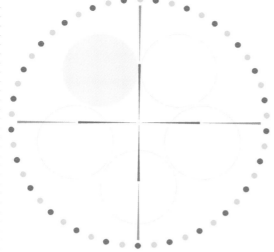

g0v Civic Tech Community

Containing a deadly pandemic through co-design and digital democracy

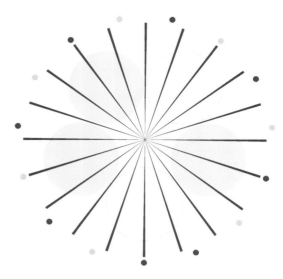

Help Delhi Breathe

Raising awareness for air pollution in Delhi and demanding solutions

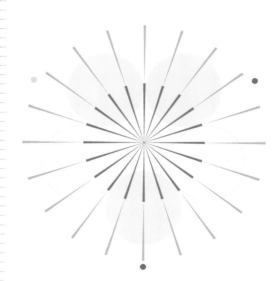

Kamu Chatbot

Answering easy questions with technology so that humans have time to field the hard ones

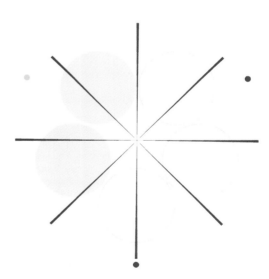

Pakistan Sign Language

Improving literacy and access to personalized learning for hearing-impaired children

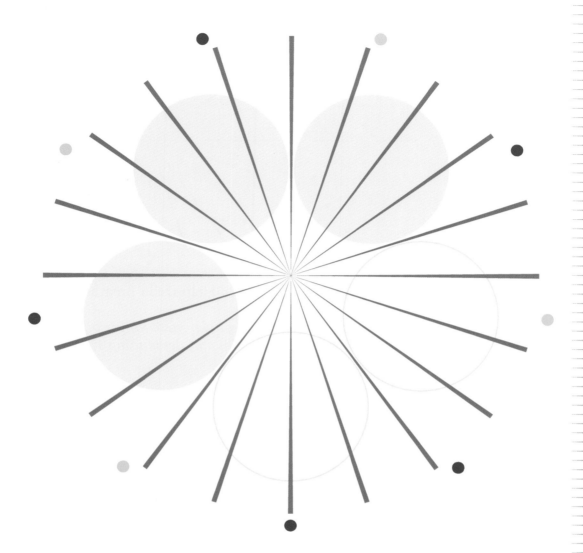

Duration
   January 2018–August 2019

Location
   Footscray, Australia

Categories
   Health and Wellness

Designer
   Craig Walker Design +
    Innovation

Partners
   Australia Post Community
    Design Lab

Key Contributors
   Amanda Brown
   Sandie Pullen
   Katrina Caris
   Jeremy Walker
   Andrew Broughton

Designer Organization Type
   ● For-Profit

Team Size
   ● 8–10

Design Quotient
   ● 41–60%

Project Costs
   ▷ $100k–$500k

Source of Funding
   ▬ Government

Funding Mechanisms
   Fee for Service

Impact Measurement Methods
   Quantitative: Financial Viability,
    Including Funding/Revenue
    Generated, Growth in Product/
    Service Adoption or Usage,
    Number of Inquiries, Observed
    Formation of New Social
    Networks

Mediums
   Digital: Website
   Physical: Posters, Information
    Guides
   Organizational: Service

Australia Post Neighbourhood Welcome Program

Connecting newcomers to their community and combating social exclusion

Australia Post has a Community Design Lab that works to combat issues such as social exclusion, illiteracy, and mental health issues by co-designing with local communities to develop new services that support those who are marginalized and vulnerable. If this sounds unusual for a post office, that's because Australia Post is not your average post office. They are the nation's largest retail network and a very well-known brand countrywide.[1] Australia Post believe they have both a responsibility and a unique opportunity to make positive change.

Working with Craig Walker Design + Innovation, a design consultancy, Australia Post launched the Neighbourhood Welcome Program, which seeks to make it easier for newcomers to make local connections after relocating. The project was conceptualized as "essential services" for newcomers.

In conceptualizing these services, the team were required to incorporate both a social and commercial impact, using or creating services that could be delivered through the post office network across Australia. Participation became a focal point of their efforts. The team identified an opportunity to create a new service that would help Australia's large immigrant population increase their participation in the local community and improve their ability to integrate economically as well, through jobs and entrepreneurship.

Working closely together, Australia Post Community Design Lab and Craig Walker built a research team to better understand the problem. First, they identified places across the country that had well-documented problems and issues relating to social inclusion and exclusion and then narrowed their focus on two key locations, Tasmania and Western Melbourne. As the first phase of field research began, the design team interviewed residents, community groups, local experts,

APCoLab, Nicholson Street in Footscray, Melbourne

Images: courtesy Craig Walker Design + Innovation

and local government to learn about the key issues driving social exclusion. This method was inspired by the "Powers of Ten" approach by American designers Charles and Ray Eames: understanding the issue at a range of scales to inform how they might solve the problem at a personal and community level. After spending ten days travelling around the communities and gathering insights, the design team gathered to synthesize their research and map emergent themes and needs.

Their collaboration resulted in a new welcome service. When someone files a change of address, Australia Post is notified that this person may need assistance in connecting with their local community. The new resident receives a flyer in their mailbox that invites them to collect a welcome box at their post office which contains information and offers for nearby organizations. The service also taps these local organizations to serve as Welcoming Spaces, where new community members can receive orientation from Australia Post staff members appointed as "Community Connectors."

The model was heavily prototyped with local community groups, shops, and residents, as the team worked through multiple iterations of the box, Welcome Space training and introduction, as well as the overall service model and business case for investment. A critical component of testing was the ability to measure both the potential commercial value (the volume of engagement with the post offices) alongside the social value through indicators such as the level of usage in Welcome Spaces and volume of new connections and inquiries. The Neighbourhood Welcome Program was rolled out via a free website showing local communities how to create their own Welcome Spaces.

1   Australia Post, "Australia Post Annual Report 2019," 2019, https://auspost.com.au/content/dam/auspost_corp/media/documents/publications/2019-australia-post-annual- report.pdf.

A Welcome Space at Konjo, a local café

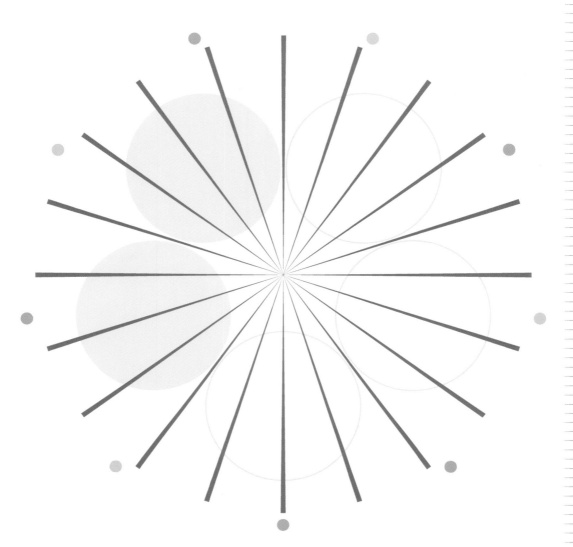

Duration
2010–2016

Location
Surakarta (Solo), Indonesia

Categories
Environment
Social Justice
Policy

Designer
Kota Kita Foundation

Partners
UN-Habitat

Key Contributors
Ahmad Rifai
John Taylor
Michael Haggerty
Bima Pratama Putra
Fuad Jami

Designer Organization Type
● Non-Profit

Team Size
● 8–10

Design Quotient
● 41–60%

Project Costs
▻ $100k–$500k

Source of Funding
➤ Government

Funding Mechanisms
Grant

Impact Measurement Methods
Quantitative: Participants/
Stakeholders Trained, Web/
Mobile Analytics

Mediums
Digital: Website
Physical: Posters

Design for Social Innovation

Solo Kota Kita

Strengthening the participatory budgeting process by expanding access to hyper-local data

Between 2005 and 2010, citizen participation in Musrenbang decreased—an annual participatory budgeting forum held by residents in Surakarta (Solo), Indonesia. The Kota Kita Foundation, an urban development NGO based in Indonesia, identified that this was because the process was too rigid, lacked information, and resulted in proposals that were not being addressed. Adding to the challenge, it was overly representative of the vocal few who determined the development proposals at the village level. Joko Widodo (also known as Jokowi), then mayor of Surakarta but now the president of the Republic of Indonesia, asked why "there are only a few people who are always actively speaking in the forum... where are the other members of the community?"

In 2010, Kota Kita began working with (then) Mayor Widodo and local leaders in Surakarta to address this challenge by increasing participation in the Musrenbang. They began by collecting data about the city's many neighborhoods which would provide an informational resource meant to draw new people into the Musrenbang participatory budgeting process, and ultimately into a fuller engagement of community self-actualization that is fair and equitable.

As a team of designers, urban planners, NGO workers, and architects, Kota Kita established a community-based approach of collecting and sharing data about the urban environment with residents and local government. They combined a decentralized survey with simple technology to better understand the assets and issues in each of Surakarta's neighborhoods. The process has four steps: data collection, mapping, analysis, and distribution.

Mayor Jokowi reviews the mini atlas during its launch

First, Kota Kita sends community facilitators to collect data from local neighborhood managers who operate within the smallest unit of local administration, known as a Ketua.

Once the survey is completed, the team uses geographic information systems (GIS) to create visual maps of the city and the data they collected through their unique process. This allows Kota Kita to map, for example, where poverty is high in Surakarta and where it is low, and to understand the confluence of different demographic data.

The team then analyzes the data and maps to understand how each neighborhood is developing, how it compares to the rest of the city, and how indicators are distributed within a given neighborhood. Data is collected on a wide variety of topics, from access to water, sanitation, poverty levels, to the number of children enrolled in school.

The Solo Kota Kita team records their analysis in a visually compelling "mini atlas" in the form of a poster that is distributed through neighborhood leaders and newspaper kiosks so that the data collected is reflected back to the community. Designed as an accessible and visually compelling document, the mini atlas shows how neighborhoods work and illustrates patterns of social and economic problems and opportunities. This process supports evidence-based advocacy for improving public services, tailoring urban-planning decisions to the community, and encouraging data interpretation skills and self-representation. For a city-wide view, Solo Kota Kita has created a website showing the data from

every neighborhood in Surakarta, which has been accessed by 33,000 people since its launch in 2010.

The use of mini atlases has contributed to "evidence-based advocacy for improving public services, tailoring urban planning decisions to the community while encouraging data interpretation skills and self-representation," according to the team. Proposals from the community include initiatives such as improving public toilets, drainage, and sewers, as well as community health services. Having the data from the mini atlas as supporting evidence has empowered citizens to more effectively advocate for these proposals during the Musrenbang.

The Solo Kota Kita team of community facilitators has collected data for all 51 neighborhoods in Surakarta twice. The first survey was completed in 2010 and took five months to complete. The survey was conducted again in 2012 to update the database, this time using a new SMS tool that allows residents to send data to the team via mobile phone, cutting the data collection time to only two months.

Since developing this methodology, the team has also worked with local governments and NGOs to apply the survey methodology in several other Indonesian cities, including Banjarmasin, Makassar, Padang, and Pekalongan.

"*Community data should be accessible not just to city government, but to residents, who also need to know what is going on in their RT and neighborhood. During Musrenbang, people can use data to understand the real conditions in their neighborhoods. What they propose in Musrenbang should be based on real needs and actual conditions—not just speculation. Information is absolutely important.*"

Mayor Jokowi (Mayor of Solo 2005–2010)

Images: Kheng Wee

Positioning for Growth

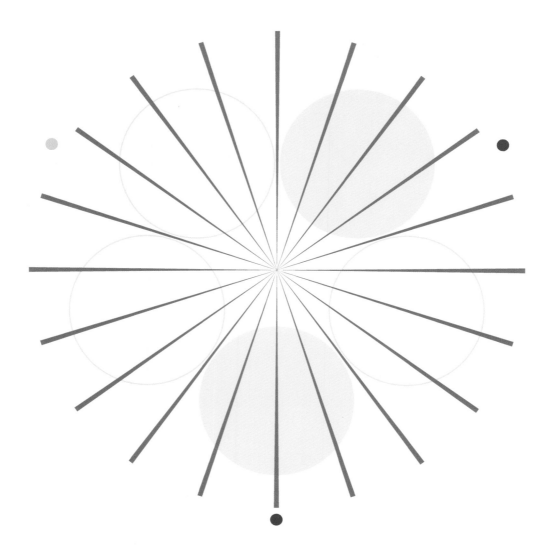

Duration
   October 2014–present

Location
   Workshops in Istanbul, Panama
   City, Panama; Dar es Salaam,
   Tanzania; Dakar, Senegal; Bali,
   Indonesia; Rabat, Morocco;
   NYC, USA, to create hubs
   in Africa, Central Asia, East
   Asia, Latin America and the
   Caribbean, the Middle East,
   and South Asia

Categories
   International Development

Designer
   Reboot

Partners
   CIVICUS
   Counterpart International

Designer Organization Type
   ● For-Profit

Team Size
   ● 2–4

Design Quotient
   ● 21–40%

Project Costs
   ▭ $100k–$500k

Source of Funding
   ▬ Government

Funding Mechanisms
   Unspecified

Impact Measurement Methods
   Qualitative: Assessment
      of Change to Internal
      Organizational Practices,
      Observed Impact on Policy

Mediums
   Experiential: Training
   Organizational: Innovation Lab

Civil Society Innovation Hubs

Countering threats to civil society through a network of regional "hubs"

In response to President Barack Obama's 2013 "Stand with Civil Society" ini-tiative,[1] USAID (United States Agency for International Development) and the Swedish International Development Cooperation Agency (Sida) set out to de-velop a global network of innovation "hubs." Rather than determining the design and driving the creation of the hubs from the top-down, the funders sought to work with civil society organizations as partners. Reboot, a non-profit design studio that works to advance social justice and equity, was asked to devel-op and co-facilitate the design process for these hubs, which they did in collabo-ration with CIVICUS, a global alliance dedicated to strengthening citizen action. Reboot contributed process and strategy knowledge, while CIVICUS provided con-tent expertise.

To lay the foundation for the network of hubs and build a proactive ethos for this new initiative, the team engaged with hundreds of civil society organiza-tions in a co-creation process to define key features and parameters of the hubs. Three principles guided this effort: 1) build trust and interpersonal connections to help the group respond together to the challenges; 2) disrupt traditional power dynamics by focusing on individual experiences and perspectives rather than on their professional representation; and 3) define a clear vision and to help ground participants while providing a flexible process to empower them.

The initiative was launched during a three-day workshop in Istanbul in 2015 including 45 civil society participants from 23 different countries. This was followed by six regional workshops. These workshops utilized a mixed set of working modalities in an attempt to be adaptive and to remove personal bias from the collaboration. Some workstreams and activities were pre-designed, while others shifted in response to the evolving dialogue and participant suggestions. Reboot framed conversations to draw on the experiences of less privileged voices,

and asked the more-powerful actors to be transparent around their interests and resources. Over time, participants took on increased leadership over the process and self-organized into working groups, with Reboot's facilitators stepping back.

Over the course of these workshops, the participants co-developed the design for each of the hubs by identifying and designing the programming, membership structure, operational structure, governance model, and local partners. After the workshops, Reboot served as an advisor to support the hubs' ongoing strategy, design, and innovation efforts through an incubation period. Many of the hubs incorporated co-creation strategies learned through the workshops as a cornerstone of their local innovations strategies and work with constituents.

With six civil society innovation hubs up and running since 2015, a seventh has launched in the Pacific, emerging from a youth co-design workshop in Fiji in 2017. The organic emergence of this additional hub is a testament to the participatory, co-creative approach that Reboot and CIVICUS hoped to initiate with the design of their workshops.

As funders, USAID and Sida were so enthusiastic about the co-creation process that they engaged a historian to document it on a website[2] and "capture its magic" so that it can be shared with other donor initiatives that seek to work in a bottom-up, collaborative manner. The process has since been used in strategic planning and design initiatives with other partners, including UNDP, the MacArthur Foundation, and the global open knowledge and open contracting movements.

Design for Social Innovation

**Images: Reboot
Design LLC**

1   "FACT SHEET: US Support for Civil Society," September 23, 2014, https://obamawhite-
       house.archives.gov/the-press-office/2014/09/23/fact-sheet-us-support-civil-society.
2   www.csiilearn.org.

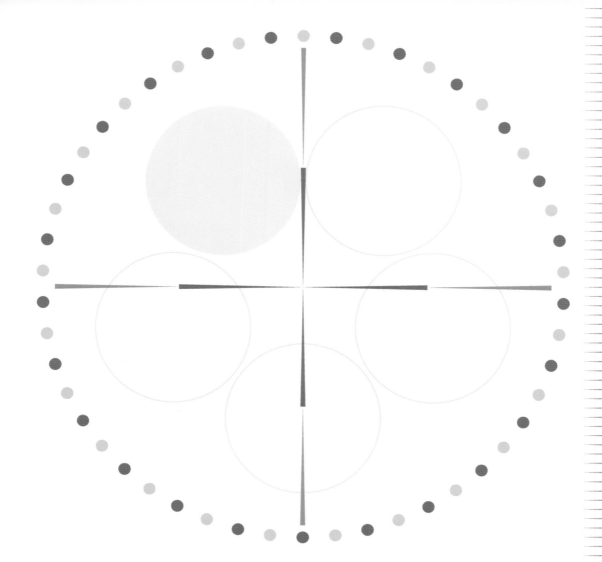

Duration
  2019–2020 (<12 months)

Location
  Taipei and Tainan, Taiwan

Categories
  Civic Tech
  Health and Wellness

Designer
  g0v (pronounced "gov zero")

Partners
  Digital Ministry, Government of
    Taiwan

Designer Organization Type
  • Civil Society

Team Size
  • 50 +

Design Quotient
  • 0–20%

Project Costs
  ▷ <$1k

Source of Funding
  ▬ Government
  ▬ Crowd Funding

Funding Mechanisms
  Crowd Funding

Impact Measurement Methods
  Qualitative: Participant/Client/
    User Feedback
  Quantitative: Web/Mobile
    Analytics

Mediums
  Digital: App, Chatbot, Social
    Media Communications

g0v Civic Tech Community

Containing a deadly pandemic through co-design and digital democracy

As of summer 2020, the COVID-19 pandemic had affected nearly every country on earth, causing more than 900,000 deaths and a global economic recession. In most parts of the world, the pandemic exposed over-burdened public healthcare systems, fragile supply chains, and slow-to-react governments. Amidst the turmoil, a collaboration between government and citizen activists in Taiwan demonstrated a different kind of approach to navigating the crisis.

g0v, a group of civic-minded hackers and entrepreneurs in Taiwan, came together in 2012 with the aim of empowering their fellow citizens with digital tools to participate in their democracy. The group they founded has evolved to harness its members' capabilities to create meaningful engagements with society.

By the time the COVID-19 pandemic hit in 2020, gov's civic-tech community had grown to more than 1,000 contributors, including web developers, programmers, hackers, activists, designers, students, and artists. Built upon their core values of open-source, free access, and co-creation, members had successfully implemented innovative projects independently and in collaboration with the Taiwanese government.

Due to its proximity to China, the original epicenter of the virus outbreak, it was anticipated that Taiwan would be impacted sooner and harder than the rest of the world. By the end of January, panic buying of face masks began with crowding and long queues outside convenience stores as supplies ran out. To control hoarding, the government instituted mask rations and simultaneously released open-source data of mask availability in pharmacies to organize the process.

As public anxiety persisted, members of the g0v community realized that their family and friends were trying to exchange information on mask availability through messaging groups. They quickly mobilized to bolster the country's pandemic efforts. With the help of digital minister Audrey Tang, g0v and the

wider open-source communities hosted a large "Face Mask Hackathon" online. Using real-time inventory data from the National Health Insurance Administration, programmers released a new prototype of the Face Mask data map within 72 hours. More than 100 digital tools, including inventory maps, chatbots, audio tools, and interactive apps, were further released within days of the initial launch in February 2020.

The apps became so popular that some of them crashed from overload, like one chatbot, BuyFaceMask, that received 2,000 queries a minute at its peak on February 6.[1] Encouraged by public adoption, the government provided bandwidth and back-end support to expand these resources to the entire country, bringing the collaboration between formal and informal bodies to a new level of integration.

Subsequently, using feedback from the platform, the government was able to co-design a distribution system for masks that could rapidly respond to pharmacists' and citizens' inputs. Usage analytics highlighted areas where people were still trying to get access to masks or gaps like the need for some stores to operate 24/7 to cater to those who worked odd hours. As a result, the Taiwanese government's work on epidemic prevention was based on actionable, fast feedback from their civic society, rather than relying on announcements from global public health organizations.

As supply stabilized, queries made to the apps declined, a sign that people were no longer struggling to find masks. By April, the ramped-up domestic mask

Images: g0v.tw   production was not only meeting local demands, but Taiwan donated 16 million masks to global relief efforts. While the Face Mask initiatives were vital to the pandemic effort, a multitude of other tools also emerged from these collaborations, such as a voluntary, self-reporting app for symptomatic citizens that served as a guide for tracking high-infection regions.

Even as much of the global economy grappled with lockdowns, schools and businesses in Taiwan could remain open due to low infection rates and transparent access to critical information. Beyond their contributions toward stemming a deadly pandemic, the gov movement has forged a new model of interaction between civil society and government. Their effort on this project demonstrates the potential for digital democracy, deployed with a bottom-up, iterative, multifocal approach as a complement, or even alternative, to traditional top-down administrative approaches.

> ## *"Ask not why nobody is doing this. First, admit that you are that 'nobody.'"*

g0v mantra

1   "Questions on Gov and Taiwan Covid Success—HackMD," 2020, https://hackmd. io/-m-WjkzJQl6tLvADMCWtcw.

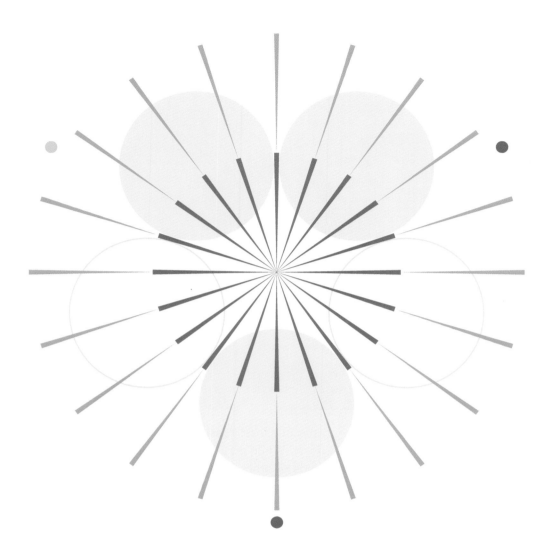

Duration
    August 2017–present

Location
    Helsinki, Finland

Categories
    Policy
    Migration

Designer
    Inland Design

Partners
    Migri (Finnish Immigration
        Service) (2017–2019)
    Ministry of the Interior (2020–
        present)

Key Contributors
    Susanne Miessner
    Mariana Salgado
    Pia Laulainen

Designer Organization Type
    ● Government

Team Size
    ● 2–4

Design Quotient
    ● 81–100%

Project Costs
    ⊏▷ $100k–$500k

Source of Funding
    ▬▬ Government
    ▬▬ Self-Funded

Funding Mechanisms
    Self-Funded

Impact Measurement Methods
    Qualitative: Participant/Client/
        User Feedback
    Quantitative: Response Rate,
        Surveys

Mediums
    Digital: Chatbot
    Experiential: Training
    Organizational: Service

Design for Social Innovation

Kamu Chatbot

Answering easy questions with technology so that humans have time to field the hard ones

Finland receives about 4,500 immigrants each year, but that number increased significantly after Europe's asylum crisis began in 2015. That year, the country received 32,476 asylum seekers, most of them from Iraq, but also from Afghanistan, Somalia, and Syria. The Finnish Immigration Service, known as Migri, was overwhelmed by the number of people who needed support. Inland Design, a design and innovation lab that was part of Migri from 2017 to 2019, co-designed a chatbot called Kamu to field initial inquiries.

It was created when Migri's customer service realized they could only answer 21% of calls from immigrants who inquired about application status. Inland Design's goal was to minimize phone calls by efficiently addressing some of the recurring questions that Migri's customer service was answering again and again. For example, "processing time" inquiries made up 37% of phone calls, so this became the figure that the team wanted to tackle first. Kamu was coded to learn and continually enrich its content so that it can be more useful.

The intention of Kamu begins with the name, which translates to "pal" or "friend" in English, hinting at the level of comfort and trust that the Inland Design team hoped to establish between their chatbot and its correspondents. Kamu's personality was developed with the aid of careful research spanning a couple months. First, Migri's customer service experts were asked to imagine the main personality traits that they use in their daily work with Migri's customers. Next, immigrants were asked what kind of personality would be most appropriate, choosing from a list of evocative examples such as "teacher," "mechanic," "boss," and "best friend." Based on the collective responses, the team developed and tested customer service personality profiles modeled on three of these

characters before eventually settling on the "teacher" as the best choice. Co-design with customer service personnel and immigrants was used to arrive at the final design of the Kamu chatbot.

After its introduction, Kamu was extended to provide information beyond the one silo of immigration services. The chatbot could also connect users with information regarding taxes and registering new businesses, common questions for individuals looking for ways to settle into their new home. "The big idea was that at some point we have a national network of chatbots. You do not need to know who does what, but you ask any national agency and they connect you with the right chatbot," according to project leader Mariana Salgado.

After the introduction of Kamu, Migru's response rate for incoming calls increased from 21% to nearly 70%. To institutionalize the design approaches and mindsets that were utilized during the creation of the Kamu chatbot, Inland Design created a broader service design training initiative. Civil servants from around the country attended in-person training in Helsinki and then went on to become part of a network of service design ambassadors that the Ministry of the Interior and Inland Design could call upon for future projects.

Co-design session with Migri's customer service specialists in Kuhmo, Finland

Image: Suse Miessner, Inland Design

"The big idea was that at some point we have a national network of chatbots. You do not need to know who does what, but you ask in any national agency and they connect you with the right chatbot."

Mariana Salgado

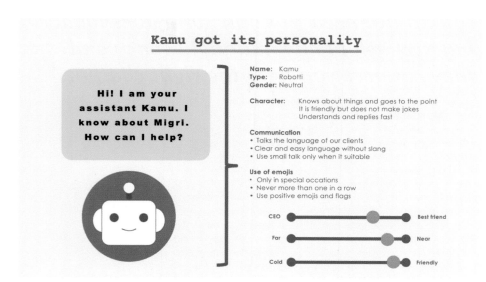

Synthesis of the personality work done for the Kamu chatbot

Images: Inland Design

Maahanmuuton superasiakaspalvelija

Tarvitsemme apuasi ymmärtääksemme paremmin, minkälainen on erinomainen asiakaspalvelija maahanmuuttoon liittyvissä kysymyksissä. Mielestämme asiakaspalvelua tulisi tarjota digitaalisten kanavien (chat, puhelu) kautta.

1. Listaa viisi adjektiivia (tai halutessasi enemmän), jotka kuvaavat mielestäsi erinomaista maahanmuuton asiakaspalvelijaa.

1. Nopea
2. Asiantun Konkreettinen
3. Informatiivinen
4. Ystävällinen
5. Ymmärtävainen

2. Mitkä ovat hänen pääasialliset ammatilliset tavoitteensa ja kiinnostuksen kohteensa?

1. Tr Ymmärtää asia monipuolisesti
2. Kehittää sosiaaliset taidot
3. Kehittää asiakaspalvelu taidot

3. Mitkä asiat turhauttavat häntä eniten töissä? Asiakkaiden persoonalliset ongelmat
2. Kiire
3. Asiakkaiden £jatkurat (turhat) tiedustelut oleskeluluvan valmistumisesta

4. Miten superasiakaspalvelijasi viestii asiakkaidensa kanssa?

- ⊗ chat
- ◯ ääni
- ⊗ asiakasportaali
- ⊗ puhelin
- ⊗ sähköposti
- ◯ muu: _____

5. Miten hän puhuu sinulle asiakkaana? Valitse 1.

opettaja	vanhempi	paras ystävä	automekaanikko	taiteilija	vanhempi
asiantunteva	ymmärtäväinen	välittävä	tietää kaikki	luova	asiantunteva
uskottava	ohjaava	luotettava	yksityiskohdat		ohjaava
luennoiva	tietämätön	omaa mielipiteitä	lyhytnäköinen	ei piittaa säännöistä	luennoiva

Miksi valitsit juuri tämän vaihtoehdon?

Tr Minulle on tärkein, että asiakaspalvelijalla on tiedot kyseisistä aiheesta, eli kova asiantuntemus. Lisäksi hänen tehtävä on ohjata minut asiointiprosessissa

in **land** co-designing public services
www.inland.studio

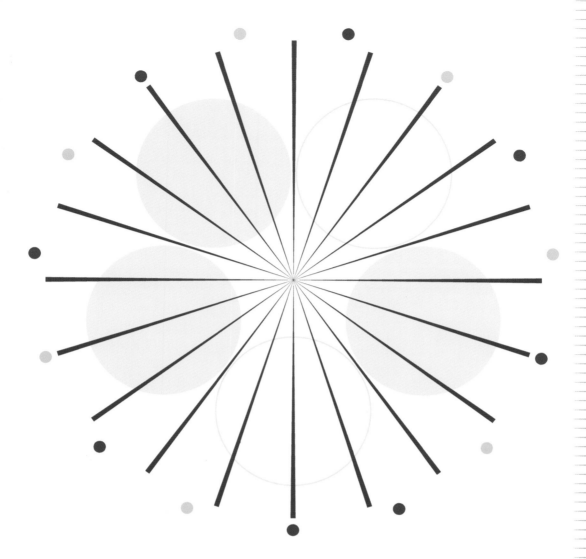

Duration
  2016–present

Location
  New Delhi, India

Categories
  Environment

Designer
  Purpose PBC

Partners
  My Right to Breathe GSCC
  Haiyya
  Chintan
  URJA
  Lung Care Foundation
  Centre for Environment and
    Energy Development
  Jhatkaa
  Delhi Trees SOS

Designer Organization Type
  • For-Profit

Team Size
  • 11–20

Design Quotient
  • 21–40%

Project Costs
  ▷ $100k–$500k

Source of Funding
  ▬ Foundation/Non-Profit/
    Endowment

Funding Mechanisms
  Grant

Impact Measurement Methods
  Qualitative: Observed impact on
    policy
  Quantitative: Event Attendance,
    Web/Mobile Analytics

Mediums
  Digital: Social Media
    Communications, Chatbot
  Physical: Billboard
  Spatial: Exhibition

Help Delhi Breathe

Raising awareness for air pollution in Delhi and demanding solutions

Air pollution causes 1.6 million deaths per year in India, which is home to 14 of the world's 20 most polluted cities.[1] In Delhi alone, 30,000 people die prematurely every year due to toxic air. Despite significant press coverage of the city's air pollution, growing demand by its citizens, and commitments by the government, there remains a lack of awareness around the causes and potential solutions. Political will to take action remains limited.

Members of the Purpose Climate Lab—a team of climate campaigners, strategists, and creatives within Purpose India—have lived and worked in Delhi's polluted air for years and initiated a project to improve air quality. They support climate campaigns and cultural interventions through digital communications strategies.

The team convened and mobilized a group of civil society organizations, citizen groups, medical associations, content creators, media, and youth groups to demand and implement solutions for Delhi's air pollution crisis. They began with a mapping exercise to understand which organizations and voices were critical to the issue. As the effort grew, an ongoing campaign was developed, Help Delhi Breathe, which fills a gap in public mobilization by organizing individuals and stakeholders alike. The campaign aims to raise awareness about the health impacts of pollution and encourage residents of Delhi to demand policies that curb it. The Purpose Climate Lab developed online and offline platforms that allow citizens to engage and take action. This included publicizing the need for better air-quality reporting, using Right to Information applications to obtain information from the government about Delhi's plans for electric buses, and conducting policy research with technical experts to understand the policy petitions that would be required to lobby the government for renewable energy.

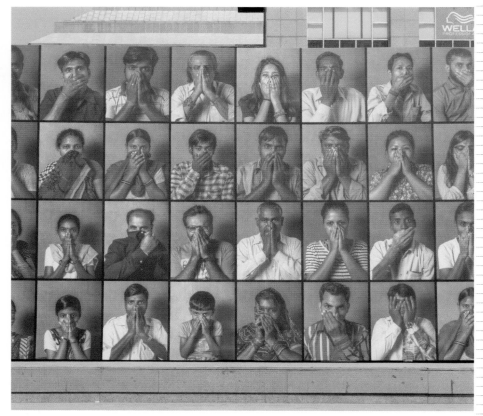

The project's ability to engage fresh audiences has been driven by innovative tactics and creative content that reimagines the issue of air pollution to make it relatable and accessible. Organizing exhibitions, creating installations, and creating digital tools to monitor air quality enabled Help Delhi Breathe to reach a range of local citizens, medical experts, youth, and communities.

Two examples help illustrate the breath of this work. The team designed a WhatsApp chatbot called "Smokey" that relays the government's real-time air-quality data for cities in a more accessible format. They also designed a "Breathing Billboard" featuring a massive set of lungs made from HEPA air filters. As the lungs were exposed to air pollution, they changed in color, creating a striking visual indicator.

These interventions helped the campaign reach new audiences by giving individuals new material to share with their networks. For example: practitioners spread the message of the importance of clean air during International Yoga Day, numerous influencers posted about the global strikes at Climate Week, while Red FM—India's leading radio station—profiled children attending the strike. The project's list of partners is still growing, and the team will continue to seek new partners. Throughout these various messaging campaigns, the team incorporated testing and perception surveys to study how the public responded to campaigns and adjust accordingly.

The "Breathing Billboard" of Delhi reached more than 300 million people in ten days through extensive media coverage. Overall, the campaign has reached nearly 50 million people digitally and has engaged with over 2.6 million people.

Policy impact included a commitment from the central government for a national clean air plan. Delhi became the first state to develop the Graded Action Response Plan, which is a set of predefined pollution mitigating actions—such as halting construction or closing schools—that is automatically triggered when different levels of particulate matter are detected in the air. Pushing citizens to demand solutions also contributed to the approval of a solar power policy for Delhi, and to the commitment of 1,400 electric buses.

1   "World Most Polluted Countries in 2019–PM2.5 Ranking | AirVisual," 2019, www.iqair.com/world-most-polluted-countries.

**Informing
students about
the air quality
index**

**Photograph of
the Breathless
Exhibition**

Design for Social Innovation

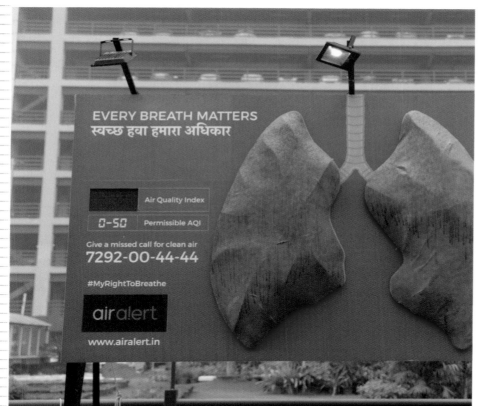

The "breathing" lungs of a billboard installation grew black with exposure to Delhi's air

Protests mobilized participants of all ages

Images: Purpose PBC

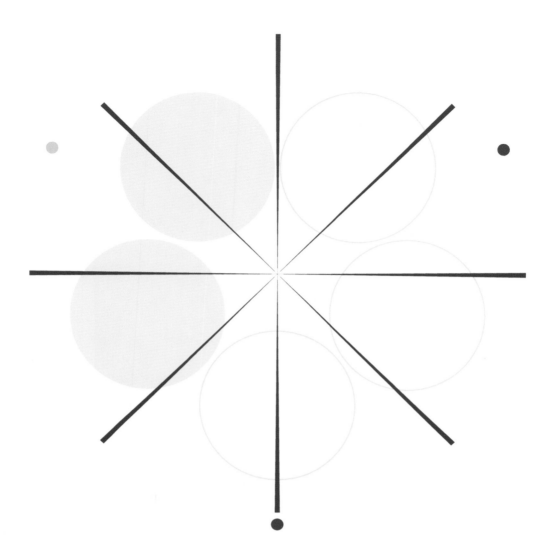

Duration
Aug 2017–May 2018

Location
Karachi, Hyderabad, and
Nawabshah, Pakistan

Categories
Education
Minority Representation and
Inclusion

Designer
Designist

Partners
Family Educational Services
Foundation (FESF)

Designer Organization Type
• For-Profit

Team Size
• 2–4

Design Quotient
• 81–100%

Project Costs
▭▻ $1k–$25k

Source of Funding
▬▸ Foundation/Non-Profit/
Endowment

Funding Mechanisms
Fee for Service

Impact Measurement Methods
Qualitative: Awards Received
Quantitative: Growth in Product/
Service Adoption or Usage

Mediums
Digital: Software
Physical: Device

Design for Social Innovation

Pakistan Sign Language

Improving literacy and access to personalized learning for hearing-impaired children

The literacy rate of Pakistan's more than 1 million deaf children lags far behind that of their hearing peers. According to the Wise Qatar Foundation, less than 5% of Pakistan's deaf children attend school, with the rate being much lower for deaf girls. A cycle of low educational achievement can lead to social marginalization, gaps in job-specific transferable skills and lowered economic prospects later in life. The schools that deaf children attend do not have enough resources to help them learn sign language efficiently. For example, instructional DVDs and USB sticks are often scarce within a school, having to be shared between multiple teachers, and some schools lack the necessary computers to begin with. Even when these devices can be acquired, the instructional media is rote and does not enable students to learn effectively through personalization or search functions.

To address this problem, the Family Educational Services Foundation (FESF), a non-profit organization based in Karachi, partnered with Designist, a human-centered design organization to create an accessible platform for Pakistan Sign Language (PSL). The mission of the FESF's Deaf Reach Program works to provide access to resources for language development by harnessing digital technologies that transform deaf education. The design team's objective was to design an easy-to-use digital platform that enabled hearing-impaired people and allies to gain access to the dictionary and learning tools. In order to be distributed nationwide, the language needed to be published on a website and in 1,000 Raspberry Pis—a small computer that costs less than US$40.

To take the dictionary into the digital era, they needed to understand current human behavior around teaching sign language in classrooms. The team made a total of five visits to three deaf schools in Karachi, Hyderabad, and

Nawabshah to observe and conduct interviews with stakeholders. Through a process of co-creation with the students and teachers, they identified key challenges at stake in learning PSL digitally and non-digitally. Building on the challenges already outlined above, the transformative opportunity was to create a system that could be personalized to the learner and their teacher in terms of needs and pacing.

The resulting PSL digital dictionary includes 7,000 words and is now used nationwide. Designist created a navigation system that utilizes easy-to-understand categories and includes a search function. In the past, teachers created lesson plans and then searched DVDs and USBs to find the correct words for their specific class, requiring them to manage a jumble of physical media. Now, using a single computer interface, teachers are able to search for words and create playlists to prepare for each class session, as well as access new PSL stories that can be used in the learning process. Likewise, students can do the same for self-guided learning by creating and storing their own playlists and favorite stories.

While the intervention improves outcomes for classrooms and individuals it also started a feedback loop at a national level by creating a venue for students to request new signs for words that are not currently in the PSL dictionary.

As of early 2020, 1,000 PSL Learning Units (PLUs) including mini-computer, monitor, and software have been distributed to 192 schools across 90 cities. This represents a community of 63,492 individuals, including students, teachers, and families. While many of the PLU are currently utilized as a supplementary

Design for Social Innovation

tool, some schools have already started using PLUs as the primary medium of instruction in their classrooms. A significant number of institutes have designated a time slot during school hours for the dedicated use of the PLU, recognizing its benefits in improving language development, general knowledge, and math. The impact of this project has been acknowledged locally through an award from Pakistan Software Houses Association (P@SHA) and earned global recognition by receiving the World Innovation Summit for Education (WISE) Award in 2018.

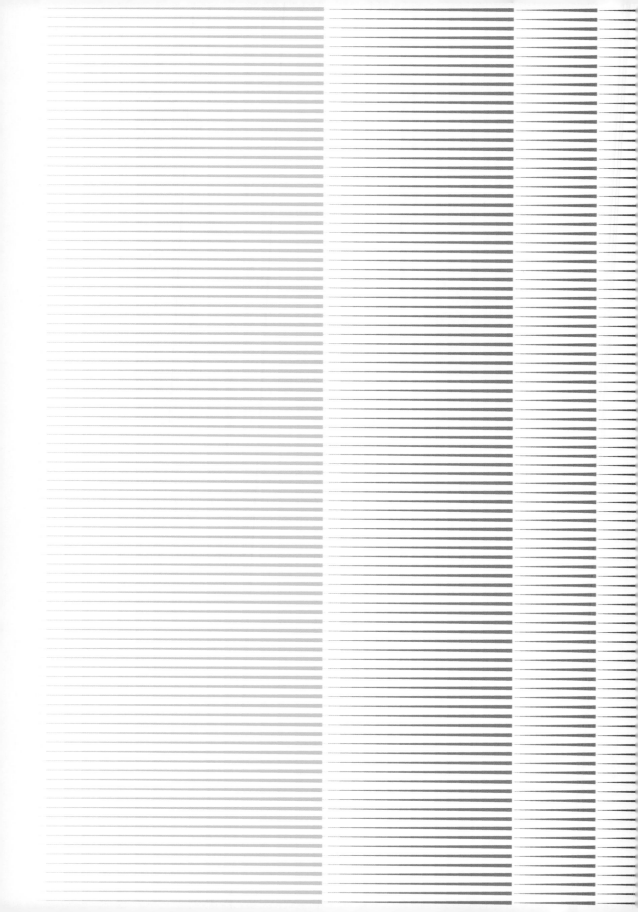

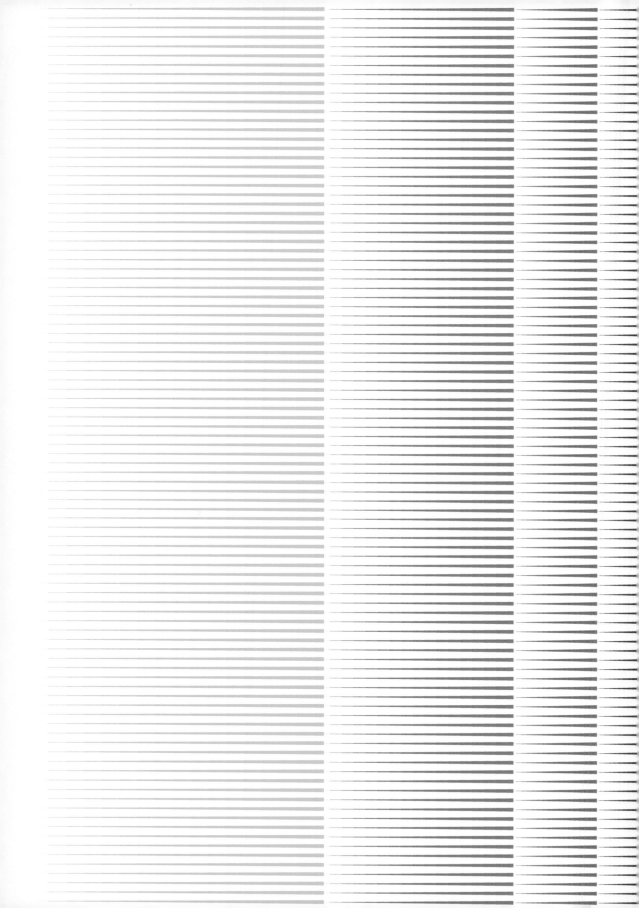

Methodology

Our goal has been to provide a snapshot of this moment in the evolution of design for social innovation (DSI). To this effort we brought a commitment to presenting plural definitions of design for social innovation, yet there was no escaping from the pervasiveness of our respective cultural lenses and their effect on our editorial choices. We cast a wide net looking for cases that would surprise us and challenge our assumptions (and to some extent the length of our editorial process is evidence of this), but ultimately the limitations of an editorial project of this nature kept us from achieving more than a purposeful sampling of what's happening in the field.

We had some working principles: strive to end up with cases from diverse geographies; showcase different funding and organizational models; show variance in budgets and scale of implementation; celebrate a broad spectrum of practitioners, design disciplines, social issues, and design outputs. Despite these objectives, we knew that the final selections for the book would be at best a non-comprehensive sample. So, in accepting, from the beginning, that our book would be full of omissions and lacking significant projects and voices equally deserving of our consideration, we embraced methodological rigor as a way into the publication.

Broadly defined, methods consist of a series of elements and structural scaffolding that help determine with coherence the conclusions we draw from the "blooming, buzzing" phenomena that we typically observe in the world.

Using projects as the unit of analysis that connect the what, who, and how of design for social innovation, we chose three research questions to provide us with the necessary scaffolding from which to build from. These were:
What are the business models behind these social innovation design practices?
Are there insightful characteristics, commonalities, and differences that we could draw from to identify patterns? How are the teams responsible for these projects accounting for positive impact?

With this framing as a start, and openly acknowledging that DSI is evolving in real time with incredible force and dynamism globally, we assembled an international editorial advisory team composed of 14 design researchers, educators, and practitioners from whom we sought wisdom and counsel. We shared with them the initial logic underlying our approach. Over a series of individual and group conversations and exchanges they helped identify opportunities and anticipated pitfalls to guard against. They also lent recommendations for individuals and organizations to consider approaching. In scoping the book, we also called on additional colleagues in our various design networks and institutions to act as critical sounding boards and provide further guidance. In many ways, this early pooling of perspectives jump-started our initial outreach process and data collection phase.

We adopted a constructivist and "practitioners' first lens" for the research design for the book. We loosely followed a mixed methods research process that allowed us to deploy our intuition and combine qualitative and quantitative techniques to collect data that came back in both words and numbers. We mixed survey and case study techniques. Case study development is a preferred strategy whenever one has little control over events and when the focus is on understanding from a qualitative perspective contemporary phenomena within a real-life context. The case study methodology also represents a research approach that allows one to capture the richness of organizational behavior, even though conclusions may not always be generalizable.

Data Collection Process and Case Study Development

To counter this limitation of the case study method, we designed two surveys. The first was a short-form questionnaire that collected primary data to decide if the project would be worth investigating further. We sent this questionnaire to the initial leads identified through our international advisors and networks. Importantly, we leveraged a bottom-up strategy for data collection by deploying this first survey via a website that announced the book and amplified the effort via social media.

After this initial outreach and launching the call for cases, we collected 182 potential cases in the first four months. With our assistant editors' support, we came together in a workshop to categorize and code all submissions, identifying strengths and gaps. Post-workshop, we did one more round of targeted outreach before arriving at the final selection of the 45 cases featured in the book.

We deployed a second survey, or "Case Study Inquiry Form" (see page 396), for the projects selected. This questionnaire was designed to be easily understandable to those practicing design and working on design-led projects. It was meant to isolate variables and attributes about the projects that we could quickly code as responses came in. The survey included open-ended questions, where respondents provided answers in their own words, and closed-ended questions, where they were asked to choose from a list of answer choices that typically corresponded to numerical data.

Design for Social Innovation

We organized the instrument in sections (outlined below) designed to encourage ease of response:

Overview
Process
Business Strategy
Impact
Your Design Context
Images, Statistics, Quotes

Project teams were asked to complement survey responses in various ways. They often included additional files to tell us more about their research process, shared especially valuable activities, and commented on their partners, and stakeholders' roles. They also offered insights into barriers and spoke to the sometimes overlooked operational dimensions of their projects. A comprehensive picture of the diversity of design outputs (or, as we came to call them, mediums) connected to these practices emerged from our analyses. The lists below capture the main categories we identified through our coding.

DIGITAL	EXPERIENTIAL	PHYSICAL	SPATIAL	ORGANIZATIONAL
App	**Education**	**Beehive**	**Exhibition**	**Business**
Chatbot	**Event**	**Billboard**	**Interior Space**	**Policies**
E-Book	**Training**	**Book**	**Repurposed**	**Incubator**
Network	**Workshop**	**Calendar**	**Buildings**	**Innovation Lab**
SMS		**Device**	**Urban Design**	**Non-Profit**
Social Media		**Furniture**		**Service**
Communica-		**Game**		
tions		**Information**		
Software		**Guide**		
Website		**Journal**		
		Medical Device		
		Posters		
		Rainwater Har-		
		vesting System		
		Teaching Aid		
		Training Manual		

The questionnaire also allowed us to collect insights related to the nature of DSI in our respondents' specific geographic context. Questions in this section covered designers' educational and professional trajectories. They also sought to isolate common barriers to practicing in a social innovation context: funding sources, procurement, time constraints, access to local design expertise, perceptions about design value, etc. Additionally, we invited respondents to situate their work within common social innovation intervention categories such as environment, education, economy, policy, humanitarian affairs, international development, social justice, and to share demographic data.

Regarding the important implementation focus of our book, we asked respondents to reflect on the kinds of impact they could self-report about their projects through qualitative and/or quantitative measures. The lists on page 394 show the self-reported techniques (edited slightly for clarity and consistency) that each project team communicated to the editors. As aggregate lists, these give the reader a glimpse of the variety of methods that designers are using to assess, learn from, and improve their work.

QUALITATIVE METHODS	QUANTITATIVE METHODS
Adoption by the Organization and/or Other Organizations	Academic Publications
Assessment of Change to Internal Organizational Practices	Cost Savings
	Evaluative Assessment
Awards Received	Event Attendance
Evaluative Case Study	External Impact Evaluator
Focus Groups	Financial Viability, Including Funding/ Revenue Generated
Mystery Client Visits	Growth in Product/Service Adoption or Usage
Observational Research	
Observed Community Participation	Headcount/Time of Participation
Observed Formation of New Social Networks	Jobs Created
	Key Environmental Indicators
Observed Impact on Policy	Number of Financially Viable Projects
Participant/Client/User Feedback	Number of Inquiries
Stakeholder Interviews	Number of Projects Initiated
Surveys	Observed Formation of New Social Networks
Team Reflections	Participants/Stakeholders Trained
	Project Replication/Citation by Other Groups
	Quantity or Area of Spaces Created
	Randomized Controlled Trial
	Response Rate
	Surveys
	Verified Sharing of Learning Experiences
	Volume of Media Coverage
	Web/Mobile Analytics

In the process of developing the cases, we decided to do a post-hoc analysis using the Sustainable Development Goals (SDGs), the United Nations' framework for advancing global progress to end extreme poverty, reduce inequality, and protect the planet by 2030. We examined the SDGs and their indicators to surface patterns and relevant connections with the social issues addressed by the projects. Given our very small sample size, other than identifying expected overlaps with the SDGs in the challenges DSI is being called to address, our findings were not conclusive.

Case Study Analysis and Writing

Once the final set of cases were selected, our team drafted the text with input from the case study respondents. This integration of case study methods with survey design enabled us to get insights into the essential factors, processes, and relationships that defined each project. Our analyses integrated the questionnaire data with a qualitative approach to discovery and exploration that allowed us to make meaning and inferences from some of these projects' complex contexts.

The responses from our long-form questionnaire/case study template became the foundation for the write-up of each project. Initially, we organized these in a loose structure that elevated project highlights such as context, intention, outputs, and implementation results—all key dimensions that inform our book's

Design for Social Innovation

focus on the sustainability of design for social innovation practices. Subsequent exchanges and interviews with respondents complemented the survey data; our respondents also filled in gaps and provided sign-off that final case study drafts accurately represent their work. The narratives that now populate the book are the result of an average of three rounds of editing and review by the entire editorial team.

By nature, case studies only provide us with a bounded view of the richness of a project and its real-world context. We mean *Design for Social Innovation: Case Studies from Around the World* to be a "snapshot," in a very real sense, of how the practice of design for social innovation is evolving as a whole.

Reproduced below is the survey instrument utilized to request information from case study teams. Respondents completed this document in PDF or online via a web form. Follow-up by email was used to clarify and expand upon the initial contribution.

Overview
Provide short responses to each of these

Title of Project

Name of your organization or studio

Additional way to contact you (email address, WhatsApp, WeChat, Skype, Zoom, etc.) If email is not the best way to reach you, please tell us what you prefer instead. *Don't forget to share your username*!

In a few words, summarize what you did, who your solution focused on, and the impact that it had or will have. For example: "Design parks to help people become more healthy" or "Educate young women to prevent unsafe sex."

Date(s) & Duration (of your engagement with the project)

Geographic Location (Country and City/Town)

Partner or Client. Short description of them and their mission.

Team Members. How many people worked on the project: 1 2–4 5–7 8–10 10–20 20–49 50+

Link(s) Provide a website that allows people to learn more about the project

About how many in your team were designers? (Define "designer" however you see fit)

What aspects of your project do you consider most innovative? We're interested in spreading knowledge among the global community of designers. Answering this helps us understand how to focus on your work:

☐ Research Methods   ☐ Community Engagement
☐ Outputs/Deliverables/design "solutions"   ☐ Other:
☐ Impacts

Process (< 225 words)
Now we would like to understand how you worked through your project, from defining the challenge to the final development.

Research (< 75 words)
Describe how you learned about the main problem or challenge.
» Were any research activities helpful?
» Did your partners, clients, end-users, or stakeholders help you with this?
» Did you use any quantitative methods?

Objective of Design (< 75 words)
What's the main problem or challenge you addressed? Was your goal to:
1. design a new product or service or refine an existing one;
2. alter or create a system to deliver a new or better solution;
3. influence the attitudes and behaviors of a culture, community, or organization?

Outputs (< 75 words)
Describe the final design.
» How did you know that it was the right intervention?
» Did you use any unique tools or methods?
» Which aspects of your approach were unique to your culture, region, or the particular challenge?

Business Strategy
In addition to the project itself, we want to learn about the ways that designers around the world are making this a sustainable business practice. These questions help us understand that part of your work.

Business Model
If the project was done in-house, please try to approximate in the total the salary and project costs. If the project was completed through a consultancy-type relationship, please approximate your fee.

☐ Less than $1K   ☐ $500k–$1mm
☐ $1K–$25K   ☐ $1mm+
☐ $25K–$100K   ☐ Other:
☐ $100K–$500k

Funding: Where did the money come from? Select all that apply.

☐ Fee for Service   ☐ Foundation / Charity / Endowment
☐ Grant   ☐ Crowdfunding
☐ Government   ☐ More than one funding source
☐ Equity investment   ☐ Other:
☐ Private Company

Design for Social Innovation

Impact (< 65 words)

Help us see the goals and affects of your project.

How did you measure impact?
Were the impacts quantitative or qualitative? Over what period of time do you measure? Was the impact direct or indirect?

What do you think is the PRIMARY category of impact for your project?
- ☐ Health and Wellness
- ☐ Environment
- ☐ Humanitarian Affairs
- ☐ Education
- ☐ International Development
- ☐ Social Justice
- ☐ Identity (gender, culture, race)
- ☐ Economic
- ☐ Policy
- ☐ Other:

If there is a SECONDARY category of impact for your project, please select as many as apply.
- ☐ Health and Wellness
- ☐ Environment
- ☐ Humanitarian Affairs
- ☐ Education
- ☐ International Development
- ☐ Social Justice
- ☐ Identity (gender, culture, race)
- ☐ Economic
- ☐ Policy
- ☐ Other:

Your Design Context (< 65 words)

This book explores how design is being used around the world to address complex challenges.

In a few words, how do you describe what you do?

In your country or region, how do designers become social innovation designers?
- ☐ Bachelor or Master programs in "traditional" design fields
- ☐ Specialized Bachelor or Master programs in design for social innovation (or related fields)
- ☐ Certificate programs in design for social innovation (or related fields)
- ☐ Through other jobs, fields, or disciplines
- ☐ International Consultants
- ☐ Other:

Based on your experience working in this region, country, or culture, what are the key challenges to your work in social innovation? Choose three.
- ☐ Funding
- ☐ Measuring impact
- ☐ Time constraints
- ☐ Buy-in from senior leadership
- ☐ Procurement
- ☐ Recognition of design as a tool for social innovation
- ☐ Finding Design Talent
- ☐ Other:

In your region, which are the most common areas in which design is or can be applied as tool for social innovation? Choose three.
- ☐ Health and Wellness
- ☐ Environment
- ☐ Humanitarian Affairs
- ☐ Education
- ☐ International Development
- ☐ Social Justice
- ☐ Identity (gender, culture, race)
- ☐ Economic
- ☐ Policy

Describe any unique opportunities to working in this region, country, or culture.

What have we missed? Please share with us any additional thoughts about your experience as a designer working on social innovation (e.g. what are particular opportunities in your region).

Images, Statistics, Quotes

Please include images to help illustrate your project. By sharing these images, you give permission to the Editors of LEAP to use the images in the print publication and/or promotional materials for the publication, whether print or online.

4-6 Images and/or Illustrations
- » Research
- » Sketches/diagrams from several points/iterations during the process
- » Visual designs (print, web, environmental, motion, etc), implementation, etc

3 Compelling Project Statistics
- » Before/after, baseline conditions

3 Quotes
- » From users, partners, clients
- » Based on interviews and/or user-testing

Image Requirements
- » High resolution (300 dpi), Horizontal, Color
- » Captions for images
- » Image credit (e.g., "Photo: Photographer's Name" or "Source: websitename.com")

Note: *If you do not own the right to these images and cannot grant us permission to use them in the book and website, please include the name and contact information of the person or organization who does own the rights.*

Acknowledgments

We started the journey of putting together this publication in September 2018 with an initial ideation session that brought the four of us together face-to-face in New York City.

Two and a half years and several in-person workshop retreats and virtual meetings later, we are grateful to have counted on one another as a core editorial team. We prevailed through the many complexities of this effort, managing the many ebbs and flows that we experienced through the various phases of research, ideation, analysis, fundraising, outreach, writing, editing, and more writing—all of which were necessary to bring this book to life. We succeeded in working collaboratively, always leaning on our respective strengths while keeping a sense of intellectual curiosity and humor during moments of difficulty. This fact offers the reader a glimpse into our uncompromising commitment to this project. It also speaks to the respect and friendship we hold for one another.

Design for Social Innovation: Case Studies from Around the World reflects the work of a great many people. As a non-comprehensive compendium of design for social innovation practices shaping the field across countries and continents, the book is informed in fundamental ways by the diversity of lenses that many esteemed colleagues from around the world generously offered. They did so in the early days of our sourcing of case studies and during other critical junctures of the project. Special thanks go to our international editorial board members; we are fortunate to count some of them as roundtable discussants or participants in a few of the book's case studies: Ahmed Ansari, Christian Bason, Andrea Botero, Jesper Christiansen, Chris Ferguson, Fumiko Ichikawa, Gabriella Gómez-Mont, Mugendi K. M'Rithaa, Celia Romaniuk, Mariana Salgado, Srini R. Srinivasan, Joyce Yee, Lou Yongqi, and Jan Christoph Zoels. We are also grateful to Professor Ezio Manzini and Carla Cipolla, who advised us on potential cases from the DESIS network's substantial body of work. There were several additional colleagues that we also consulted along the way. Thank you to Shana Agid, Camilla Buchanan, Koray Caliskan, Krystina Castella, Justin W. Cook, Tom de Blasis, Chris Fabian, Dan Hill, Cynthia Lawson Jamarillo, Saloni Jha, Onur Kocan, Chris Larkin, Rachel Lehrer, Shu Yang Lin, Hoai Nam Pham,

Lara Penin, Mark Randall, Diane Rhyu, Eduardo Staszowski, Marco Steinberg, Thridev Suvarnan, Manuel Toscano, and Jocelyn Wyatt. Thanks to Steven Butler for your early guidance on the social media strategy to solicit case study submissions. Finally, a word of profound gratitude to each of our roundtable discussants for dialoguing with us and lending your knowledge and critical perspectives, which provide the essential backbone to this publication. We also direct our gratitude to the many individuals associated with the different organizations represented in our 45 case studies. Many of you participated in and supported multiple rounds of editing as we shaped the narrative synthesis and culled the data that each case study features. To all, we say thank you.

This project would never have happened without our larger editorial team's support and contributions, particularly a dedicated group of individuals from two of our three home institutions, Parsons School of Design, The New School, and ArtCenter College of Design. Connected to the community of alumni from the School of Design Strategies at Parsons are assistant editors Isabella Gady and Jenny Liu: we thank you for being such vital contributors at every stage of this publication. Thank you to editorial case study assistant Andrea Noble for your sustained collaboration during the first round of case study editing. We extend our appreciation to editorial data assistant Vasuta Kalra: your partnership on data analysis brought essential clarity to our manuscript; thank you for your critical eye as well in the final editorial review stages. To the incredibly talented editorial research team that supported us and contributed to the book in so many crucial ways, we appreciate your support. Mohammad Sial, we are indebted for your care in sifting through a large number of images and making sense of which could best enrich each case study's narrative; many thanks as well for your overall editorial support. Stephanie Soussloff, we are thankful for your insightful research about the case studies in the context of the thematic streams of the United Nations Sustainable Development Goals. Last but not least, rounding out the editorial research team, our thanks also go to Nidhi Singh Rathore, an alumna from the Media Design Practices program at ArtCenter College of Design, for your crucial research contributions and outreach efforts.

We must also recognize that this expanded editorial team's involvement was made possible in part by key institutional support. Specifically, we are indebted to Parsons and seed funding from faculty research grants and school and cross-college-level-based awards that Mariana Amatullo and Andrew Shea were able to dedicate to the publication's development. We also wish to acknowledge the overall encouragement of many faculty and staff colleagues at Parsons, ArtCenter, and the University of Michigan—too numerous to list here—that have advised us and championed our efforts during every step of this journey. Thank you all!

Catalytic support for many aspects of *Design for Social Innovation: Case Studies from Around the World* and the accompanying website for the publication has benefited from the generosity of the Sappi Ideas that Matter award. Our special thanks go to Patti Groth for her early vote of confidence in this publication's promise and to the judges of the 2019 edition of the Sappi Ideas that Matter (ITM) award, as well as to Deb Aldrich and Laura Des Enfants of D'NA

Company. We remain humbled by this prestigious recognition and accompanying support. We are delighted to join more than 500 grant winners that Sappi has recognized over the years for driving positive change through their design work. Thank you to Brendan Griffiths for your help to shape the website's vision, with the contributions of a terrific team of students from the School of Art, Media, and Technology at Parsons.

The graphic design of this volume is graced by the exceptional talent of Lupi Asensio and Martin Lorenz, the partners behind TwoPoints.Net. It is always a joy to trust publication projects to them. They have a knack for elevating any content one hands them with the rigorous aesthetic, craft, and intelligence that characterizes their versatile practice. We are incredibly thankful for your patience with our changing timelines and the many constraints we have asked you to honor during this project's arc. An essential word of gratitude also goes to our publisher, Routledge. We are very proud to see our book added to their expansive library of important publications.

Finally, we must give immense credit to each of our life partners and immediate families. They have sustained us with their love and support, day in and day out, throughout the hard work we have dedicated to this book, a process that has also meant our spending considerable time away from them. Thank you for your unwavering partnership. Team members also welcomed two babies during this project; welcome, Eloise and Frederick.

This book has grown out of almost two decades of our respective learning trajectories and practices. To our former students, colleagues, and community partners who are shaping the field of DSI around the world: your creativity and dedication continue to be a source of profound inspiration. We remain indebted to all of you.

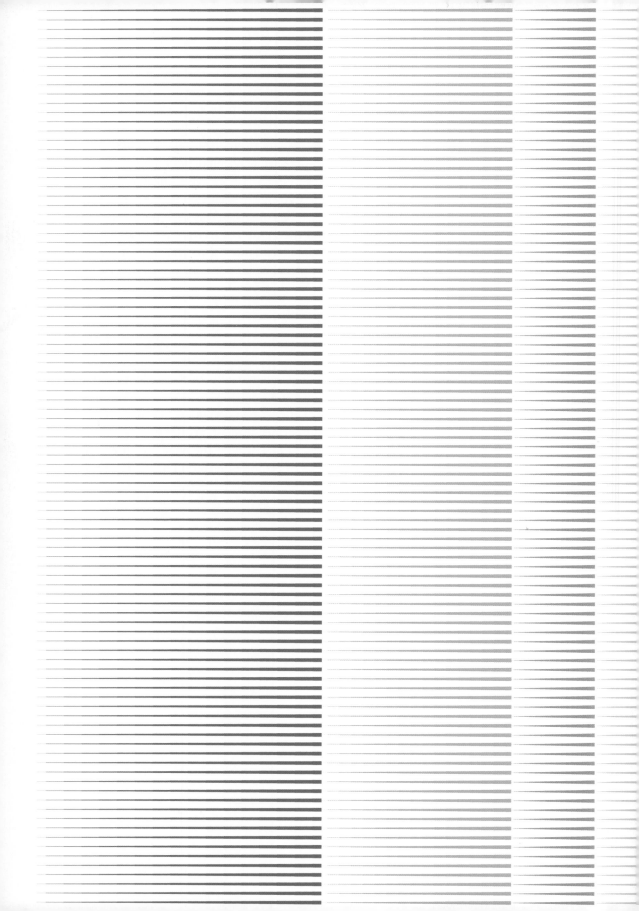

Shana Agid is an artist/designer, teacher, and activist whose work focuses on relationships of power and difference in visual, social, and political cultures. She is the Dean at the School of Art, Media, and Technology and an Associate Professor of Arts, Media, and Communication at Parsons School of Design. Shana is a co-developer of Working with People (working-with-people.org), a keyword-based curriculum and website for developing critical pedagogical frameworks for collaborative practices. His design work focuses on exploring possibilities for making self-determined services and campaigns through teaching and design research. She is also a book artist and letterpress printer. Shana has an MFA in Printmaking and Book Arts, an MA in Visual and Critical Studies from California College of the Arts (CCA), and a Ph.D. in Design from the Royal Melbourne Institute of Technology (RMIT).

Ahmed Ansari is the Director, Ph.D., and Assistant Professor in Integrated Digital Media in the Dept. of Technology, Culture & Society, at New York University. His work and research are situated at the intersection of design studies, critical cultural studies, and the philosophy of technology, with interests in decolonizing knowledge production in design and creating alternatives to present-day systems utilizing local cosmologies and genealogies of knowledge. He is also an educational consultant for universities, and has developed curricula for design programs in Karachi, Pakistan, and is a founder of the Decolonising Design platform.Ansari received his Ph.D. in Design Studies and Masters in Interaction Design from Carnegie Mellon University and Bachelors in Communication Design from IVSAA, Karachi.

Christian Bason, CEO, Ph.D., leads the Danish Design Centre, a publicly funded institution that advances the value of design for business and society. Previously he was Director of MindLab and business manager with the consultancy Ramboll. Christian is the author of seven books on innovation, design, and leadership, including *Leading Public Design* (2017), and has published in *Harvard Business Review,* and *Stanford Social Innovation Review*. He teaches executives at, among others, the University of Oxford's Saïd Business School, the European School of Administration, and Copenhagen Business School. He is M.Sc. in political science and a Ph.D. in design leadership.

Tessy Britton is Director of Participatory City, an initiative that is building a large urban Demonstration Neighborhood in a London borough of 200,000+ residents. Working closely with the local authority and many other collaborators, the intention is that over a five-year period, this neighborhood will become a model of equality, well-being, and sustainability. Prior to the commencement of this demonstration, Tessy has researched and prototyped new ways to support widespread practical participation of the kind that works with the fabric of daily life.

Stuart Candy (@futuryst) helps people think about possible worlds by bringing them to life. He wrote the first Ph.D. dissertation on intersections of the futures field with design, "The Futures of Everyday Life" (2010), and has extensively taught, consulted, written, and devised interventions and frameworks to amplify social foresight in diverse cultural, educational, scientific, and governance contexts. Partner organizations include the International Federation of Red Cross and Red Crescent Societies, UNESCO, University of Oxford, NASA JPL, IDEO, the Smithsonian Institution, and the US Conference of Mayors. Candy is co-creator of the award-winning imagination game The Thing From The Future (2015) and co-editor of the landmark open-access collection Design and Futures (2019). He currently serves as Associate Professor of Design at Carnegie Mellon University in Pittsburgh, Pennsylvania, where he is responsible for leading the integration of foresight throughout the curriculum, and Visiting Professor of Future Strategy at KAIST in Daejeon, South Korea.

Nandana Chakraborty is currently working as a Design Thinking Lead in Research and Innovation with Tata Consultancy Services (TCS). Previously, she was associated with Digital Impact Square, A TCS Foundation Initiative, as a Design Lead for Social Innovation. She has a formal education in Communication Design from the National Institute of Design, Ahmedabad. She has worked in Public health, Transportation and Mobility, Education system, and Assistive technology innovations through applied Human-centered research integrating with technology and entrepreneurship during her career span. Her interest lies in participative and co-creative innovation practice and process, transportability and impact of social interventions, and understanding the science of human behaviors. Her personal spectrum of interest lies in different mediums of paintings, Indian classic vocals, reading about personal development, and yoga. She also loves sharing her doodled Sketch notes to capture personal reflections on various conferences, webinars, workshops attended, and books read.

Jan Chipchase is the founder of Studio D, a discreet international consultancy working at the intersection of research, design, strategy, brand, and public policy. It always takes a team.

Vivek Chondagar is currently working as an Innovation Champion with Tata Consultancy Services. He was associated with Digital Impact Square as a Design Lead for Digital Social Innovation in his previous role. He has a formal education in engineering, design, and psychology. In the past, he has worked with the aerospace, automotive, and railway industries. He has been a fellow at Venture Studio Ahmedabad University, where he worked on a next-generation bicycling system for cities. He has been actively associated with social organizations working on art & craft preservation, climate change, and mental health across India. His interest lies in implementing the human-centered design process to realize the impact of a product or service. He is a reader, a long-distance runner, and has a deep interest in different musical instruments.

Jesper Christiansen is co-founder of States of Change, a non-profit global public innovation learning collective supported by leading innovation organizations and expert practitioners from around the world. It is dedicated to supporting governments and institutions to reinvent themselves and drive culture change to deal more effectively with the problems we face today (www.states-of-change.org). Before this, Jesper was Head of Strategy & Development of Innovation Skills at UK global innovation foundation Nesta and Head of Research and Programme Lead at Danish cross-government innovation unit MindLab. Over the past decade, Jesper has been working with leading innovation practitioners, governments, and international institutions to support their strategic innovation work and build better capacity for dealing with complex problems. Jesper holds a Ph.D. in Anthropology and is the author of multiple publications and resources aimed at understanding and supporting the practice of public innovation and creative problem-solving.

Debbie Aung Din is co-founder of Proximity Designs, a social business operating in Myanmar that delivers affordable and innovative products and services for farm families living in poverty. Aung Din has been engaged in design and economic research in Myanmar since 1995. She has also lived and worked in Mississippi, Cambodia, and Indonesia. She has worked for NGOs, USAID, the UN, and the World Bank. Aung Din holds a MA from Harvard University in public policy and development economics. She received social entrepreneurship awards from the Schwab Foundation (World Economic Forum) and the Skoll Foundation.

Proximity Designs is a non-profit social business that has operated in Myanmar since 2004 and focused on the agriculture sector. Proximity has developed a unique platform composed of financing, farm technologies, and agronomy advice, which delivers affordable and innovative products and services to small farmers in their journey out of poverty. Products and services are specially designed to boost farm productivity and increase household incomes by an average of US$250 per year. Proximity's operations serve more than 100,000 new customers annually. Since 2004, Proximity small-farm services have spanned over 10,000 villages and enabled 3.2 million people in rural Myanmar to grow their farm enterprises and afford basic food, health care, and education for their families.

Robert Fabricant is co-founder and Partner at Dalberg Design, which has studios in Dakar, London, Mumbai, Nairobi, and New York. His team brings an agile approach to human-centered design (HCD) and systems thinking to clients in social impact and civic engagement. Robert joined Dalberg after a long career at the forefront of human-centered design. Most recently, he was Vice President of Creative for frog Design where he incubated and led "frog Impact", working with key partners in public health, financial inclusion, mobile technology, and disaster response to leverage the power of design and technology to accelerate positive behavior change. Robert has an MPS in Design and Technology from NYU and writes and speaks extensively about design and social impact. He holds multiple patents and is the co-author of the book *User Friendly: How the Hidden Rules of Design Shape the Way We Live, Work and Play* (2020). Robert has won numerous design awards from Fast Company, Core77, and IDSA and has been named one of the top 100 public interest designers working globally today. He serves on the board of Praekelt.org, a leading tech company in South Africa that develops population-scale mobile applications to drive behavior change.

Sarah Fathallah is an independent designer, researcher, and educator specializing in the application of design to the social sector. She has worked on projects of various sizes with non-profits, governments, and social enterprises, on topics ranging from civil and human rights to healthcare, education, and financial inclusion. Her clients have included the International Domestic Workers Federation, the International Rescue Committee, and Open Society Foundations, to name a few. Sarah's design work has been honored by the Core77 Design Awards, the International Design Excellence Awards (IDEA), ONE Prize, and the GSMA mWomen Design Challenge. Sarah is a co-founder of Design Gigs for Good, a free community-driven resource to help more people use the tools of design to create positive social change. Sarah is a graduate of Sciences Po Paris, where she studied International Business and Middle Eastern and Mediterranean Affairs. She also studied design innovation at the Paris

Est d.school, user experience design at General Assembly, and participatory design at MIT.

Alexandra Fiorillo is the Founder of GRID Impact, a global social enterprise behavioral research and design collective. GRID uses participatory research and collaborative design practices to help create equitable and inclusive systems and programs in the global social impact space. Alex is particularly passionate about applying human-centered design, behavioral science, and innovative technologies to achieve social impact and is energized by leading projects that bring people with diverse experiences together. Alexandra earned her Master's in development economics from Columbia University, and she holds a Bachelor's in Economics and Latin American Studies from Connecticut College. She was a Fulbright Scholar in Ecuador, where she researched and evaluated microfinance and social enterprise projects among indigenous communities. She teaches behavioral design with the Copenhagen Institute for Interaction Design.

Gabriella Gómez-Mont is the founder and principal of Experimentalista and was the founder and former director of Laboratorio para la Ciudad (2013–2018), the award-winning experimental arm of the Mexico City government. Gabriella is also a journalist, visual artist, curator, director of documentary films, and a creative advisor to cities, universities, and companies. She has received several international recognitions, such as the Audi Urban Future Award (Germany), the Best Art Practice Award (Italy), as well as the TED City 2.0 Prize (USA + UK). She was one of the three people worldwide to receive the Creative Bureaucrats Award (2018) by the German government and the *Der Spiegel* newspaper, the Young Creators National Grant (Mexico), Jumex Contemporary Art Foundation (Mexico), and the IMCINE National Film Grant (Mexico). Her work has been showcased in international publications such as *The New York Times*, *The Guardian*, *Forbes USA*, *Wired* magazine, *Fast Co.*, and *Metropolis*, among others. She is a Yale World Fellow, MIT Director's Fellow, a Georgetown University Global Cities Initiative Visiting Fellow, TED Senior Fellow, an Institute for the Future Fellow, a Salzburg Seminar Fellow, a Fabrica Alumni, and a World Cities Summit Young Leader.

Fumiko Ichikawa is co-founder and managing director of Think-and-Do Tank Re:public, based in Japan. Fumiko's professional background mixes human-centered design and innovation. At Re:public, she leads Tokyo's studio, working with clients such as Panasonic, Sony, Japan Patent Office, and the National Ministry of Environment to understand and envision civic futures, and how citizens can be the decision-makers of their lives and in the cities they live. She also works with multiple municipalities, where her role is to support local governments and institutions, focusing on digital transformation, education, innovation ecosystem development, and circular economy. She started her career in user experience and ethnographic research working for multiple global companies. She is now a director for the board of a circular design firm called fog and serves as a mentor for 100 BANCH in Shibuya. She is a member of multiple committees supporting social ventures and local economic development.

Indy Johar is an architect, co-founder of Project 00 and Dark Matter Labs, and a Senior Innovation Associate at the Young Foundation. Indy has co-founded multiple social ventures such as Impact Hub Birmingham, Hub Westminster, and Open Systems Lab. Indy is a thought leader in systems change, the future of urban infrastructure finance, outcome-based investment, and the future of governance. He has led discussions on strategic design for policy and a new economy in forums such as Demos, the Centre for Social Justice, Helsinki Design Lab, the European Parliament, LSE, the Royal Academy, the Royal Society of the Arts, and the Royal Institute of Chartered Surveyors. He has written for national and international journals on the future of design, social systems, and venturing. Indy is a Fellow of the RSA, Demos Associate, ResPublica Fellow, and a JRF Anti-Poverty Strategy Programme Advisory Group member. He is a non-executive director of Wiki-House Foundation, RIBA Trustee, and an Advisor to the Mayor of London on Good Growth. He is a lecturer at various institutions worldwide, such as the University of Bath, TU-Berlin, the Architectural Association, University College London, Princeton, Harvard, MIT, and The New School.

Chris Larkin is the Managing Director—Impact at IDEO.org, where she supports design teams in developing services and products that can have lasting social impact. She brings systems thinking, social and behavior change expertise, and measurement to the creative design process and builds designers' capacity to leverage these tools. With a background in social and organizational psychology, Chris has worked in the fields of social impact research, evaluation, and programming for the past 15 years. She is particularly interested in the transformative role of design, as well as approaches that harness media, branded communications, and digital technologies. Before joining IDEO.org, Chris led research and evaluation with several creative organizations in the international development sector, including BBC Media Action and Girl Effect.

Panthea Lee is the Executive Director of Reboot. She is passionate about driving unlikely but courageous collaborations between communities, activists, and institutions to advance social justice. Panthea is a pioneer in leading multi-stakeholder processes to tackle complex social challenges, with experience doing so in 30+ countries, with partners including UNDP, Wikimedia, Open Government Partnership, CIVICUS, MacArthur Foundation, and governments at the national, state, and local levels. The global co-creation initiatives she's led have resulted in bold new efforts to protect human rights defenders, tackle public sector corruption, advance participatory democracy, reform international agencies, and strengthen independent media. Her contributions to equity-centered design have been recognized by Fast Company and Core77. Her work has been featured on Al Jazeera and in *The Atlantic*, *The New York Times*, *MIT Innovations*, and *Stanford Social Innovation Review*. She advises the OECD Network on Innovation Citizen Participation and Greenpeace; and serves on the boards of RSA US, Development Gateway, and People Powered: The Global Hub for Participatory Democracy.

Ramia Mazé is a Professor in Design for Social Innovation and Sustainability at London College of Communication, University of the Arts, United Kingdom. She has been an editor of the leading journal *Design Issues* since 2016. Previously, in Finland, she was a professor and head of education in the Department of Design at Aalto University and, before that, in Sweden, she worked at Konstfack College of Arts, Crafts, and Design, KTH Royal Institute of Technology, the national doctoral school Designfakulteten, and the Interactive Institute. A designer and architect by training, her Ph.D. is in interaction design. She has led, published, and exhibited widely through major interdisciplinary and international practice-based design research projects, most recently in social and sustainable design, design activism, and design for policy. She specializes in participatory, critical, and politically engaged design practices, as well as "research through design" and feminist epistemologies.

Fatou Wurie is an accomplished social justice advocate with 10+ years of interdisciplinary experience in gender, public health, and innovation. She works at the nexus of humanitarian action and development to tackle issues of equity, inclusion, and accountability in service of diverse and affected communities. Currently, at UNICEF global, Fatou is an Emergency Specialist for Digital Engagement, working on a people-centered agenda and supporting the scale-up of safe and accessible reporting channels for sexual exploitation and abuse. During the West-Africa Ebola outbreak, Fatou co-founded the Survivor Dream Project (SDP), a local non-profit for Women and Girl survivors of Ebola and Sexual Violence. Prior, she was the Regional Advocacy Advisor for UK-Aid funded campaign on maternal and newborn health. Fatou speaks and lectures on grassroots movements and social, gender, health justice issues. She is a communicator operating on the ethos that storytelling can be employed as a tool for healing and global justice.

Joyce Yee is a Professor of Design and Social Innovation at the School of Design, Northumbria University, UK. Joyce's research explores how design is used to support, enable and drive change by creating innovative practices in organizations. She co-founded the Designing Social Innovation in Asia-Pacific network (www.desiap.org) in 2015 with Yoko Akama. DESIAP is a virtual learning network for social innovation practitioners using design to support their work. She has co-authored books on the future of design practice. Her last book, *Transformations* (2017), documented how design can support culture change and innovation in organizations. Her recent research includes an investigation into the societal impact of creative districts in Thailand and the development of an evaluation framework to measure impact in social innovation programs.

Ayah Younis is a human-centered designer and a children's literature writer with ten years of experience in education in museums. She works with Ahlan Simsim, a program by the International Rescue Committee, to design relevant and easy-to-adopt programs for children and caregivers realizing innovative and user-centered delivery modalities. Previously, she held the position of Education and Programs Manager at the Children's Museum Jordan (CMJ) in Amman, where she designed and managed the implementation of playful learning experiences for children and facilitators in science, art, literature, and technology. Younis contributed to the designing and implementation of CMJ strategy and local and regional flagship projects. Ayah has designed and delivered several workshops for children and youth in Jordan and the Middle East. Ayah Younis has authored seven children's books and presented a research paper on children's literature. Younis holds a B.Sc. in Industrial Engineering from the University of Jordan in Amman.

EDITORS

Mariana Amatullo is an Associate Professor of Strategic Design and Management at Parsons School of Design; she is an affiliated faculty member with the Parsons DESIS Lab and the university's Graduate Minor in Civic Service Design and serves as the Vice Provost for Global Executive Education and Online Strategic Initiatives at The New School, New York. Mariana is the current President of Cumulus, the international association of colleges and universities of design, art, and media. Previously, Mariana co-founded and led the award-winning social innovation department, Designmatters, at ArtCenter College of Design in Pasadena, California. Mariana's academic research and publishing bridge the design and management fields and examine the role of a design attitude as a cognitive approach to social innovation and organizational learning. Her editorial projects include *LEAP Dialogues: Career Pathways in Design for Social Innovation* as lead editor and the open-source *LEAP Dialogues: The Educator's Guide*. A Global Fellow with the Royal Society for the Arts (RSA) and Salzburg Global, Mariana is the recipient of numerous awards, including the Inaugural DELL Award for Outstanding Social Innovation Education (2012). Mariana lectures internationally about design and social innovation and serves on several juries and executive and advisory boards, including the Vera List Center for Arts and Politics. Mariana holds a Ph.D. in Management from Case Western Reserve University, an M.A. in Art History and Museum Studies from the University of Southern California, and a Licence en Lettres Degree from the Sorbonne University, Paris, where she also studied Art History at L'Ecole du Louvre. A native of Argentina and the child of a diplomat, Mariana grew up around the world.

Bryan Boyer is co-founder of the architecture and strategic design studio Dash Marshall where he runs the studio's strategic design practice, working with clients such as Google, Sidewalk Labs, IKEA, Bloomberg Philanthropies, and the Museum of Modern Art to envision future cities and urban experiences. The studio was named a Next Progressive studio by *Architect* magazine (2020) and Top 50 firms by *AN Interior* magazine (2020). In addition to practice, Bryan is a founding Director of the Bachelor of Science in Urban Technology degree at the University of Michigan's Taubman College of Architecture and Urban Planning and Assistant Professor of Practice in Architecture. He joined the University as an Eliel Saarinen visiting professor 2019–2020. Previously, Boyer was a co-founder of Helsinki Design Lab at the Finnish Innovation Fund, one of the first design teams working at a national level inside government. His editorial projects include *LEAP Dialogues: Career Pathways in Design for Social Innovation* (2016), *Brickstarter* (2013), *Helsinki Street Eats* (2012), *Legible Practices* (2013), and *In Studio: Recipes For Systemic Change* (2011). Bryan serves on the board of directors for Public Policy Lab in New York City and is based in Detroit, MI. He holds a Master of Architecture degree from the Harvard Graduate School of Design and a Bachelor of Fine Arts in Interior Architecture degree from the Rhode Island School of Design.

Jennifer May finds innovation at the intersections of design, art, education, and social change. Jennifer is currently the Executive Director for Designmatters, the social innovation department at ArtCenter College of Design, where she oversees a dynamic portfolio of external partnerships, curricular and extracurricular programs, including the Designmatters Minor in Social Innovation, and an active slate of special initiatives and publications exploring how design and art can effect change in the areas of sustainable development, social entrepreneurship, health, public policy, and social justice. She serves on the advisory committee for Shine-LA, a cross-sector initiative led by Cedars-Sinai Research Center for Health Equity, focusing on raising physical activity levels among Angelenos over the next ten years. Jennifer was Managing Editor of *LEAP Dialogues: Career Pathways in Design for Social Innovation*, an award-winning publication on new practices in social innovation, and editor of the open-source *LEAP Dialogues: The Educator's Guide*. She was named an Impact Maker to Watch in Los Angeles in 2020 and was part of the inaugural LEAD LA cohort for Coro Southern California. Jennifer earned her M.B.A. with honors from USC Marshall School of Business, where she was a Society and Business Lab Graduate Fellow and Forté Fellow.

Andrew Shea founded and is the creative director of MANY Design, a studio that designs strategies and artifacts that support progressive social agendas, sustainable economic endeavors, and the environment. MANY's work has been featured by Fast Company, Slate, Print, How, 99% Invisible, Communication Arts, and AIGA, among others. Andrew is Associate Director and Assistant Professor of Integrated Design at Parsons School of Design, The New School. He has also taught at Pratt Institute, Maryland Institute College of Art, and the City University of New York. Andrew was an editor of *LEAP Dialogues: Career Pathways in Design for Social Innovation* (2016), and he authored *Designing for Social Change: Strategies for Community-Based Graphic Design* (2012). His design writing has also appeared in *Core77*, *AIGA*, *Entrepreneur* magazine, and *Design Observer*, who included one of his essays in *Culture Is Not Always Popular: Fifteen Years of Design Observer* (2018). Andrew regularly speaks about design at schools, conferences, and events like TEDx Transmedia. He has served on juries organized by AIGA, Worldstudio, the Center for Urban Pedagogy, and Sappi. He received a Master of Fine Arts in Graphic Design from Maryland Institute College of Art and a Bachelor of Arts in Politics & Philosophy and Creative Nonfiction Writing from the University of Pittsburgh.

ASSISTANT EDITORS

Isabella Gady is a Design Strategist, Researcher, and Public Policy Practitioner. She has worked locally, nationally, and internationally co-creating organizational change and innovation processes, leading program and service development, and facilitating multi-stakeholder engagement and participatory strategies. Fueled by the desire to imagine better futures for all, she fuses elements from many disciplines with design - combining research, organizational development, and strategy. Her methods draw from anthropology, the behavioral sciences, and psychology to bring new solutions and ways of working to complex public sector challenges. Isabella has worked with organizations including the United Nations, UN Women, the City of New York, Ideo.org, 3x3 Design, Snowcone and Haystack, and Spark Microgrant. She co-founded the New York Digital Diplomacy Chapter and served as Spokeswoman and Special Advisor for International Development at the Austrian Federal Ministry for Europe, Integration and Foreign Affairs. Isabella holds an MS in Strategic Design from Parsons School of Design in New York and an MA (Magistra FH) in Economic Sciences from the University of Applied Sciences St. Poelten, Austria. She is a published author and researcher investigating public sector innovation, a part-time faculty at Parsons School of Design, and an accredited coach.

Jenny Liu is a design researcher who combines participatory ethnography, behavioral science, prototyping, and storytelling in her practice. Her work advocates for greater inclusion of underrepresented voices, from warehouse employees to family caregivers to low-income senior Americans, to nudge complex systems to be more caring and equity-centered. Her clinical and behavioral research origins inform her critical and analytical stance to developing innovative and evidence-based products, services, and programs. She has worked on projects with non-profits, consulting firms, and technology companies, such as Dalberg Design and the International Rescue Committee, in sectors ranging from financial inclusion to public health. She has been part of project teams that have received recognition from Fast Company, MIT Media Lab, and Massachusetts General Hospital. She has an MFA in Transdisciplinary Design from Parsons School of Design and a BA in Neuroscience and Biology from Washington University in St. Louis.